Reading Luke–Acts

in the Pentecostal Tradition

READING LUKE–ACTS
IN THE PENTECOSTAL TRADITION

MARTIN WILLIAM MITTELSTADT

CPT Press
Cleveland, Tennessee USA

Reading Luke–Acts in the Pentecostal Tradition

Published by CPT Press
900 Walker ST NE
Cleveland, TN 37311
email: cptpress@pentecostaltheology.org
website: www.pentecostaltheology.org

Library of Congress Control Number: 2010923185

ISBN-10: 0981965172
ISBN-13: 9780981965178

To my professors

Ronald Kydd,

Ed Neufeld,

&

William Kurz, S.J.

CONTENTS

Preface ix
Abbreviations.. xiii

Introduction: Twentieth Century Trajectories
Getting Started.. 1
Terms and Parameters 4
Luke–Acts Research in the Twentieth Century 7
Trajectories of Pentecostal Theology in the Twentieth
    Century.. 11

History and Trajectory of Pentecostal Contributions to
Luke–Acts Research.. 18
Chapter 1: Stage 1—Pre-1970... 18
    1.1 Acts Sets the Standard... 19
        1.1.1 Charles Parham 20
        1.1.1 Azusa Street... 22
        1.1.2 Early Pioneers 26
    1.2 Acts as the Center of Dissent.. 31
        1.2.1 The New Issue 31
        1.2.2 Tongues and the Bible Evidence 34
    1.3 Acts and Preservation.. 38
    1.4 Summary.. 43
Chapter 2: Stage 2—The Dunn Factor: Pentecostals Enter the
    Academic Marketplace... 46
    2.1 Responses 49
        2.1.1 Gordon Fee 49
        2.1.2 Roger Stronstad 51
        2.1.3 Howard Ervin 55
        2.1.4 James Shelton... 56
        2.1.5 Robert Menzies... 58
        2.1.6 Max Turner... 60
        2.1.7 Summary 63

2.2 Pressing Issues 64
   2.2.1 Cessationism 64
   2.2.2 Spirit Baptism 68
   2.2.3 Hermeneutics..77
   2.2.4 Summary...79
Chapter 3: Stage 3—Out of the Shadows....................81
   3.1 The Triumph of Narrative Theology 82
   3.2 Missiology...92
   3.3 Healing & Exorcism 98
   3.4 Women..103
   3.5 Spiritual Formation 106
   3.6 Oneness Theology 110
Chapter 4: Stage 4—Old Story, Enduring Message: Luke–Acts for
   the Twenty-first Century....................................114
   4.1 Social Justice/Ethics....................................115
   4.2 The Good News of Peace 122
   4.3 Suffering and Persecution............................126
   4.4 Ecumenism and Interreligious Dialogue.........131
   4.5 Global Readings: 'To the Ends of the Earth'....138
   4.6 Luke–Acts in a Postmodern Age...................143

The Current Status of Luke–Acts Research:
Observations and Possibilities....................................150
   An Open Door..151
   Pentecostals and World Christianity.................152
   The Politics of the Gospel 154
   The Gospel and Vocation 155
   Luke, Acts and/or Luke–Acts..........................156
   Untapped Possibilities.....................................160

A Not So Final Word..162

Appendix: Commentaries & Pastoral Tools 165
Bibliography 170
Author Index..206
Scripture Index...211

PREFACE

Why another work on Luke-Acts and by a Pentecostal nonetheless? While potential readers have good reason to ask this question, I believe this work fills a significant gap in Pentecostal scholarship on Luke-Acts. Any Pentecostal with a reasonable amount of history in the tradition knows of the insatiable passion of Pentecostals for Luke-Acts. Since the Lukan stories serve as a primary launching point for Pentecostal theology and experience, zeal for Luke-Acts comes as no surprise. Early Pentecostals draw heavily upon Luke-Acts via testimonies, sermons, short pamphlets, and ministerial training textbooks. In the latter part of the twentieth century as Pentecostals enter the world of academia, the sheer volume of Pentecostal scholarship in biblical studies remains heavily tilted toward Luke-Acts. And Pentecostal theologians, whether systematicians or historians, recognize quickly the substantial dependence on Luke-Acts for the development of identity and doctrine.

In recent years, though numerous non-Pentecostal Lukan scholars have produced helpful trajectories of Lukan scholarship, they pay little attention to Pentecostal contributions. Similarly, though Pentecostal theologians have tendered useful histories of the development of Pentecostal theology, no one, to date, has attempted to combine these approaches. In this work, I seek to fill this important lacuna and offer the first comprehensive history of interpretation of Lukan scholarship by Pentecostals. At the very least, I provide the first thoroughgoing bibliography of their work. While the extensive bibliography at the end of this volume makes Pentecostal contributions more visible, I tender a larger purpose. I walk readers through the early generations of Pentecostalism when Pentecostals remained on the sidelines of Lukan scholarship but used their work to shape, preserve, and sustain the tradition. Slowly the adolescent Pentecostal movement begins to produce scholars who not only enter academia but also bring much needed credibility to the broader ecclesial and scholarly community. Readers may be amazed at the extensive scholarship of Pentecostals in Lukan studies. My contribution consists of a structural analysis of approximately one hundred years of research from infancy to maturation as well as suggestions for future research.

I believe this work should prove valuable for a mixed readership. First, I write for fellow Pentecostals. I am optimistic that Pentecostal scholars and students engaged in research on Luke-Acts, Pentecostal history, or theology will benefit greatly from this collection of rich resources already available at the hands of Pentecostal scholars. As the current generation of scholars becomes more familiar with the Pentecostal story, I envision that they will build on the foundation already laid down and lead the movement in its second century of existence. I also write for clergy and informed lay readers. Over the years, as I embarked on research for sermons (and essays, whether as a student or scholar), I often missed out on the munificent scholarship of Pentecostals. I hope my attempt at historical and thematic trajectories will avert such unawareness and make Pentecostal scholarship more available to Pentecostal preachers and teachers. Though I retain great respect and appreciation for Lukan scholarship furnished by those outside of the Pentecostal tradition, Pentecostals should also benefit from the solid research advanced by their own scholars. In light of this, readers will quickly become aware of the consistent pastoral appeal in Pentecostal scholarship. Pentecostal scholars write unashamedly to defend, stir, and stimulate those within their own tradition both theologically and experientially.

Second, I write for scholars and students outside of the Pentecostal tradition. As Pentecostals come of age, the time is ripe for mutual growth to arise out of serious dialogue. Pentecostals have much to contribute to the broader Christian community, and I trust this work will help profile their valuable research. But learning and growth must move in both directions. As Pentecostals become more visible to the larger academic community, they will embrace Luke's vision for the people of God as a result of mutual engagement with thinkers from all Christian traditions. Such debate expresses well the spirit of the academy.

As I offer this volume to the above communities, I pause to thank many people for their participation in this endeavor. I thank John Christopher Thomas for the necessary spark. In 2005, the Biblical Studies track of the Society for Pentecostal Studies (SPS) hosted a panel discussion of my recently published PhD dissertation *Spirit and Suffering in Luke-Acts: Implications for a Pentecostal Theology* (2004) at the 34th annual meeting at Regent University (Virginia Beach, VA). During the session Chris remarked that Pentecostals seemed to be making great strides in Lukan scholarship and suggested that someone ought to write an SPS paper that chronicles the history and status of interpretation through Pentecostal lenses. I took up the challenge. I (and Chris!) could have hardly imagined the wealth of information already produced by Pentecostals. Any hope of writing a fifteen to twenty page SPS paper quickly faded; the bibliography alone soon exceeded standard SPS boundaries for length. I persisted and produced an essay (well beyond typical length restrictions) and presented it at the 36th annual SPS meeting at Lee University (Cleveland, TN) in 2007. Chris intended to publish the essay in the *Journal of Pentecostal Theology*. Given the length of the paper, he suggested it be published in two parts or, better yet, turn the essay into a full monograph. Once again, I took the challenge and produced this volume, twice the length of the original essay. I also thank my SPS colleagues, too many to name, for their valuable feedback at the 2007 session.

Thanks to Glenn Bernet (Vice President of Academic Affairs) and Gary Liddle (Theology Department Chair) at Evangel University for granting me a sabbatical in the spring of 2008. Thanks to my colleagues in the Evangel University Theology Department for their inspiration and enthusiasm; I see in them daily examples of fulfillment of the academic vocation. I reflect with gratitude on the many students I have taught over the years. I cannot measure the insights and stimulation from countless Luke-Acts students at Evangel University, Tyndale Seminary (Toronto), Assemblies of God Theological Seminary, and various church-related Sunday School and Bible study contexts. Thanks to Dale Jensen, research librarian at Evangel University. Dale is a bloodhound; whatever I needed, he found! I also acknowledge Darrin Rodgers and his staff at the International Flower Pentecostal Heritage Center in Springfield, MO; Glenn Gohr, in particular, searched diligently for materials, helped on minute details, and did so with lightning speed, joy and passion. I am also grateful to two Evangel University colleagues, James Edwards and Wave Nunnally, and my friend Matthew

Paugh for their careful reading of the manuscript. I benefited greatly from their attention to detail. I owe an enormous thank you to Jessica Johnson, my recent student worker at Evangel University. Though an undergraduate, JJ served more like a graduate research assistant. She was a diligent hunter, gatherer, copyist, typist, editor, and formatter (!!!). I thank my wife Evelyn, as well as my children Rachel, Sarah, and Andrew for their encouragement and gracious understanding during long periods of study. I pray that our family remains steadfast on the journey of discipleship envisioned by Luke.

Finally, I express heartfelt gratitude to three mentors through the course of my educational journey. These New Testament teachers not only shared of their tremendous knowledge of the Lukan story, but did so with inspiring zeal: Ronald Kydd (Central Pentecostal College, Saskatoon, SK), Ed Neufeld (Providence Seminary, Otterburne, MB), and my doctoral director, William Kurz, S.J. (Marquette University). It is not without coincidence that my title stems from Kurz's *Reading Luke-Acts*, a pioneering work on Luke as a literary artist. Through their lives and scholarship, these wonderful men exemplify Luke's vision that the people of God might continue what 'Jesus began to do and teach' (Acts 1.1). I dedicate this volume to them.

ABBREVIATIONS

AJPS	*Asian Journal of Pentecostal Studies*
APTS	Asia Pacific Theological Seminary
CBQ	*Catholic Biblical Quarterly*
CPCR	*Cyberjournal for Pentecostal-Charismatic Research*
Encounter	*Encounter: Journal for Pentecostal Ministry*
EPTA	European Pentecostal Theological Association
IBR	Institute of Biblical Research
JBL	*Journal of Biblical Literature*
JEPTA	*Journal of the European Pentecostal Theological Association*
JPT	*Journal of Pentecostal Theology*
JPTSup	Journal of Pentecostal Theology Supplement Series
JSNT	*Journal for the Study of the New Testament*
JSNTSS	Journal for the Study of the New Testament Supplement Series
NIDPCM	*New International Dictionary of Pentecostal and Charismatic Movements*
NovT	*Novum Testamentum*
NTS	*New Testament Studies*
NTTS	New Testament Tools and Studies
TrinJ	*Trinity Journal*
TynB	*Tyndale Bulletin*
VoxEv	*Vox Evangelica*
ZNW	*Zeitschrift für die neutestamentliche Wissenschaft und die Kunde der alteren Kirche*

INTRODUCTION:
TWENTIETH CENTURY TRAJECTORIES

In contrast to magisterial Protestantism, which tends to read the New Testament through Pauline eyes, Pentecostalism reads the rest of the New Testament through Lukan eyes, especially with the lenses provided by the book of Acts.

(Donald Dayton)[1]

When we look for the biblical roots of the baptism in the Spirit, we discover that the Pentecostals and their predecessors based their views almost exclusively on the Gospel of Luke and the Acts of the Apostles.

(Walter J. Hollenweger)[2]

GETTING STARTED

I often hear concerning Pentecostalism that no tradition in the history of Christianity exemplifies more the notion of a canon within a canon. When it comes to finding a corner in Scripture, Pentecostals may be at the top of the list. Since their unassuming arrival at the beginning of the twentieth century, the Pentecostal movement enters the twenty-first century as the fastest growing movement in Christendom. Through the first century of their existence Pentecostals found their theological and practical identity by way of their reading of Luke–Acts.[3] The citations above serve as two of many

---

[1] Donald W. Dayton, *Theological Roots of Pentecostalism* (Peabody: Hendrickson, 1987), p. 23.

[2] Walter J. Hollenweger, *The Pentecostals* (Peabody: Hendrickson, 1972), p. 336.

[3] I should add that all traditions are susceptible to a canon within the canon. Indeed while some are implicit, others are explicit. There is perhaps no better (or worse) example than Martin Luther from the preface of the first edition of his German New Testament:

statements that set the stage for the centrality of the Lukan narratives for Pentecostal theology and praxis. Whether sermons, testimonials, and devotional material or journal articles, theses, dissertations, and books, the sheer volume demonstrates their passionate and utter reliance upon Luke–Acts for theology and praxis. Given this proclivity to Luke–Acts, it comes as a surprise that no extensive analysis of Pentecostal contributions to Lukan scholarship appears to date.[4] In an attempt to fill this gap, I offer the first comprehensive collection of Pentecostal materials with primary or significant attention focused upon Luke–Acts. From this collection, I propose an integrated historical and theological trajectory concerning Pentecostal interpretation of Luke–Acts. I conclude with general observations on the past one hundred years and suggest possibilities for future scholarship.

In the introduction, I begin with the development of non-Pentecostal Luke–Acts scholarship in the twentieth century because it is valuable for all thinkers. Since non-Pentecostal surveyors/bibliographers tend to ignore, out of lack of interest or awareness, the work of Pentecostal/Charismatic scholars, I have thought it important to draw attention to this insider thought. Both of these

---

From all this you can rightly judge between all the books, and distinguish which are the best. For St. John's Gospel and St. Paul's Epistles, especially that to Romans, and St. Peter's first Epistle, are the true marrow and kernel of all the books; which properly also might be the first, and each Christian should be counseled to read them first and most, and make them as common by daily reading as his daily bread … briefly St. John's gospel and his first Epistle, St. Paul's Epistles, especially those to the Romans, Galatians, Ephesians, at St. Peter's first Epistle: these are the books which shew the Christ, and teach all which is needed and blessed for these to know, even if you never see or hear any other book or any other doctrine. There is the Epistle of James a right strawy Epistle compared with them, for it has no character of the Gospel in it.

This citation does not serve primarily as a critique but points to the inherent nature of worshipers and/or interpreters to settle individually and collectively on certain portions of the canon.

[4] I should note that this effort is a significant revision and expansion of a Society for Pentecostal Studies paper by the same title: 'Reading Luke–Acts in the Pentecostal Tradition: The History and Status of Luke–Acts Research' (paper presented at the annual meeting of the Society for Pentecostal Studies, Cleveland, TN, March 2007). See also 'Scripture in the Pentecostal Tradition' (paper presented at the annual meeting of the Society for Pentecostal Studies, Pasadena, CA, March 2006), repr. in Michael Wilkinson (ed.), *Canadian Pentecostalism: Transition and Transformation* (Montreal: McGill/Queens University Press, 2008).

schools of scholars are important for understanding the evolution of Pentecostal tradition. Non-Pentecostals have ignored insider scholarship for three quarters of a century, even though quality commentary has been developing over the past thirty-plus years. Furthermore, the phenomenal numerical growth of global Pentecostalism should cause scholars to pay greater attention to the theological evolution of this relatively young movement. At the same time, I suggest that there is continuity between the insider trajectories of Pentecostal history with the emergence of Pentecostal Luke–Acts scholarship. In other words, self-identity correlates well with its use of Luke–Acts.

The body of this project consists of four chapters. I propose a historical trajectory of Pentecostal scholarship on Luke–Acts based upon four primary developments. I suggest that the earliest stage runs from the origins of the movement to 1970. During the initial stage (1900-1970), interpretation of Luke–Acts proves integral to the emerging Pentecostal community. Leaders look consistently to the Lukan narratives for evidence and affirmation of the charismatic experiences of the participants, the standardization of primary doctrine, navigation of the movement through dissent, and subsequent preservation. However, unlike subsequent periods, this first era remains pre-critical; Pentecostal literature appears primarily in the form of homilies and teaching resources. Preachers and teachers write for fellow Pentecostals, typically parishioners and students preparing for ministry. A new era begins in 1970 due to the monumental work of James Dunn whose challenges to Pentecostal interpretation propel Pentecostals into the intellectual marketplace.[5] Dunn examines Luke's view of *Baptism in the Spirit* and equates Spirit baptism with regeneration. Given Pentecostal adherence to post-conversion experience of Spirit baptism, Dunn becomes a target for Pentecostal response (see sections 2.1 and 2.2). Though Dunn's subtitle, *A Re-examination of the NT Teaching on the Gift of the Spirit in Relation to Pentecostalism Today*, makes clear his disagreement with the Pentecostal position, he surely could not have foreseen the impact of his 1968 doctoral dissertation. Published shortly thereafter, this work goes through numerous printings and launches not

---

[5] James D.G. Dunn, *Baptism in the Holy Spirit: A Re-examination of the New Testament Teaching on the Gift of the Spirit in Relation to Pentecostalism Today* (London: SCM Press, 1970).

only his career but also lures Pentecostals into the world of critical scholarship. Dunn typifies the larger Evangelical community and becomes the primary conversation partner for Pentecostal scholars in an adolescent movement looking to 'join the big leagues'. Pioneering scholars like Gordon Fee, Roger Stronstad, James Shelton, and Howard Ervin respond directly (or indirectly) to Dunn and consequently bring Pentecostal theology and praxis into the academic marketplace. Questions concerning Spirit baptism give rise to further interest surrounding hermeneutics and the prevalent disposition of Evangelicals and Fundamentalists toward cessationism. While the beginnings of this second stage are clear, its ending remains imprecise. In the third period, Pentecostals come of age and move not only out of a pre-critical era and the shadows of Dunn but also beyond a defensive mode. The ascendance of literary criticism not only allows but encourages Pentecostal advancement. As Pentecostals move from the fringe of Lukan scholarship to main stage, they bring their longstanding interest in Lukan motifs such as missions, healing, and women into the scholastic marketplace. In the fourth and final period, Pentecostals now well acquainted with the academic landscape join other Lukan scholars in addressing questions surrounding social justice and peacemaking, ecumenical and interreligious dialogue, globalization and postmodernism. Indeed, given the numerical explosion of Pentecostals around the world, entry into these discussions comes as no surprise.

After offering a history of Luke–Acts scholarship, I present provisional observations and reflections on the trajectory of Pentecostal research as well as possibilities for further research in Lukan studies. The comprehensive bibliography follows the numerical and categorical outline of the monograph.

TERMS AND PARAMETERS

Before embarking upon a background to the history of interpretation, it remains prudent to discuss various terms and boundaries for this study. First, I refer to 'Luke' as the author of Luke–Acts unless noted otherwise. While debate concerning authorship and the identity of Luke persists, first generation Pentecostals seldom discuss this question. These Pentecostals see little reason to doubt the traditional position; the author of the Third Gospel and Acts is Luke the physician, converted Gentile, and traveling companion of Paul. As the generations pass, Pentecostal scholars become more aware of critical questions surrounding date and authorship, but remain by and large committed to the traditional view. Given the consistent adherence of Pentecostals to historical reliability of the New Testament, this comes as no surprise. In many of the articles or shorter monographs, Pentecostal scholars pay little or no attention to the question of authorship thereby assuming implicit agreement with the view above. Others offer a short statement often in a footnote affirming their affinity with the traditional view. When addressed in commentaries, most commentators generally speak to questions of authorship as part of the standard introductory section. For the most part, these commentators stand in continuity with their Pentecostal forefathers and argue for Lukan authorship via 1) the weight of internal evidence, particularly the 'we' passages (we/us/our) beginning in Acts 16.10; 2) the external evidence from Marcion to the Muratorian Canon, from Clement of Alexandria to Origen and Eusebius; and 3) Paul's references to Luke as 'the beloved physician' in Col. 4.14, a 'fellow worker' in Phlm. 24, and the only remaining coworker in 2 Tim. 4.10-11.

Second, I use the term 'Pentecostal' in a broad and inclusive manner. The earliest designation refers to the turn of the twentieth century 'classical Pentecostals', namely, those of the Apostolic Faith movement; these individuals generally follow a Restorationist vision and hold to traditional Spirit baptism with tongues as the 'Bible evidence'. As the renewal spreads, a new influx of adherents begin to receive and claim the label 'Charismatic'; beginning in the late 1950's, participants from mainline denominations begin to come into a Pentecostal-like experience. These Charismatics usually do not form new denominations but remain within their established Protestant, Catholic, or Orthodox traditions. The trajectory of Luke–Acts scholarship in the Pentecostal tradition includes solid representation across the entire Pentecostal/Charismatic spectrum.[6] Finally, in light of my inclusive approach to Pentecostal identity, I made an extensive search for books and monographs on Luke–Acts as well as a thorough investigation of Pentecostal/Charismatic

---

[6] See the various categorical articles in Stanley Burgess and Eduard M. Van Der Maas (eds.), *New International Dictionary of Pentecostal and Charismatic Movements* (rev. and exp. edn; Grand Rapids: Zondervan, 2002).

journals produced across many denominational, cultural, and continental lines. The extent of my search in order of earliest appearance includes comprehensive searches through the following Pentecostal journals:

Paraclete: A Journal Concerning the Work of the Holy Spirit (1967-1995)

Pneuma: The Journal of the Society for Pentecostal Studies (1979-)

Journal of the European Pentecostal Theological Association (1982-)

Journal of Pentecostal Theology (1992-)

Cyberjournal for Pentecostal-Charismatic Research @ www.pctii.org/ cyber/ (1997-)

Asian Journal of Pentecostal Studies (1998-)

Australasian Pentecostal Studies @ www.aps.webjournals.org (1998-)

PentecoStudies: The Online Journal for the European Research Network on Global Pentecostalism @ www.glopent.net/pentecostudies (2002-).

Encounter: Journal for Pentecostal Ministry @ www.agts.edu/ encounter/about.html (2004-).[7]

I made a thorough search of any related papers presented at the annual Society for Pentecostal Studies Conferences and any essays from various Pentecostal-based compilations and *Festschriften.*[8] I also include various articles under topics such as hermeneutics or Spirit baptism because of immediate connections to Luke–Acts. Of course, for Pentecostals, Luke–Acts remains the storm center on topics such as biblical interpretation and the ongoing work of the Spirit in the life of the believer. Lastly, contributors to the discussion include both insiders and outsiders; Pentecostals in conversation with non-Pentecostals. The size and breadth of the bibliography points to the significant impact of Pentecostals to date and should serve both scholars and students as an open window into the world of Pentecostal scholarship on Luke–Acts.[9]

---

[7] All subsequent references to these journals will follow SBL or abbreviated formats. See the list of abbreviations.

[8] A significant number of papers originally presented at annual meetings of the Society for Pentecostal Studies find their way into various journals and collected works. Some remain as presented; others undergo revision.

[9] I must pause to acknowledge the limitations of my research. First, I have undoubtedly failed to discover every piece of relevant material. Therefore, I cannot claim total comprehensiveness. Second, I admit that many works defy simple categorization; I will undoubtedly be accused of heuristic analysis. Finally, the

LUKE–ACTS RESEARCH IN THE TWENTIETH CENTURY

As the twentieth century nears its end, numerous scholars engage in attempts to chart scholarly trajectories of Luke–Acts research and ensuing implications for ecclesial communities. An early and invaluable work by Ward Gasque originally published in 1975 under the supervision of the influential F.F. Bruce provides a lucid trajectory of twentieth century history of interpretation. Gasque marches quickly through the eighteenth century only to slow down in order to chronicle the nineteenth century clash between the oft-called German liberals and British conservatives. Gasque cites this interpretative clash as the milieu for twentieth century debate with the primary point of conflict focusing on historical reliability of Luke.[10] By tracing the influential Tübingen scholar F.C. Baur, whose work gives rise to *Tendenzkritik* ('tendency criticism') and the careful British historians, Sir William Michael Ramsey and J.B. Lightfoot, Gasque narrates the desire to control questions of historicity. These historical questions remain a crucial concern throughout the century and set the tone for new questions.

Gasque also discusses the emergence of several scholars via the colossal five-volume encyclopedic analysis of Acts edited by F.J. Foakes Jackson and Kirsopp Lake (1919-1933).[11] One of the principal contributors, Henry J. Cadbury becomes an influential proponent for the unity of Luke–Acts as a two-volume work. In his best known work, Cadbury challenges the scholarly majority, namely, those satisfied to study the Third Gospel alongside the other Synoptic Gospels and in isolation from Acts. The title, *The Making of Luke–Acts*, sums up Cadbury's thesis: 'Acts is neither an appendix, nor an afterthought', but 'an integral part of the author's original

---

trajectory I propose indicates my own sense of the history of Luke–Acts interpretation in the Pentecostal tradition. As a Pentecostal insider I concede biases and blind spots, some of which are due to the pros and cons of my personal experience. At the same time, of such is the life of a Pentecostal.

[10] Ward Gasque, *A History of the Interpretation of the Acts of the Apostles* (rev. edn; Peabody, MA: Hendrickson, 1989). Before Gasque, see Andrew J. Mattill and Mary B. Mattill, *A Classified Bibliography of Literature on the Acts of the Apostles* (NTTS 7; Leiden: Brill, 1966). They amass an impressive bibliography on works published through 1961.

[11] F. J. Foakes-Jackson and Kirsopp Lake (eds.), *The Beginnings of Christianity* (5 vols.; London: MacMillan, 1919-1933).

plan and purpose'.[12] Gasque classifies Cadbury as a kind of proto-redaction critic who strives to identify literary methodologies in order to get at Lukan personality and purpose.[13] Building upon the work of Cadbury, many Lukan scholars continue convergence of historical and literary concerns and embrace thoroughgoing analysis of 'Luke: The Historian and Theologian' culminating in a monumental work by I. Howard Marshall in 1970.[14] Gasque's template for twentieth century interpretation proves important for the current study. At least four observations are noteworthy:

1. Prior to 1970, Pentecostals remain pre-critical and thus unnoticed. Though conservative in their understanding of historical reliability, they remain removed from the academic drama for it seems to them an unrewarding venture.

2. However, these same Pentecostals are already reading Luke–Acts through proto-literary lenses yet basically oblivious to the emerging critical methodologies around them. Ironically, when Pentecostals move into the academic marketplace, their pre-critical reading and application of Luke–Acts as exemplary for Christian faith and praxis will serve them well.

3. In the first edition, Gasque concludes with celebration and optimism a growing scholarly field with fresh focus on the purpose, drama, structure, and theology (including soteriological,

---

[12] Henry J. Cadbury, *The Making of Luke–Acts* (New York: Macmillan, 1927), p. 9. Note also the work of C.K. Barrett, 'The Third Gospel as a Preface to Acts? Some Reflections', in F. Van Segbroeck *et al.* (eds.), *The Four Gospels, 1992:* Festschrift Frans Neirynck (*Bibliotheca Ephemeridum Theologicarum Lovaniensium*, vol. 2, ed. F. Van Segbroeck, C.M. Tuckett, G. Van Belle, and J. Verheyden; Louvain: Leuven University Press, 1992), pp. 1451-66.

[13] Cadbury proves influential for the next generation of scholarship not the least being German theologian Martin Dibelius. See *Studies in the Acts of the Apostles* (ed. Heinrich Greeven; trans. Mary Ling; New York: Scribner, 1951). See also the recent collection of Dibelius' earlier essays, *The Book of Acts: Form, Style and Theology* (ed. K.C. Hanson; Minneapolis: Fortress Press, 2004). While early Pentecostals seem unfamiliar or uninterested in Dibelius, current Pentecostal scholars recognize his enduring influence. See my review of Martin Dibelius, *The Book of Acts: Form, Style and Theology*, Pneuma 27.2 (2005), pp. 393-95.

[14] I. Howard Marshall, *Luke: Historian and Theologian* (Exeter: Paternoster Press, 1970). The simultaneous publications by Marshall and Dunn (*Baptism in the Spirit*) provide mutual impetus for the emergence of Pentecostal scholarship. Pentecostals benefit from Marshall's conclusion that Luke is in fact a historian and theologian and begin to challenge Dunn's reading of Luke–Acts through Pauline lenses (see section 2).

christological, ecclesiological, and pneumatological analyses) of Acts. At the same time, given the year of its publication, Gasque is unable to introduce Pentecostals to his readers. By 1975 Pentecostals have not yet been able to position themselves for entry into this broader scholarly community. Substantial responses to Dunn do not appear before Gasque's first edition (see 2.2—'The Dunn Factor').

4. In the second edition, revised in 1989, Gasque includes an addendum on Luke–Acts research from the mid 1970s through the 1980s. Gasque cites Roger Stronstad as the lone Pentecostal. It is surely not coincidental that Gasque served as the director for Roger Stronstad's trailblazing thesis (see 2.2.1.2), but it is also hard to imagine that Gasque could have envisioned the impact of his student's thesis. Most important at this stage is Gasque's single reference to a Pentecostal scholar. In fairness, Pentecostal contributions remain only a footnote through the first seventy-five years of the twentieth century.[15]

Other surveys to appear shortly after Gasque's revised edition include surveys of Luke (1989) and Acts (1991) by Mark Allan Powell, Joel Green and Michael McKeever (1994) and a summary of recent theological efforts on Acts by Jacob Jervell (1996) and Todd Penner (2004). These surveys/synopses of Lukan studies continue to relegate Pentecostal scholars to the margins. Like Gasque, Powell discusses only Stronstad in his work on Acts; Jervell and Penner make no reference to Pentecostal scholars.[16] Finally, note the limited enlargement of Pentecostal awareness in the collection by Green and McKeever (1994). They include Pentecostal dialogue partners James Dunn and Max Turner and Pentecostal scholars James Shelton, Roger Stronstad, and Robert Menzies.[17]

---

[15] Gasque, *History of the Interpretation*, p. 334.

[16] Mark Allan Powell, *What are They Saying About Luke?* (New York: Paulist Press, 1989) and *What are They Saying About Acts?* (New York: Paulist Press, 1991); Jacob Jervell, *The Theology of the Acts of the Apostles* (New Testament Theology; ed. James D.G. Dunn; Cambridge: Cambridge University Press, 1996); and Todd Penner, 'Madness in the Method? The Acts of the Apostles in Current Study', *Currents in Biblical Research* 2.2 (2004), pp. 223-93. Powell references only Stronstad (*Acts*, pp. 51-52).

[17] Joel B. Green and Michael C. McKeever, *Luke–Acts and the New Testament Historiography* (IBR Bibliographies 8; Grand Rapids: Baker Books, 1994), pp. 53-56, 60.

While Gasque serves as the premier analyst of Luke–Acts scholarship on the first seventy-five years of the twentieth century, the meticulous French scholar François Bovon eventually assumes the position as primary surveyor. In three successive revised editions published in 1975, 1983, and 2005, Bovon demonstrates unparalleled breadth on the proliferation of scholarship on Luke–Acts.[18] And further, while Gasque and others give minimal reference to the emergence of Pentecostal scholars, Bovon offers slow but sure recognition of Pentecostal scholarship. Bovon concludes his most recent survey of Lukan scholarship (3rd edition 2006) with a chapter entitled 'Luke the Theologian from 1980-2005' where he reflects briefly upon his gradual awakening to Pentecostal scholarship particularly with respect to contributions on the role of the Holy Spirit in Luke–Acts. He pleads guilty:

> As a first conclusion to these pages on the Spirit I note that the number of books published marks the arrival of Pentecostal scholars in the field of New Testament scholarship. As a second conclusion, I regret that I have not investigated whether or not this wave of publication represents true scholarly progress. In my survey published in 1976, I suggested that the study of Lukan pneumatology had reached an end. Was I wrong?[19]

A look at Bovon's journey leads to the following observations:

1. In his 2005 edition, Bovon recognizes the contributions of the following Pentecostal scholars: Roger Stronstad (see 2.1.2), James Shelton (see 2.1.3) and John Michael Penney (see 2.2.1 and 3.2) under the category of Luke and the Holy Spirit, Matthias Wenk under Luke and social justice (see 3.6), and dialogue partners James Dunn (see 2) and Max Turner (see 2.1.6).

2. Since the majority of early contributions by Pentecostals appear not as book length monographs but journal articles, Bovon

---

[18] François Bovon, *Luc le théologien: Vingt-cinq ans de recherches (1950-1975)* (Paris: Delachaux et Niestle, 1978); *Luke the Theologian: Thirty-Three Years of Research (1950-1983)* (trans. K. McKinney; PTMS 20; Allison Park: Pickwick Publications, 1987); *Luke the Theologian Fifty-Five Years of Research (1950-2005)* (3rd edn; Waco: Baylor University Press, 2006).

[19] Bovon, *Luke the Theologian Fifty-Five Years*, p. 540, where he reflects upon his earlier conclusions from 'Orientations actuelles des études lucaniennes', *RTP* 26 (1976), p. 173.

captures only a small percentage of early Pentecostal scholarship. In fact, this is a self-imposed and necessary weakness of his survey. Bovon includes only selective journal articles and admits that any attempt to include the majority of journal articles on Lukan scholarship would be an insurmountable task.[20]

3. But perhaps most importantly, Bovon's statement above symbolizes an academic community now postured for the arrival of Pentecostals. Bovon signals that Pentecostal scholars appear ready to move from the margins to mainstream scholarship.

It is also noteworthy that before their entry into the broader academic marketplace, Pentecostal scholars create their own opportunities through establishment of their own journals. While these journals still provide valuable opportunities for Pentecostal publication (not the least being articles on Luke–Acts), their scholars begin deliberate entry into the broader marketplace and put forward their first substantial contributions to Lukan scholarship outside of the tradition. Indeed, the final quarter of the twentieth century marks the legitimate arrival of Pentecostal scholars in the broader academic world.

TRAJECTORIES OF PENTECOSTAL THEOLOGY IN THE TWENTIETH CENTURY

Before I move to Pentecostal scholarship specifically on Luke–Acts, a look at several general trajectories of Pentecostal theology proves sensible. During the final decades of the twentieth century, Pentecostals begin self-examination of their entry into the academic marketplace. While these insider trajectories do not focus upon Luke–Acts (indeed, this is the gap I attempt to fill), reflections upon the academic emergence of Pentecostals find strong correlation to the evolution of Lukan scholarship. Three scholars from the Church of God (Cleveland, Tennessee) provide an important point of depar-

---

[20] Bovon, *Luke the Theologian Fifty-Five Years*, p. 504. Since the length of the 3rd revised edition comes close to seven hundred pages, Bovon's self-imposed limits affirm that he is not opposed to Pentecostal scholarship or any other tradition. Concerning many of the articles not referenced in this book, he refers readers to *New Testament Abstracts*, the *Elenchus Bibliographicus* of *Biblica*, the *International Zeitschriftenschau für Bibelwissenschaft und Grenzgebiete*, the *Religious Index* online and the Tübingen CD-ROM of Periodicals.

ture. In the inaugural 1992 publication of the *Journal of Pentecostal Theology*, co-editors Steven Land, Rickie Moore, and John Christopher Thomas suggest an outline for the materialization of the broader theological relationship between Pentecostals and the academy. They propose three generations of development.

1. The first generation produces only a few scholars who complete graduate degrees. These Pentecostals work primarily as educators in a Pentecostal environment that does not yet encourage interaction between their faith and critical theological scholarship. Noted conservative scholar Bernard Ramm echoes this typical assessment of the growing Pentecostal movement: '[Pentecostalism] has not been a reflective movement. Little systematic theology has been developed ... The ordinary educational system was very mediocre with some sad results, but programs are improving ... [The Pentecostal Movement] is generally anti-intellectual'.[21] In concert with Land, Moore, and Thomas, Pentecostal theologian Frank Macchia offers a more positive assessment: 'the major purpose of Pentecostal denominational schools has rarely been to produce a body of critical theological scholarship but to train ministers for evangelism and pastoring within the limited confines of denominational priorities and values'.[22] Ramm's statements seem harsh yet, in fairness to Pentecostals describe a Restoration movement in its infancy.

2. The second generation begins to witness Pentecostal ideology and experience as fodder for descriptive historical analyses and/or social scientific study. Pentecostals begin as objects of study rather than contributors to the academic community. The growth of the movement warrants the outside interest of historians, while the nature of Pentecostal experience proves intriguing to social and behavioral scientists. However, Pentecostals

---

[21] Bernard Ramm, 'Varieties of Christian Belief: Acts, Chapter Two', *Eternity* 45 (1982), pp. 45-46. It is also worth noting that in this short synopsis of Pentecostalism, Ramm also identifies the strong connection between Pentecostals and Acts; the movement 'draws its theology from the Gospel of Luke and the book of Acts rather than Paul's great letters' (p. 46).

[22] Frank Macchia, 'The Struggle for Global Witness: Shifting Paradigms in Pentecostal Theology' in *The Globalization of Pentecostalism: A Religion Made to Travel* (ed. Murray Dempster, Byron Klaus and Douglas Petersen; Irvine, CA: Regnum Press, 1999), p. 9.

would not remain the objects of history; this second generation begins to produce the first round of Pentecostal historians. According to Augustus Cerillo and Grant Wacker, while early Pentecostal historians proffer simplistic, one-dimensional, and overly celebratory origins by overstating the providential and supernatural development of the movement, such studies offer a glimpse of the new movement even if through a glass darkly.[23] In other words, Pentecostals begin self-analysis, albeit pre-critical.

3. By the third generation, Pentecostals begin to produce critical theological research across the entire range of theological sub-disciplines.[24] Indeed, the inaugural publication of *JPT* by Sheffield Academic Press heralds the arrival of Pentecostal scholarship. The editors embody a new era where Pentecostals offer fresh insights to old but ever evolving issues including theological method, hermeneutics, ethics, and practical theology. It comes as no surprise that this third stage parallels my location of the beginnings of serious Pentecostal scholarship on Luke–Acts among these theological sub-disciplines. What is more, the editors demonstrate their recognition of the centrality of Luke–Acts; the inaugural editorial includes a commitment for essays in the second or third issues to address Pentecostal responses in Lukan studies to Dunn's *Baptism in the Spirit*.[25]

In 1998, John Christopher Thomas, in his Presidential address for the Society for Pentecostal Studies, adds a fourth and current generation; he observes that the increasing number of Pentecostals in graduate theological training provide new freedom with regard to

---

[23] Augustus Cerillo and Grant Wacker, 'Bibliography and Historiography of Pentecostalism in the United States', *NIDPCM*, pp. 382-405. See also David D. Bundy, 'Bibliography and Historiography of Pentecostalism Outside of North America', *NIDPCM*, pp. 405-417.

[24] Rickie Moore, John Christopher Thomas and Steven Land, 'Editorial', *JPT* 1 (1992), pp. 3-6.

[25] The editors deliver as promised. In the third issue, James Dunn offers a synopsis on the current status of 'Baptism in the Spirit: A Response to Pentecostal Scholarship on Luke–Acts', *JPT* 3 (1993), pp. 3-27. Ensuing responses to Dunn occur in the sixth and seventh issues by William Atkinson, 'Pentecostal Responses to Dunn's *Baptism in the Holy Spirit*: Luke–Acts', *JPT* 6 (1995), pp. 87-131, and 'Pentecostal Responses to Dunn's *Baptism in the Holy Spirit*: Pauline Literature', *JPT* 7 (1995), pp. 49-72.

Pentecostal research. Pentecostal students and scholars benefit not only from a hermeneutical shift from modernity to postmodernity, but also significant demographic increases making them the largest student constituency at many institutions.[26] The explosive growth of Pentecostalism not only produces interest from outside the tradition but also leads to slow but steady development of their scholars from within the young tradition.

Asian scholar Wonsuk Ma suggests a similar trajectory.[27] The first era runs through the late 1970s and is marked by literalistic and apologetic interpretation as well as devotional readings with a strong eschatological/mission impulse. Not surprisingly, Ma cites a personal conversation with Assemblies of God scholar William Menzies who cites Pentecostal dependence upon the Lukan narratives as 'intuitively assumed rather than intelligently argued'.[28] The second era continues through the 1980s and signals the appearance of trained Pentecostal scholars whose works begin to appear in various forums, journals, books, theses, and dissertations. Scholars during this era succeed due to increasing acceptance of narrative for communication of traditions and truth within the broader academic world. Once again, Ma refers to Pentecostal use of the Lukan narratives in order to establish normative practice. The third era marked by the emergence of twenty-first century post-modernity proves opportunistic for Pentecostal scholars. In order to sustain momentum, Pentecostal academicians join scholars across traditional lines and address pressing concerns such as social justice, women in ministry, racial reconciliation, the vibrancy of missions, institutionalization, and ecumenism.

Paul Lewis offers a comparable fourfold reconstruction of the first hundred years:[29]

1. The period of formulation (1901-1929) begins with the events of Topeka and continues to the death of Charles Parham. Pen-

---

[26] John Christopher Thomas, '1998 Presidential Address: Pentecostal Theology in the Twenty-First Century', *Pneuma* 20 (1998), pp. 3-4.

[27] Wonsuk Ma, 'Biblical Studies in the Pentecostal Tradition: Yesterday, Today, and Tomorrow', in *The Globalization of Pentecostalism* (ed. Murray W. Dempster *et al.*; Irvine, CA: Regnum Books, 1999), pp. 52-69.

[28] Ma in conversation with William Menzies (April 5, 1996) in Seoul, Korea.

[29] Paul Lewis, 'Reflections on a Hundred Years of Pentecostal Theology', *CPCR* 12 (February 2003): http://www.pctii.org/cyberj/cyberj12/lewis.html.

tecostals of this period adamantly declare continuity (and restoration) with God's work in the early church and in their day.

2. The period of entrenchment and adaptation (1929-1967) ends with the advent of the Charismatic movement. During these years, Pentecostals such as Myer Pearlman, P.C. Nelson, and E.S. Williams entrench theological endeavors. These three Assemblies of God theologians produce pastoral texts that function more like doctrinal guidebooks; they are generally not interested in critical reflection or contemporary socio-cultural concerns. Once again, an Assemblies of God theologian echoes Lewis' appraisal. Russell Spittler surmises: 'For classical Pentecostals, "systematic theology" is an elegant name for doctrine. And doctrine consists of a concise statement of biblical truth presented in a logical order and marked by gathered scriptural support'.[30]

3. The period of challenge (1967-1984) begins with the Charismatic movement and ends with advent of the Third Wave movement. Lewis cites major challenges to Pentecostals that focus upon key hermeneutical and exegetical passages in Acts by the likes of James Dunn and Frederick Bruner and, on a popular level, John Stott and J.I. Packer.[31] Positively, these challenges pave the way for Pentecostal entry into the intellectual marketplace. Ironically, Pentecostals remain on the margins until forced to begin defense of their theological positions and practices.

4. The period of reformulation (1984-) constitutes a re-envisioning of the Pentecostal movement. Pentecostals begin to produce their own academic journals. They defend, debate, and dialogue across traditions on key issues including the potential for a 'Pentecostal hermeneutic', the challenges of dispensational

---

[30] Russell P. Spittler, 'Theological Style among Pentecostals and Charismatics', in *Doing Theology in Today's World* (ed. John D. Woolbridge and Thomas Edward McComiskey; Grand Rapids: Zondervan, 1991), p. 297.

[31] Dunn, *Baptism in the Spirit*; Frederick Dale Bruner, *A Theology of the Holy Spirit: The Pentecostal Experience and the New Testament Witness* (Grand Rapids: Eerdmans, 1970); John R.W. Stott, *The Baptism and Fullness: The Work of the Holy Spirit Today* (London: Inter-Varsity Press, 1964). See also the later yet popular critiques by J. I. Packer, *Keep in Step with the Spirit* (Old Tappan, NJ: F.H. Revell, 1984) and John MacArthur, *Charismatic Chaos* (Grand Rapids: Zondervan, 1992).

and cessationist theology, and in the arena of Spirit baptism, both initial evidence and the doctrine of subsequence.[32]

When I compare the trajectories by Thomas, Ma, and Lewis, the first two reflect more accurately the developments over the last twenty years. Undoubtedly, while Lukan scholarship within the Pentecostal tradition remains focused upon hermeneutics, cessationism, and questions surrounding Spirit baptism, Pentecostals begin to come of age (see stage 4). Thomas' and Ma's farsighted projections appear closer to the mark, for Pentecostals begin to make inroads beyond their tradition. Concerning all three trajectories, one thing is clear. Given the central role of Luke–Acts in the history of the Pentecostal movement, it is not surprising that these trajectories are generally consistent with the emergence of Luke–Acts scholarship in Pentecostalism. I turn now to the pre-critical stage where Pentecostals solidify their identity via the Lukan narratives.

---

[32] See also the related trajectories of Pentecostal theologizing by Douglas Jacobsen, 'Knowing the Doctrines of Pentecostals: The Scholastic Theology of the Assemblies of God, 1930-1955' (paper presented at the annual meeting of SPS. Guadalajara, Mexico, November 1993) and his *Thinking in the Spirit: Theologies of the Early Pentecostal Movement* (Bloomington: Indiana University Press, 2003); Henry Lederle, *Treasures Old and New* (Peabody: Hendrickson, 1988); and Henry Lederle *et al.*, *What is Distinctive about Pentecostal Theology?* (Pretoria: University of South Africa, 1983). Further resources include Gerald Flokstra, 'Sources for the Initial Evidence Discussion: A Bibliographic Essay', *AJPS* 2 (1999), pp. 243-59; and Walter J. Hollenweger, 'The Critical Tradition of Pentecostalism', *JPT* 1 (1992), pp. 7-17.

HISTORY AND TRAJECTORY OF PENTECOSTAL CONTRIBUTIONS TO LUKE–ACTS RESEARCH

CHAPTER 1

STAGE 1—PRE-1970

PENTECOST HAS COME!
Los Angeles Being Visited by a Revival of Bible Salvation
and Pentecost as Recorded in the Book of Acts ...

THE OLD-TIME PENTECOST.

*This work began about five years ago last January, when a company of
people under the leadership of Chas. Parham, who were studying God's
word tarried for Pentecost, in Topeka, Kan. After searching through the
country everywhere, they had been unable to find any Christians that had
the true Pentecostal power. So they laid aside all commentaries and notes
and waited on the Lord, studying His word, and what they did not understand they got down before the bench and asked God to have wrought
out in their hearts by the Holy Ghost. They had a prayer tower in which
prayers were ascending night and day to God. After three months, a sister who had been teaching sanctification for the baptism with the Holy
Ghost, one who had a sweet, loving experience and all the carnality
taken out of her heart, felt the Lord lead her to have hands laid on her
to receive the Pentecost. So when they prayed, the Holy Ghost came in
great power and she commenced speaking in an unknown tongue. This
made all the Bible school hungry, and three nights afterward, twelve students received the Holy Ghost, and prophesied and cloven tongues could
be seen upon their heads. They then had an experience that measured up
with the second chapter of Acts.*

(William Seymour)[1]

---

[1] William Seymour (ed.), *The Apostolic Faith* 1.1 (Sept. 1906) 1:1-2.

SUNDAY—Bible Classes and Sunday School 9:30 a.m.

Regular Services for worship, preaching and testimony

at 11 a.m., 3 p.m. and 7:30 p.m.

WEEK DAYS—Tuesday, Wednesday, Thursday, and Friday

Bible Study 11 a.m. to 1 p.m. Night meetings 7:30 p.m.

All Day Meeting on the last Thursday of each month

when the ordinances are administered.

On the previous day (Wednesday) we always have a baptismal service.

*In connection with the Mission there are two or three
street meetings every night.*

*In the Sunday morning Bible Class we are going through
the Book of Acts.*

(Stanley Horton)[2]

1.1 ACTS SETS THE STANDARD[3]

The advertisement above comes from the inaugural edition of the
Upper Room published in 1909 and provides a snapshot of the critical importance of Acts for early Pentecostal theology and praxis.
The announcement states the obvious: Sunday preaching 'through
the book of Acts'. However, a close reading of the structure of
their meetings is telling. Renewal meetings include daily instruction,
fellowship, the Lord's Table, conversions, and monthly baptismal

---

[2] The headline of the inaugural issue of *The Upper Room* (June 1909) cited by
Stanley Horton, *Reflections of an Early American Pentecostal* (Baguio City: APTS
Press, 2001), p. 95.

[3] The following three categories (2.1.1–2.1.3) are adapted from Gary McGee's
'Historical Backgrounds', in Stanley Horton (ed.), *Systematic Theology: A Pentecostal
Perspective* (Springfield: Logion Press, 1994), pp. 9-38. McGee also integrates a
number of the works cited below into his own analysis of the initial evidence
debate (Gary McGee [ed.], *Initial Evidence: Historical and Biblical Perspectives on the
Pentecostal Doctrine of Spirit Baptism* [Peabody: Hendrickson, 1991]). See also the
helpful historical trajectory of the role of tongues upon early Pentecostal interpretation by Neil Hudson, 'Strange Words and Their Impact on Early Pentecostals: A Historical Perspective', in Mark J. Cartledge (ed.), *Speaking in Tongues: Multi-
Disciplinary Perspectives* (*Studies in Pentecostal and Charismatic Issues*. Waynesboro: Paternoster Press, 2006), pp. 52-81.

services illustrate deliberate resemblance to the daily routine of the apostolic community described in Acts 2.42-47.[4] In other words, instruction from Acts provides focal practice; in this case, reenactment of the original church. This example serves as one of many representations of the primitivist worldview of early Pentecostals, their attempt to recover the apostolic community in word and deed.[5]

1.1.1 CHARLES PARHAM

Charles Parham, leader of the short-lived Topeka revival of January 1901, stands as an early Pentecostal pioneer to believe that Luke the Evangelist is far more than a historian. The writings of Luke the theologian lead a ragtag band from Kansas on a search for fresh power and experience parallel to that of the apostolic community. When asked about the early days of the revival, Parham offers the following rejoinder: 'For if it is in the Bible, Ye need not believe it, but if it is in the Word of God, Ye *must* receive it'.[6] Using Acts, Parham leads his Bethel Bible School students to seek out and experience tongues as the Bible evidence of the Baptism of the Holy Ghost. In one of the best known stories of Pentecostal origins, Parham provides a first-hand account:

> In December of [1900] we had our examination upon the subject of repentance, conversion, consecration, sanctification and the soon coming of the Lord. We had reached in our studies a problem. What about the 2nd Chapter of Acts? ... having heard so many different religious bodies claiming different proofs as the evidence of their having the Pentecostal Baptism, I set the students at work studying out dilligently [*sic*] what was the Bible evidence of the Baptism of the Holy Ghost.

---

[4] The importance of (Luke-)Acts remains a constant in Pentecostal preaching and teaching. See the recent analysis by Joseph Dutko, 'This-Worldly Explanations for Otherworldly Growth: Vitality in an Ozarks Megachurch' (MA thesis, Missouri State University, 2008). In gathering the passages used for 10 years of preaching at James River Assembly in Springfield, Missouri, Dutko calculates more than one hundred fifty sermons on the Third Gospel and more than seventy on Acts (47).

[5] See Grant Wacker, *Heaven Below: Early Pentecostals and American Culture*. (Cambridge, MA: Harvard University Press, 2001).

[6] Charles Parham in Robert L. Parham (ed.), *Selected Sermons of the Late Charles F. Parham, Sarah E. Parham: Co-Founders of the Original Apostolic Faith Movement* (Baxter Springs, KS: Apostolic Faith Bible College, 1941), p. 93. Original emphasis.

Parham leaves his students with this assignment and sets out for three days of ministry. Upon his return on the morning of the watch night service in 1900, he recalls:

> To my astonishment they all had the same story, that while there were different things [which] occurred when the Pentecostal blessing fell, that the indisputable proof on each occasion was, that they spake with other tongues.[7]

That same night Parham prays over sister Agnes N. Ozman and 'she began speaking in the Chinese language and was unable to speak English for three days'. Only a few nights later, Parham receives his baptism of the Holy Spirit. According to biographer James Goff, Parham 'found that the second floor of the building resembled a veritable 'upper room' with visual, as well as audible, evidences of an Acts 2 outpouring'.[8]

The events of this initial Pentecostal revival evoke commentary on several fronts. First, the recounting of the events: while Parham tells that his students come independently to a unanimous decision about the Bible evidence, in actuality, Parham likely comes to this conclusion sometime in the fall of 1900 and then primes his students toward his conclusions.[9] Second, Parham also concludes that the tongues experienced express *xenoglossa*, real languages previously unknown to the recipient. According to Parham, the same real languages given to the apostles on the Day of Pentecost in Acts 2 in order to evangelize foreign Jews become available to initiate a new wave of world evangelism. In utilitarian fashion, Parham dissects the experience; Spirit-filled recipients need only to identify their language as an affirmation of God's call and move on to the mission field.[10] Finally and perhaps most importantly, while Parham's

---

[7] Sarah E. Parham, *The Life of Charles F. Parham* (Joplin, MO: Tri-State Printing Co., 1930; repr., Birmingham, AL: Commercial Printing Co., 1977), pp. 53-54.

[8] James R. Goff, *Fields White Unto Harvest: Charles F. Parham and the Missionary Origins of Pentecostalism* (Fayetteville: University of Arkansas Press, 1988), p. 67.

[9] Goff, *Fields White Unto Harvest*, p. 67.

[10] Goff, *Fields White Unto Harvest*, pp. 73-74. For example, see Parham's *Everlasting Gospel* (Baxter Springs, Kansas: Apostolic Faith Bible College, 1911) where he states emphatically that Spirit baptism does not produce 'the chattering and jabbering, wind-sucking, holy-dancing rollerism going on over the country, which

concept of 'missionary tongues' fails miserably, his deduction of tongues as the Bible evidence for Spirit baptism prevails. In spite of an otherwise dubious legacy, Parham's recognition of tongues as demonstrable evidence for baptism in the Holy Spirit becomes the norm for Pentecostal theology and experience.[11]

1.1.2 AZUSA STREET

History reveals that the doctrinal impact of the Parham-led Topeka meetings far outweighs any applied impact. While Parham declares the need for worldwide evangelism based upon missionary tongues as the fulfillment of Pentecost, his short-lived Bethel Bible School sends no students to the field. However, Parham's later investment in the life of a young African-American student named William Seymour (while in Houston) produces the spark that leads to the Azusa Street revival in Los Angeles (1906-1909).[12] Seymour, under the short-lived blessing of Parham, becomes leader of a 'Revival of Bible Salvation and Pentecost as Recorded in the Book of Acts' and presumably chief editor of the Azusa Street periodical, *The Apostolic Faith*. Following the opening caption *Pentecost Has Come* (cited above) of the inaugural newsletter in September 1906, Seymour writes: 'Pentecost has surely come and with it the Bible evidences are following: many being converted and sanctified and filled with the Holy Ghost, speaking in tongues as they did on the day of Pentecost'.[13] In this same issue, Seymour (and presumably the leaders of the revival) outlines his position: 'The Baptism with the Holy Ghost is a gift of power upon the sanctified life; so when we get it we have the same evidence as the Disciples received on the Day of Pentecost (Acts 2.34), in speaking in new tongues. See also Acts 10.45,

---

is the result of hypnotic, spiritualistic, and fleshly controls, but a real sane reception of the Spirit in baptismal power, filling you with glory unspeakable and causing you, without any effort, to speak freely in foreign languages' (p. 55).

[11] The young Assemblies of God fellowship rejects an early challenge to tongues as Bible evidence by F.F. Bosworth (see 1.1.2). When the Pentecostal message comes to mainliners in the 1960's, these 'Charismatics' enjoy the intimacy of the Spirit but many chose not to hold to the classical Pentecostal position designated as 'initial evidence'.

[12] The tumultuous relationship between Parham and Seymour is well documented. See Cecil M. Robeck, 'Azusa Street Revival' and 'Seymour, William Joseph' in Stanley Burgess (ed.), *NIDPCM* (Grand Rapids: Zondervan, 2002), pp. 344-50; 1053-58 and his recent history *The Azusa Street Mission and Revival: The Birth of the Global Pentecostal Movement* (Nashville: Thomas Nelson, Inc., 2006).

[13] Seymour, *The Apostolic Faith*, 1.1 (Sept. 1906) 1.1.

46; Acts 19.6'.[14] Still another narrative demonstrates this straight-forward approach:

> In Luke 24.49, Jesus told His disciples to 'Tarry ye in the city of Jerusalem, until ye be endued with power from on high'.

> And being assembled together with them, commanded them that they should not depart from Jerusalem, but wait for the promise of the father, which, saith he, ye have heard of me. For John truly baptized with water, but ye shall be baptized with the Holy Ghost not many days hence. When they therefore were come together, they asked of him, saying, Lord, wilt thou at this time restore again the kingdom to Israel? And he said unto them, It is not for you to know the times of the seasons which the Father hath put in his own power. But ye shall receive power after that the Holy Ghost is come upon you: and ye shall be witnesses unto me both in Jerusalem, and Judea, and in Samaria, and unto the uttermost part of the earth'.—Acts 1.4 -8. They obeyed this command, and Acts 2.4 states, 'And they were all filled with the Holy Ghost, and began to speak with other tongues, as the Spirit gave them utterance'. We see here that they ALL spoke in other tongues.

> If you will now turn to Acts 10 and read the story of Peter and Cornelius, you will see that the speaking in tongues was the sign or evidence to Peter that the Gentiles had received the Holy Ghost. Peter preached the Word, and they were cleansed through the Word, as the disciples before the Day of Pentecost. This was a hard dose for Peter to take, he being a Jew and having been taught that the Gentiles were dogs and unclean. God had previously given Peter a vision of a great sheet let down from heaven, filled with all manner of unclean animals, with the command, 'Rise, Peter, slay and eat'. The preaching of Jesus to the Gentiles was part of the eating, but Peter obeyed, and Pentecostal signs followed (Acts 10.46): 'For they heard them speak with tongues and magnify God'.

> If you will now turn to Acts 19.1-6, you will find that about twenty-nine years after Pentecost, Paul found some disciples at

---

[14] Seymour, *The Apostolic Faith* 1.1 (Sept. 1906) 2.1.

Ephesus that had not received their Pentecost. He preached the Word and explained to them their great privileges in the gospel, 'And when Paul laid his hands upon them, the Holy Ghost came on them: and they spoke with tongues and prophesied' Acts 19.6.

How foolish so many of us have been in the clear light of God's Word. We have been running off with blessings and anointings with God's power, instead of tarrying until Bible evidence of Pentecost came.[15]

According to early Pentecostal evangelist and Oneness advocate Glenn Cook, Seymour referenced Acts 2.4 in every sermon.[16]

In a similar vein, Azusa Street participants promoted Acts as standard. Frank Bartleman publishes *How 'Pentecost' Came to Los Angeles* in 1925.[17] He pieces together notes from his diary as well as various clippings from previous articles to chronicle the events of 1906-1909. One sample from an earlier article first appeared in the *Way of Faith* (August 1, 1906):

'Pentecost' has come to Los Angeles, the American Jerusalem. Every sect, creed, and doctrine under Heaven is found in Los Angeles, as well as every nation represented ... Men are now in trouble of soul everywhere, and the revival with its unusual phenomena is the topic of the day. There is terrible opposition manifested also ... Persecution is strong. Already the police have been appealed to break up the meetings ... We can do little but look on and pray ... Next to old Jerusalem there is nothing like it in the world. (It is on the opposite side, near half way around) ... All nations are represented, as at Jerusalem. Thousands are here from all over the Union, and from many parts of the world,

---

[15] Seymour, *The Apostolic Faith* 1.1 (Sept. 1906) 2.1 in an exhortation entitled 'Tongues as a Sign' (paragraph divisions original). Kenneth Archer refers to this early Pentecostal hermeneutic as the 'Bible Reading Method' ('Early Pentecostal Biblical Interpretation', *JPT* 18 [2001], p. 49. Previously a paper presented at the annual meeting of the Society for Pentecostal Studies. Kirkland, WA, 16-18 March 2000).

[16] Cited by Cecil Robeck in 'Seymour, William Joseph', p. 1055.

[17] Frank Bartleman, *How 'Pentecost' Came to Los Angeles—As It Was in the Beginning* (Los Angeles: the author, 1925). Reprinted first as *Another Wave Rolls In* (Northridge, CA: Voice Publications, 1962) and then as an Azusa Street centennial edition, *Azusa Street: An Eyewitness Account* (Gainesville, FL: Bridge-Logos, 2006).

sent of God for 'Pentecost'. They will scatter the fire to ends of the earth ... Surely we are in the days of restoration, the 'last days', wonderful days, glorious days ... They are days of privilege, responsibility, and peril.[18]

Bartleman situates the revival in continuity not only with the Day of Pentecost in Acts 2, but also the larger scope of Acts, amidst global witness, opposition, and the last days.[19]

Elmer Fisher, founder of the Upper Room Mission, a local Los Angeles church spawned by the revival, writes with a polemical tone. In 'Stand for the Bible Evidence', he states:

We have found the Holy Spirit endorses those who stand for the Bible evidence. The Evidence that is given us in the Word of God will stand. The evidence of the full Pentecostal baptism in the Holy Ghost and fire, according to Acts 2.4 is that they 'Spake in other tongues as the Spirit gave them utterance'. Also in Acts 10.44-48 when the Spirit was poured out upon the gentile converts in the home of Cornelius, the Jews who came in from Joppa with Peter knew that the Holy Ghost had been given to them. 'For (because) they heard them speak with tongues and magnify God'. Again in Acts 19.6 when Paul laid his hands upon the twelve disciples at Ephesus 'The Holy Ghost came upon them and they spake with tongues and prophesied'.

He continues:

Don't allow any of the counterfeits of the Devil or the failures of men to cause you to lower the standard of the Word of God, that those who receive the full baptism of the Holy Ghost will speak in tongues as the Spirit gives utterance, always'.[20]

Undoubtedly, Fisher's comments reflect internal hesitation concerning tongues as initial evidence as early as 1909 at the peak of the

---

[18] Bartleman, *Azusa Street*, pp. 70-71.

[19] In 1915 Bartleman reflects on the revival: 'Nine years ago the Holy Spirit began to lead us into the book of Acts and show us the meaning of that Word that had been hidden since the back sliding of the church in the early centuries' ('Present Day Conditions', *Weekly Evangel* 5 [1915], p. 3).

[20] Elmer Kirk Fisher, *The Upper Room* 1.1 (June 1909), p. 3. The article was reprinted in the June 15, 1909 issue of the *Bridegroom's Messenger*, p. 2. Cited by his grandson, Stanley Horton, *Reflections*, pp. 92-93.

Azusa Street Revival. Fisher relies solely on Acts for his support of Bible evidence.

The marvel of the Azusa Street Mission continues to capture the imagination of Pentecostals. Some forty years after the Azusa Street revival, historian Carl Brumback recounts the providential origin of the Assemblies of God. In the foreword, J. Roswell Flower suggests a rhetorical question: 'Is it possible for the church of the twentieth century to revert to the principles of the church of the first century, and to expect that the miraculous leadership of the Holy Spirit, so explicitly recorded in the Acts of the Apostles, may be realized in the church today?' Brumback boldly proclaims his 'latter rain' answer: 'the church ended in Acts 28, went underground for 1900 years and reemerged at Azusa Street'.[21]

While scholars carry on the debate for the origins of the Pentecostal movement, sociologist Michael Wilkinson presents a compelling argument for the 'Azusa Street Revival'. Wilkinson coins the notion of Pentecostal 'Azusa-ization', a process whereby Pentecostals look for their identity in relation to this historic event.[22] In other words, regardless of the multiple possibilities for the origins of the movement, Pentecostals find at Azusa an archetype. Pentecostals embrace Azusa's Acts-like post-conversion encounter with the Holy Spirit (specifically, Spirit baptism and the gifts of the Spirit). Jesus, the consummate man of the Spirit, serves not only as an example, but also releases this same Spirit upon the church. New and fresh life of the Spirit serves as the foundation for radical Christianity driven by a passion for evangelism at any cost.

1.1.3 EARLY PIONEERS

An early sampling of Pentecostal pioneers illustrates their consistent dependence upon Acts. During these formative years, several prominent pioneers concurrent with the Azusa Street revival demonstrate unswerving loyalty to a Lukan standard. In what may have been the first book-length exposition of a Pentecostal theology,

---

[21] Carl Brumback, *Suddenly … from Heaven: A History of the Assemblies of God* (Springfield, MO: Gospel Publishing House, 1925), p. 6. This language emerges consistently as early and latter rain (see various titles from section 1.1.3).

[22] Michael Wilkinson, 'Religion and Global Flows' in Peter Beyer and Lori Beaman (eds.), *Religion, Globalization and Culture* (Boston: Brill Academic, 2007), pp. 375-89. This view certainly reflects the emergence of North American Pentecostalism.

Pentecostal preacher and an eventual superintendent of the Pentecostal Holiness Church, George Floyd Taylor vigorously defends the new teaching according to the pattern in Acts:

> Look up all the accounts given in Scripture of any receiving the Baptism, and you will not find any other manifestation mentioned on that occasion without the manifestation of tongues ... Show us any other Scriptural manifestation and we will accept it. Show us one account of an apostolic service of which the Book says, 'They were filled with the Holy Ghost, but did not speak with tongues'.[23]

Similarly, Joseph H. King, founder of the Pentecostal Holiness Church, explains:

> The Book of Acts is the only one in the Bible that presents to us the Pentecostal baptism from an historic standpoint; and it gives the standard by which to determine the reality and fullness of the Spirit's outpouring, since in every instance where the Spirit was poured out for the first time this miraculous utterance accompanied the same, so we infer that its connection with the baptism is to be regarded as an evidence of its reception.[24]

Still others relied heavily upon personal testimony to uphold the standard. Popular itinerant evangelist Maria Woodworth-Etter writes her autobiography with the telling co-title of 'Acts of the Holy Ghost'.[25] The lesser-known Evangelist Levi Lupton begins publication of his newsletter *The New Acts* in 1904 only to receive the baptism of the Holy Spirit in December, 1906. In his subsequent publication in February, 1907, Lupton declares its providential title:

---

[23]George Floyd Taylor, *The Spirit and the Bride: A Scriptural Presentation of the Operations, Manifestations, Gifts and Fruit of the Holy Spirit in His Relation to the Bride with special references to the 'Latter Rain' Revival* (Falcon, NC: Falcon Printing Co., 1907), pp. 46-47. Donald Dayton published an edited reprint under the title *Three Early Pentecostal Tracts* (New York: Garland, 1985), p. 46.

[24]J.H. King, 'How I Obtained Pentecost', *A Cloud of Witnesses to Pentecost in India* 2 (September 1907), p. 50.

[25] Maria Woodworth Etter. *Acts of the Holy Ghost or The Life, Work and Experience, of Mrs. M.B. Woodworth-Etter, Evangelist. Complete, Including Sermons* (Dallas: John F. Worley Printing Co., 1912).

The New Meaning of the Name. That which will occupy our columns will be to quite an extent the same as before, and as in this issue, with those large additions of that which we hope will be even more interesting, inspiring, and quickening to all, than that which has formerly appeared in this paper, and which, thank God, can be even more truly and fittingly chronicled under the heading of this paper than anything which we have ever before published. The name which the paper has borne for two years, we have always felt was given us of the Lord, and we are more convinced now than ever, for He, praise his name, foresaw what no man saw at the time.[26]

Lupton locates his fresh experience in the book of Acts, continuous with first century Christianity and available for his readers.

Aimee Semple McPherson, possibly the most popular voice of early Pentecostalism and founding pastor of Angelus Temple in Los Angeles and the (International) Church of the Foursquare Gospel titles a collection of autobiographical experiences, sermons, and writings, *This is That*, reminiscent of Peter's apostolic pronouncement on the Day of Pentecost.[27] She and others contribute regularly to *The Bridal Call*, which McPherson first publishes in 1917. McPherson construes the events at Angelus Temple and the campus of Lighthouse for Foursquare Evangelism Bible College as the re-embodiment of Acts.

How that Day of Pentecost stands out in the history of the Church! We are enthused, filled, thrilled—our hearts are fired as we realize the change that His blessed coming meant. The change in the Apostle Peter exemplifies the transformation that should be wrought in the heart of every believer when the Comforter comes in to abide. He will make a change in the Church, a change in the laymen, in the minister, in the evangelist, in every *one* of us.[28]

---

[26] Levi Lupton, *The New Acts*, Volume III. No. I. Alliance, Ohio (February 1907).

[27] Aimee Semple McPherson, *This is That: Personal Experiences, Sermons, and Writings of Aimee Semple McPherson* (Los Angeles: Echo Park Evangelistic Association, 1923).

[28] The examples are plentiful. See the above example from McPherson's 'The Story of My Life', *The Bridal Call*, (January 1925), pp. 12-13 and (March 1925), pp.

And concurrent with McPherson, Pentecostal educator P.C. Nelson produces his testimony. Autobiographical in nature, Nelson speaks to his Pentecostal experience and calling alongside his reading in Acts.[29]

The above noted testimonies surely carry theological freight. These storytellers encourage their readers/listeners to search the Lukan narratives and discover Pentecostal experience. So also Daniel Kerr, a formative Assemblies of God educator, argues that Luke chooses from a mass of available factual material in order to proclaim the accompaniment of tongues upon baptism in the Holy Spirit. Concerning Acts 2, Kerr writes: 'The 120 believed and, therefore, they spake in other tongues as the Spirit gave them utterance. We also believe, and we speak in other tongues as the Spirit gives utterance'.[30] Kerr continues with what can only be understood as a polemic, 'Is this not an altogether striking characteristic of the book of Acts?'[31]

Similarly, on the other side of the world, Thomas Ball Barratt, the well-known Norwegian Pentecostal pioneer, echoes Kerr's defense:

> But on the DAY OF PENTECOST we notice that they were 'ALL filled with the Holy Ghost, and began to SPEAK WITH OTHER TONGUES, as the Spirit gave them utterance'. Acts 2.4. And this experience was repeated time and again, according to the story in Acts, in the lives of others. Five cases are men-

---

16-19, where the subtitles state: 'Each month, with loving appreciation, thousands look forward to this story of Sister's McPherson's life—a reproduction of *This is That*; and 'God's Pattern for a Model Revival', *The Bridal Call* (February 1929), pp. 7-8, 30, based upon the threefold presentation of Jesus in early Acts via salvation, divine healing and baptism in the Holy Spirit. This exhortation is followed by a McPherson sermon entitled: 'Dorcas' (9-10, 31-32) where McPherson implores her listeners to be a Dorcas, a Peter, or a worker for Christ. See also the following report by Alwyn Greenwalt 'One Heart—One Soul', *The Bridal Call*, (February 1927), pp. 16-17, a comparison of the Fourth Great Foursquare Convention (January 1-10, 1926) to the day of Pentecost and the ensuing expansion of the church.

[29] P.C. Nelson, *Testimony of P.C. Nelson to His Healing and His Baptism in the Holy Spirit* (Enid, OK: Southwestern Press, 1920).

[30] D.W. Kerr, 'The Bible Evidence of the Baptism with the Holy Ghost', *Pentecostal Evangel* 11 (August 1923), p. 2.

[31] Kerr, 'The Bible Evidence of the Baptism with the Holy Ghost', p. 2. Note also an early tract by J.R. Flower, *Is it Necessary to Speak in an Unknown Tongue* (Toronto: Full Gospel Publishing House, n.d.).

tioned. In three of them it is expressly stated that they spoke in tongues on receiving the Holy Spirit. In the other two cases we have no reason to believe that they were an exception to the rule. At Samaria it is said that Simon SAW the effects of the outpouring. They evidently spoke in tongues there as in the other cases mentioned. As concerns Paul and his Baptism of Fire, he says 'I thank my God, I speak with tongues more than ye all'. 1 Cor. 14.18. He of course began to do so, as the others, when he received his Baptism. The ACTS is certainly the best book in the world to explain the Baptism of the Holy Ghost, and in each case mentioned there, they surely spoke in tongues when the FIRE FELL![32]

As Kerr, Barratt, and other early Pentecostals assess key passages in Acts, the force of the biblical data compels them to believe that of all the potential accompanying phenomena, tongues alone provides the visible evidence necessary to authenticate baptism in the Holy Spirit. Over the next half-century, various writers continue the same message. While examples are myriad, two popular preachers/authors capture this sense. Gordon Lindsay writes a five volume series entitled 'Acts in Action', where he consistently reports the connection between first and twentieth century healings, miracles, discipleship, and evangelism.[33] And evangelist T.L. Osborn writes, 'The Book of Acts is the supreme example for us today. We may read inspiring accounts of the ministry of Luther, Whitfield [sic], Moody, and scores of other great men of God, but the Book of Acts is our model'.[34]

Examination of early Pentecostal pioneers reveals that the book of Acts becomes the controlling theological and experiential document through which they read the rest of the Bible. These early Pentecostal writers seldom question whether this approach to the narrative of Acts might be aligned with traditional Protestant her-

---

[32] Thomas Ball Barratt, 'The Baptism of the Holy Ghost and Fire. What is the Scriptural Evidence?' Evangel Tract No. 953 (Springfield, MO: Gospel Publishing House, n.d.), pp. 9-10. See also his *In the Days of the Latter Rain* (London: Simpkin, Marshall, Hamilton, Kent & Co., Ltd., 1909).

[33] Gordon Lindsay, *Acts in Action* (5 vols.; Dallas: Christ For the Nations, 1975).

[34] T.L. Osborn, *3 Keys to the Book of Acts* (Tulsa: T.L. Osborn Publications, 1960), p. 11.

meneutical procedures.[35] At a popular and sermonic level, Acts as a standard for the movement does not wane. They read the Gospels through and in harmony with Acts. The epistles play a secondary and supportive role so that Acts serves as the definitive account of Apostolic Christianity. They find in Acts the necessary and primary narratives for the shaping of belief and practice.[36] As the years go by the fledgling Pentecostal movement begins to mature. Old questions linger and new challenges emerge but one constant remains; with Acts as their standard, Pentecostals march forward. Indeed, debates concerning the Acts narratives continue to produce the standard, even when it means splitting the movement.

1.2   ACTS AS THE CENTER FOR DISSENT

Just as the earliest Pentecostals rely upon Acts to standardize belief and practice, so also during the first decade(s) of institutional existence, Pentecostals turn to Acts to deal with controversy. The experiences of the upstart Assemblies of God (chartered in 1914) represent two such controversies.

1.2.1 THE NEW ISSUE

Before ending their second decade of existence, voracious study of Acts by Pentecostals unearths new theological and practical questions and thereby generates irreparable separation within the infant movement. The name of the first storm, though simple, produces more than a little damage. Deemed the 'New Issue' (1913-1916), this controversy originates amidst restorationist impulses and heavy Christological emphases of the full gospel. News spreads quickly concerning teaching on the nature of water baptism via an international Pentecostal camp meeting at Arroyo Seco (near Los Angeles) in April 1913. Canadian evangelist Robert E. McAlister concentrates on Luke's use of the singular 'in the name of Jesus' for baptisms in Acts (as in 2.38); in contrast to the Trinitarian formula

---

[35] Gary B. McGee, 'Early Pentecostal Hermeneutics: Tongues as Evidence in the Book of Acts' in Gary B. McGee (ed.), *Initial Evidence: Historical and Biblical Perspectives on the Pentecostal Doctrine of Spirit Baptism* (Peabody, MA: Hendrickson, 1991), p. 96.

[36] McGee, 'Early Pentecostal Hermeneutics: Tongues as Evidence in the Book of Acts', p. 30.

founded upon Mt. 28.19-20.[37] McAlister's sermon garners significant response, particularly from his friend Frank Ewart. One year later Ewart preaches his first sermon on Acts 2.38. Based upon a literal reading of Acts, Ewart appeals for baptism and, if necessary, rebaptism in the name of 'Jesus only' and eradication of the historic doctrine of the Trinity.

Ewart becomes an early champion of Oneness theology. His exegesis regarding water baptism proves critical. When addressing the apparent contradiction between the Matthean and Acts accounts, Ewart muses: 'Why is there no mention made of Father, Son, and Holy Ghost, in any formula of baptism known and used by the Apostles?'[38] He retorts: 'If the Apostle Peter did not obey Christ's commandment (Mt. 28.19) on the Day of Pentecost (Acts 2), then it never has been obeyed. If the words of the Master were to be taken as a formula for Christian baptism, then the Acts of the Apostles present one of the most colossal contradictions of history. In that case the church was built on a flagrant act of disobedience'.[39] By implication, Ewart attests to the superiority of Acts when interpreting other passages such as Mt. 28.19. According to Ewart, 'The apostles knew how to interpret Matthew 28.19', namely, on the basis of Acts 2.38. Thus the apostles always baptized in the name of the Lord Jesus, that is, the 'Apostolic' interpretation of Mt. 28.19 (see further section 3.8).[40]

Upon hearing McAlister, African-American Garfield Thomas Haywood becomes another early preacher to adopt the Oneness position. In an attempt to harmonize passages concerning salvation with Acts 2.38, Haywood states: 'It is our purpose to take up the subject from a Bible point of view to see whether there is an experience in the New Testament scriptures, called the birth of the Spirit, aside from the baptism of the Holy Ghost, according to the second chapter of the Acts of the Apostles'.[41] Once again, with

---

[37] See Gary McGee, 'Historical Backgrounds', pp. 18-19.

[38] Frank Ewart, *The Revelation of Jesus Christ* (Portland, OR: Apostolic Book Publishers, n.d.), p. 20.

[39] Ewart, *The Revelation of Jesus Christ*, p. 32 and also *The Phenomenon of Pentecost: A History of the Latter Rain* (rev. edn Hazelwood, MO: Word Aflame Press, 1975), p. 111.

[40] Ewart, *The Revelation of Jesus Christ*, pp. 7, 16, 39.

[41] G.T. Haywood, *The Birth of the Spirit in the Days of the Apostles* (Indianapolis: Christ Temple Book Store, n.d.), p. 5.

Acts as the controlling text, Haywood proceeds. After setting up Mt. 11.28 ('Come unto me all ye that labor and are heavy laden, and I will give you rest') as a reference to new birth (full salvation), Haywood shifts to Isa. 28.11-12 ('For with stammering lips and other tongues will he speak to his people. To whom he said, this is the rest where with ye may cause the weary to rest') and concludes that the 'stammering lips and other tongues' of Acts 2.4 links 'rest' with the baptism in the Holy Spirit as full salvation.[42] In short, if Mt. 11.28 refers to salvation and Isa. 28.11-12 as prophetic fulfillment of the Holy Spirit, then the tongues of Acts 2.4 serve as the fulfillment.[43] For Haywood (and Ewart), an accurate interpretation of Acts returns the church to its original standard; there is no difference between the birth of the Spirit and Spirit baptism.

The end results in a momentous discrepancy. While for Haywood and Ewart, their Oneness understanding of Acts serves not only to recapture an old standard, it also proves schismatic. At the conclusion of the fourth General Council in 1916, the Assemblies of God chooses to part ways with 156 of 585 ministerial delegates. The Oneness debate forces delegates to settle in one of two camps: those who believe that conversion and water baptism according to the Trinitarian formula precede a second experience of empowerment and those non-Trinitarians who maintain that the three elements of repentance, baptism in Jesus' name, and reception of the Holy Spirit (with speaking in tongues) as recorded in Acts 2.38 converge into one act of grace. The centrality of Acts in this controversy cannot be overemphasized. On the one end, Oneness Pentecostals evolve as a result of an 'unbending literalism' marked by their unwillingness to embrace doctrinal statements like that of the Trinity not directly supported by New Testament language (through exact phrases), specifically in Acts.[44] Oneness Pentecostalism materializes at least in part as a rejection of the philosophical language of human creeds that do not express Lukan understanding and language. Kenneth Archer suggests Acts functions as the con-

---

[42] Ewart, *The Revelation of Jesus Christ*, pp. 2-3, 25, 29.

[43] Haywood also looks to the account of the Gentile Pentecost in Acts 10 as a test case for his conclusions.

[44] See Russell P. Spittler, 'Are Pentecostals and Charismatics Fundamentalists? A Review of American Uses of These Categories', in Karla Poewe (ed.), *Charismatic Christianity as a Global Culture* (Columbia, SC: The University of South Carolina Press, 1994), p. 111.

trolling narrative through which early Pentecostals read Scripture. According to Archer, a 'popularistic commonsensical Bible Reading Method' provides theological synthesis between apparently contradictory passages in Acts and other New Testament passages.[45] On this occasion, a seemingly commonsensical reading by proponents of the New Issue causes an irreparable parting of the ways. On the other end, as noted above, the infant Assemblies of God originally formed with little regard for creeds and organization must produce and adopt its own Statement of Fundamental Truths in response to controversy.[46]

1.2.2 TONGUES AND THE BIBLE EVIDENCE

A second controversy strikes due to an attempt to revisit the foundational Pentecostal claim of tongues as Bible evidence for Spirit baptism. Sometime around 1918, Fred Francis Bosworth produces a pamphlet entitled 'Do All Speak in Tongues?' espousing his belief that tongues point to one of many possible indications of Spirit baptism. Bosworth cannot reconcile the separation between tongues as Bible evidence and the gift of tongues according to 1 Corinthians 12.[47] He warns further that 'not one of the inspired apostles or prophets ever taught it, and not one of the world's great soul winners ever taught it'.[48] The controversy comes to a head but also a speedy and peaceful resolution at the 1918 Assemblies of God General Council. In response to Bosworth's contentions, Daniel Kerr rouses the delegates with a convincing sermon; he reproduces the standard position that in every case of Spirit baptism in Acts recipients speak in tongues. Bosworth resigns diplomatically from the Assemblies of God in 1918 and the General Council reaffirms the teaching of the standard setting period.[49] The minutes and resolution reflect the passionate concern of the 1918 General council:

---

[45] Archer, 'Early Pentecostal Biblical Interpretation', p. 61.

[46] David Reed, 'Oneness Pentecostalism', *NIDPCM*, pp. 936-44. See also *'In Jesus' Name': The History and Beliefs of Oneness Pentecostals* (Dorset, England: Deo Publishing, 2007).

[47] F.F. Bosworth, Do All Speak in Tongues? 1 Cor. 12.30. An Open Letter to the Ministers and Saints of the Pentecostal Movement (New York: Christian Alliance Publishing Co., n.d.), p. 5.

[48] Bosworth, *Do All Speak in Tongues?*, pp. 17-18.

[49] McGee, 'Early Pentecostal', p. 110.

The afternoon session was taken up with an animated discussion on the importance of a united stand in the ministry on the truth that the full consummation of the baptism of believers in the Holy Ghost is invariably accompanied with the initial, physical sign of speaking in other tongues as the Spirit of God gives utterance, (Acts 2.4).

Brothers R.A. Brown, Joseph Tunmore, J.T. Boddy, D.W. Kerr, T.K. Leonard, W.H. Pope, J. Rosselli, F.F. Bosworth, W.T. Gaston, and many others took part, and there was the utmost enthusiasm as message after message went forth in defense of what has always been considered the distinctive testimony of the Pentecostal people.

RESOLVED, That this Council considers it a serious disagreement with the Fundamentals for any minister among us to teach contrary to the distinctive testimony that the baptism of the Holy Spirit is regularly accompanied by the initial physical sign of speaking in tongues as the Spirit of God gives the utterance, and that we consider it inconsistent and unscriptural for any minister to hold credentials with us who thus attacks as error our distinctive testimony.[50]

Before moving beyond this period of dissent, it remains judicious to remark upon the important doctrinal shift of William Seymour. Though not as controversial as the Bosworth challenge, Seymour's change of heart reflects the ultimate failure of long term transformation so-desired as a result of Spirit baptism. In the aftermath of the Azusa Street Revival, Seymour changes his position on tongues as the Bible evidence. Note the original Azusa Street position on Spirit baptism according to the Apostolic Faith Papers:

The baptism with the Holy Ghost is a gift of power upon the sanctified life; so when we get it we have the same evidence as the Disciples received on the Day of Pentecost (Acts 2.3, 4), in speaking in new tongues. See also Acts 10.45, 46; Acts 19.6; 1

---

[50] *Minutes of the Sixth Annual Meeting of the General Council of the Assemblies of God in the United States of America, Canada, and Foreign Lands held at Springfield, Missouri Sept. 4-11, 1918* (Springfield, MO: Gospel Publishing House, n.d.), pp. 7-8.

Cor 14.21. 'For I will work a work in your days which ye will not believe though it be told you'.—Hab. 1.5.[51]

Nearly a decade later as pastor of the Azusa Street Apostolic Faith Mission, Seymour drafts the 'Doctrines and Disciplines' in 1915 for his fledgling congregation. Comparable to a local church constitution, Seymour's comments reflect his disappointment. In the fourth amendment, he states:

> The Speaking in tongues being one of the 'signs following' the baptized believers and other evidences of the Bible, casting out devils, healing the sick and with the fruits of the Spirit accompanying the signs (1 Cor. 13; Mark 16.16-19; Acts 2.2-3; Acts 10.44-45-46; Acts 19.6).

Later in the document and under the category of 'Speaking in Tongues', Seymour continues:

> When we set up tongues to be the Bible evidence of baptism in the Holy Ghost and fire only, we have left the divine word of God and have instituted our own teaching … While tongues is one of the signs that follows God's Spirit-filled children, they will have to know the truth and do the truth.[52]

This position is not entirely new. In the September 1907 publication of the Azusa Street papers, Seymour expresses similar tension:

> Tongues are one of the signs that go with every baptized person, but it is not the real evidence of the baptism in the everyday life. Your life must measure with the fruits of the Spirit. If you get angry, or speak evil, or backbite, I care not how many tongues you may have, you have not the baptism with the Holy Spirit. You have lost your salvation. You need the Blood in your soul.[53]

---

[51] First published in *The Apostolic Faith* 1.1 (Sept. 1906) 1:1 and regularly thereafter.

[52] See Larry Martin (ed.), *Doctrines and Disciplines of the Azusa Street Apostolic Faith Mission of Los Angeles, California* (The Complete Azusa Street Library 7; Joplin, MO: Christian Life Books, 2000), pp. 48, 81. In this booklet, Seymour often copies verbatim from the *Doctrines and Disciplines* of various Methodist organizations as well as the 'Thirty-Nine Articles' of the Anglican Church.

[53] Seymour (ed.), *The Apostolic Faith* 1.9 (June to September 1907): 2:1.

Several scholars suggest that in the years following the revival Seymour laments the lack of racial inclusivity and character transformation. In light of such limited change, he moves conclusively to an altered position. Most important concerning this shift may be its minimal sphere of influence. While Bosworth challenges the upstart Assemblies of God, Seymour creates little reaction and continues to minister in relative obscurity. In contrast to Bosworth, Seymour's shift on Spirit baptism creates little reaction. However, the tensions expressed by Seymour and Bosworth persist throughout the twentieth century; Pentecostals return regularly to Acts in order to preserve or challenge the classical Pentecostal position.[54] While the issue of 'Bible Evidence', later termed 'initial evidence', remains essentially untouchable among the clergy, Pentecostal scholars of the ensuing century do not cease to wrestle with the Lukan narratives on this matter (2.2.2.2).[55]

---

[54] Bosworth's resignation leaves little numerical damage. Unlike the Oneness schism, only he and his brother leave the Assemblies of God. For further detail see the following primary sources on the Bosworth/Kerr debate collected in a packet by Gary McGee entitled *Readings on the Doctrine of the Initial Evidence* (Unpublished Text for Assemblies of God Theological Seminary, n.d.). The order of the primary sources cited below follow McGee's outline: E.N. Bell, 'Questions and Answers', *Christian Evangel* (August 9, 1919), p. 5; Aimee Semple McPherson, 'What is the Evidence of the Baptism of the Holy Ghost?' *Pentecostal Evangel* (November 1, 1919), pp. 6-7; Thomas Atterberry, 'They Shall Speak With New Tongues', *Pentecostal Evangel* (December 27, 1919), pp. 2-3; Daniel W. Kerr, 'Not Ashamed', *Pentecostal Evangel* (April 2, 1921), p. 5; 'The Bosworth Meetings', *Pentecostal Evangel* (April 2, 1921), p. 7; E.N. Bell, 'Questions and Answers', *Pentecostal Evangel* (May 28, 1921), p. 10; 'A Return to Pentecost', *Pentecostal Evangel* (September 2, 1922), p. 5; Daniel W. Kerr, 'The Basis for Our Distinctive Testimony', *Pentecostal Evangel* (September 2, 1922), p. 4; Daniel W. Kerr, 'The Bible Evidence of the Baptism with the Holy Ghost', *Pentecostal Evangel* (August 11, 1923), pp. 2-3; Arthur W. Frodsham, 'What Is the Use of Speaking in Tongues?' *Pentecostal Evangel* (August 11, 1923), pp. 6-7; W.T. Gaston, 'The Sign and the Gift of Tongues', *Tract No. 4664* (Springfield, MO: Gospel Publishing House, n.d.); F.M. Moffat, 'All May Speak with Tongues', *Pentecostal Evangel* (March 29, 1924), pp. 6-7; P.C. Nelson, *Did They Speak With Tongues in Samaria?* (Enid, OK: Southwestern Press, 1939). When compared to many short tracts of the day, this work is significantly longer (59 pages).

[55] It should be noted that while tongues as initial evidence function as the majority position among Pentecostals some denominations reject tongues outright or include tongues only as an evidence of Spirit baptism. See the excellent summary by Gary McGee, 'Initial Evidence', *NIDPCM*, pp. 788-90.

1.3 ACTS AND PRESERVATION

As Pentecostals move into the second and third generations, writers begin to school believers into a fuller understanding of Christian and specifically Pentecostal faith. In doing so, Acts remains prevalent. For example, in 1955, the youth department of the Assemblies of God launches a nationwide reading of Acts. Through cooperation with the American Bible Society, the Assemblies of God distributes more than 50,000 free copies of the Book of Acts to some 7000 youth groups around the nation.[56] This initiative illustrates the centrality of Acts for the preservation and perpetuation of classic Pentecostal doctrine and experience. As people of the Spirit, at least two ideals emerge: 1) Pentecostals read Acts through missiological lenses and 2) Pentecostals see the apostles and emerging church of Luke's account as exemplary for contemporary believers and churches. I offer only a small sampling from influential educators and popular ministers on the American and Canadian fronts. At a popular level, the renowned *Revivaltime* speaker, C.M. Ward produces a reflective booklet centering on the ministry of his father, A.G. Ward. The title offers only half of the intent: 'I saw the Holy Spirit move in these meetings ...'; the subtitle reveals continuity with the Acts story—'AN EYEWITNESS REPORT BY ELDER A.G. WARD of occasions when the Holy Spirit came upon the scene and turned church services into repetitions of the Book of Acts. With comments by C.M. Ward'.[57] The younger Ward provides a biographical sketch to promote both continuity with the Acts story and further pursuit of Acts-like ministry.[58]

---

[56] See 'Book of Acts Reading Set on April 24', *Springfield Newsleader* (Sunday, Feb. 20, 1955); also published as 'CA Youth Group to Sponsor Bible Reading Project', *Springfield Advertiser* (Thursday, Feb. 24, 1955).

[57] C.M. Ward, 'I Saw the Holy Spirit Move in These Meetings', *Pulpit Series 22* (Springfield, MO: Assemblies of God, 1956).

[58] See also the earlier work of Robert Chandler Dalton's *Tongues Like As of Fire: A Critical Study of Modern Tongue Movements in the Light of Apostolic and Patristic Times* (Springfield: Gospel Publishing House, 1945). Dalton includes a chapter on pre-twentieth century outbreaks of glossolalia among the Cevenal Prophets, the Camisards, and the Irvingites before embarking on a short historical synopsis on the role of Pentecostal tongues in the early part of the twentieth century. Dalton also includes a personal chapter entitled: 'My Own Personal Contact with the Glossolalia Phenomenon' where he states 'I received the promise of the Father spoken of in the Book of Acts *with like signs* ... As to the *power* it gives I can assuredly testify' (p. 52, original emphasis).

Among Assemblies of God educators, Myer Pearlman proposes a general missiological reading of Acts. He outlines the New Testament books as follows: 1) The Gospels—a manifestation of our salvation; 2) Acts—propagation of our salvation; 3) Doctrinal Books—explanation of our salvation; and 4) Revelation—consummation of our salvation.[59] Pearlman also proceeds to break Acts into three parts: '1) ascension; 2) descension; and 3) extension'. Following the ascension, Jesus pours out the promised Holy Spirit, and sets in motion the powerful proclamation of Jesus to the ends of the earth.[60] E.S. Williams, one-time general Superintendent of the Assemblies of God, repeatedly examines biblical texts as a template for contemporary Pentecostal believers. In a collection of sermons on the Gospels and Acts, several titles require only minimal commentary: in 'Two Demonstrations of Self (Lk. 15.11-32)', Williams challenges listeners to locate their lives with one of two sons in Luke's parable of the prodigal son; in 'A Model Prayer Meeting (Acts 1.12-14)', Williams offers principles and postures for prayer; in 'Points in Pentecostal Preaching (Acts 2.14-21)', he establishes Peter's Pentecost speech as a model sermon; and in 'Prevailing Qualities in God's House', an exposition of Acts 4.23, Williams presents the young church at Jerusalem as a model for today.[61] Finally, by way of a series of articles in the *Pentecostal Evangel*, Alice E. Luce, Assemblies of God missionary to India and later to Hispanics in America, suggests a specific Pentecostal strategy for world missions based upon 'Paul's Missionary Methods'.[62]

On the Canadian front, the official organ of the Pentecostal Assemblies of Canada, *The Pentecostal Testimony* regularly highlights this paradigmatic dynamic. In 1951, an unidentified writer serves as an example:

> Each of us as individual Christians, however, would do well to read again the book of Acts to see how the Holy Spirit actually operated when He first took His place in the lives of those who

---

[59] Myer Pearlman, *Through the Bible Book by Book: New Testament Gospels and Acts—Part III* (Springfield, MO: Gospel Publishing House, 1935), p. 5.

[60] Pearlman, *Through the Bible Book by Book*, p. 58.

[61] E.S. Williams, *My Sermon Notes: The Gospels and Acts* (Springfield, MO: Gospel Publishing House, 1967), pp. 101, 178, 186, 190.

[62] Alice Luce, 'Paul's Missionary Methods', *Pentecostal Evangel* (January 8, 1921), pp. 6-7; (January 22, 1921), pp. 6, 11; (February 5, 1921), pp. 6-7.

received Jesus Christ as Saviour. Then we would do well to lay aside all preconceived notions as to how we think He ought to operate, and ask the Lord Jesus Christ to show us exactly how He wants the Holy Spirit to operate in us. In this exercise we would do well to follow the scriptural injunction 'to tarry'— taking time before God in order to be so completely yielded to His will.[63]

Still in *The Pentecostal Testimony*, Aaron Lindford reflects on the events of the day of Pentecost and correlates the validity of scriptural authority and historical precedent:

And of this baptism Peter says, 'This is that'. The experience they had just received was in harmony with the words of the prophet Joel. The baptism of the Holy Spirit is not merely pragmatic, it is dogmatic. True Pentecost is doctrinally sound. The 'thisness' of experience and the 'thatness' of exposition go together. We must not stress the 'thisness' at the expense of the 'thatness'—that borders on existentialism, making subjective feeling the criterion. Nor must we emphasize 'thatness' and omit 'thisness'—that is arid dogmatism. We must have both: an experience that has for its centre the grace of God, and for its circumference the revealed word.[64]

Linford's emphasis upon the Pentecost narrative as paradigmatic for contemporary experience must not be missed; Pentecostals clearly desire to see their own reflection on the pages of Acts.

Similarly, Canadian educator Karel Marek implores Pentecostals to live according to 'Acts Chapter 29'. The subtitle sets up his thesis: 'In case you hadn't noticed recently there are only 28 chapters recorded in the Book of Acts in your Bible'.[65] In his opening paragraph with vintage Pentecostal exhortation, he declares: 'I've frequently heard of churches with a desire to 'write' Acts chapter 29. Is it not the dream of every preacher? Is this not what the world

---

[63] Author Unidentified, 'Signs and Wonders: Can the Present Church Fight the Increasing Antichristian Forces with Less Power than the Apostles of Old?' *Pentecostal Testimony* 32 (1951), p. 3.

[64] Aaron Linford, 'The Initial Sign', *The Pentecostal Testimony* 54 (1973), p. 3.

[65] Karel Marek, 'Acts 29', *The Pentecostal Testimony* 70 (December 1989), p. 24. Notice the date for Marek's article. The primary focus upon Luke–Acts as mandate and paradigm for missions in popular pastoral and homiletical literature remains strong into the present.

needs to see?' To encourage a person/church in the writing of Acts 29, Marek weaves a connection among three words in Acts: witness, Pentecost, and prayer. In order to write additional chapters to Acts, he believes churches must start with the prayers in the upper room (Acts 1). Witness as displayed from Acts chapters 2-28 follow Pentecost (Acts 2), and, of course, Pentecost repeats only through prayer (back to Acts 1).[66]

Finally, Canadian minister David Slauenwhite produces a popular pamphlet sponsored by the Pentecostal Assemblies of Canada. In prime Pentecostal fashion, Slauenwhite links Luke's first century missionary mandate to the contemporary Pentecostal mission:

> The marks of a Pentecostal church are therefore clear. Prayer is our atmosphere and is done in the Spirit with intercession for souls. Holy living is our calling, through a Spirit-filled life meant to be a witness that Jesus saves. Preaching is our method, under the anointing of the Spirit, with an evangelistic intent. Manifestations of the Spirit's presence and demonstration of His giftings are expected and encouraged, so that we may effectively reach others with the gospel.[67]

Collectively, these writers offer a consistent message. They implore Pentecostals to view not only the Lukan stories but often their own lives as 'living texts', models for a contemporary Pentecost and the ensuing results.[68]

Emphasis upon the unfinished Lukan drama continues into the Charismatic Tradition. Episcopal pioneer Dennis Bennett aptly entitles his autobiography *Nine O' Clock in the Morning* based upon Acts 2.15 and links both his experience and the emerging Charismatic movement with the Lukan narrative: 'the Acts of the Apostles ... has no conclusion'. Following narration of his participation in the Charismatic renewal, he continues: 'the last chapter of this book, too, like Acts 28, must finish open-ended'.[69] Publications for the

---

[66] Marek, 'Acts 29', p. 24.

[67] David Slauenwhite, *Fresh Breezes: An Historical Perspective on the Pentecostal Assemblies of Canada* (Mississauga: PAOC Dept. of Spiritual Life, 1996), p. 12.

[68] See also the work of the influential British Assemblies of God theologian Donald Gee, *Pentecost* (Springfield, MO: Gospel Publishing House, 1932).

[69] Dennis Bennett, *Nine O' Clock in the Morning* (South Plainfield, NJ: Bridge Publishing Inc., 1970), p. 198. Bennett appropriately titles the final chapter of his book: 'Acts Twenty-Eight'.

Episcopal Charismatic Fellowship as well as testimonies of Charismatic Baptists, and Charismatic Nazarenes express similar sentiment. *Acts 29: Where we are now in the Continuing Acts of the Holy Spirit*, *The Acts of the Holy Spirit among the Baptists Today*, and *The Acts of the Holy Spirit among the Nazarenes Today* respectively rely upon the Acts story and thereby offer testimonies to articulate and extend charismatic experience.[70] Still other publications include David Womack's *ReACTion* newsletter in 2001 with the subtitle: 'A Quarterly Newsletter Calling for a Fresh Revival of Book-of-Acts Christianity'[71] and *Acts: Today's News of the Holy Spirit's Renewal (Los Angeles)* by a Charismatic network. In the inaugural year of publication, the editor states:

> Comparing the New Testament Church with ours it seems obvious to us that one of two things must have happened. Either God deliberately deprived the Church of the power of Pentecost, with its supernatural gifts and powers, or else the church has somehow lost contact with Pentecost as a vital continuing experience.[72]

As the years go by, Pentecostal scholars also offer analytical reflection on such sermons, testimonies, autobiographies, and publications. Their conclusions reveal significant consistency; Pentecostals reinforce their identity and desire ongoing extension of Acts-like ministry. Church of God (Cleveland, TN) scholar, Steven Land identifies 'Pentecostal Spirituality' as a metaphor for journey. According to Land, the people of God are not yet where and what they ought to be; therefore, communicators use testimonies and

---

[70] The *Acts 29 Newsletter: Where we are Now in the Continuing Acts of the Holy Spirit*. The Episcopal Charismatic Fellowship publishes their inaugural conference report in 1973 and continues publishing the newsletter/bulletin through the mid 1990's. *The Acts of the Holy Spirit among the Baptists Today* (Los Angeles: Full Gospel Business Men's Fellowship International, 1971); *The Acts of the Holy Spirit among the Nazarenes Today* (Los Angeles: Full Gospel Business Men's Fellowship International, 1973).

[71] Editor David Womack continues with sporadic publications of *ReACTion: A Quarterly Newsletter Calling for a Fresh Revival of Book-of-Acts Christianity* 1-6 (2001-2006).

[72] *Acts: Today's News of the Holy Spirit Renewal* (Los Angeles: Acts Publishers). First published in 1967, this periodical includes contributing editors such as David DuPlessis, Larry Christenson, and Gerald Derstine. Foreign editors also come from the likes of Norway, Canada, Italy, Japan, Sweden, and New Zealand.

rhetoric to evoke an ever-fresh sense of adventure.[73] Similarly, Assemblies of God scholar Amos Yong reiterates the Pentecostal approach to Lukan story: 'the church faithfully improvises the performance of the twenty-ninth chapter of Acts in times and places far removed from Theophilus's original situation'.[74] Finally, while Pentecostals certainly embrace continuation of the Lukan story for the purpose of identity and extension, the concept certainly extends beyond their domain. For example, Yong references the work of the influential N.T. Wright. While not in the Pentecostal/Charismatic tradition, Wright compares the church's performance of the scriptural narrative to a group of actors' performance of an unwritten fifth act of a Shakespearean play with a four act script.[75] In short, though Pentecostals are not alone in their pursuit of preservation and extension of the Lukan story, Pentecostal scholars correctly link success to the maximization of this impulse.

1.4 SUMMARY

Kenneth Archer, in an essay on Pentecostal hermeneutics, offers a synopsis of Pentecostal interpretation reminiscent of the trajectory thus far:

> Once again, the book of Acts became the controlling theological document through which the rest of the Bible was read because Acts was the definitive account of apostolic Christianity. The Gospels were extremely important but they would be read through and in harmony with the Book of Acts. Hence, in early Pentecostal communities the Book of Acts and the Gospels

---

[73] Steven J. Land, *Pentecostal Spirituality: A Passion for the Kingdom* (JPTSup 1; Sheffield: Sheffield Academic Press, 1997).

[74] Amos Yong, *Hospitality & the Other: Pentecost, Christian Practices, and the Neighbor* (Maryknoll, NY: Orbis Books, 2008), p. 55.

[75] N.T. Wright, *The New Testament and the People of God* (Minneapolis: Fortress, 1992), pp. 140-43. See also Floyd Filson, 'Journey Motif in Luke–Acts', in *Apostolic History and the Gospel* (ed. W. Gasque and R. Martin; Exeter: Paternoster, 1970), pp. 68-77; Nicolas Lash, 'Performing the Scriptures', *Theology on the Road to Emmaus* (London: SCM, 1986), pp. 37-46; the work of Lash's student, Keith Vanhoozer, *The Drama of Doctrine: A Canonical-Linguistic Approach to Christian Theology* (Louisville: Westminster John Knox, 2005), chapters 6-7, and the recent work of Paul Borgman, *The Way according to Luke: Hearing the Whole Story of Luke–Acts* (Grand Rapids: Eerdmans, 2006).

were the primary narratives in shaping of Pentecostal belief and practice. The Epistles played a secondary and supportive role. Therefore, it was important to know which biblical book or passage has the final word on any given topic when one 'interpreted scripture in light of scripture'.[76]

Similarly, Assemblies of God historian Gary McGee argues that the pre-critical era produces at least two constants. Pentecostal conviction concerning the theological import of the Acts narrative leads to the following conclusions: 1) witness, testimony, and experience must replicate the early church; and 2) creedal statements, particularly cardinal doctrines, rely heavily on the early readings in Acts.[77] Luke–Acts surely stands as central to the standardization and preservation of Pentecostalism.

Before moving beyond this inaugural era, I offer the following transitional observations. On the one hand, Pentecostals of the pre-critical era feel little compulsion to defend Christianity in general or Pentecostalism specifically from attack by outsiders.[78] Pentecostals generally steer clear of the debate concerning the historicity of Luke–Acts that occupies center stage through the first half of twentieth century scholarship. They believe in the historical reliability of the virgin birth, the miracles of Jesus, and a bodily resurrection and ascension of Jesus. Douglas Jacobsen captures the standardizing and preservationist motivation of early Pentecostals. Speaking of early leaders like Myer Pearlman and E.S. Williams, Jacobsen surmises:

> [They] were not trying to defend the theological past either of their own fellowship or of Christianity in general from attack by outsiders; nor were they trying to adjust pentecostal faith to some one or another already established system of thought from

---

[76] Archer, 'Early Pentecostal Biblical Interpretation', p. 69.

[77] McGee, 'Initial Evidence', *NIDPCM*, pp. 789-90.

[78] Note the following exception by British Pentecostal Donald Gee. His tract on the initial evidence for Spirit baptism published by Gospel Publishing House in the early 1930's garners a response from then popular non-Pentecostal writer John R. Rice. In a chapter entitled 'Tongues Not the Bible Evidence', Rice sets out to refute Gee's tract. Rice's response serves as a microcosm of a kind of Pentecostal/non-Pentecostal soliloquy that took place through the 1960's. Donald Gee, 'The Initial Evidence of the Baptism in the Holy Spirit', Evangel Tract No. 961 (Springfield, MO: Gospel Publishing House,) and John R. Rice *Speaking in Tongues* (Wheaton, IL: Sword of the Lord, n.d.).

'outside' the pentecostal world (e.g., fundamentalism). Instead, they were in their own eclectic ways trying to organize pentecostal belief for the first time ... They were seeking to create a distinct middle-of-the-road blend of theology in the textbooks they were writing that could be used to school pentecostals into a more mature and ecumenically orthodox, but still clearly pentecostal understanding of the Christian faith.[79]

Jacobsen's synopsis certainly resonates with the exegetical intentions behind early analyses of Luke–Acts. While Pentecostals would eventually discover the value of the historical critical method, their earliest works remain primarily homiletical/devotional in character.

On the other hand, around mid-century, Pentecostals begin to take stock of outsider opinions and take advantage of an opportunity to forge a new alliance with burgeoning Evangelicals.[80] Many third generation Pentecostals welcome this opportunity and sense little or no risk. Though they would cling to the watchword, 'cooperation without compromise', Pentecostals do indeed fall prey to various methodologies and values of the older more organized and articulate Evangelical movement. The absence of Pentecostal graduate schools or seminaries forces budding Pentecostal scholars to attend Evangelical educational institutions and thereby produce not only rapid engagement but often convergence of Evangelicalism with western Pentecostalism. The new and *bona fide* generation of Pentecostal scholars relies heavily on the Lukan narratives in order to maintain its identity. However, these same scholars go beyond their predecessors; they seek to display the Pentecostal worldview on the larger academic stage.

---

[79] Douglas Jacobsen, 'Knowing the Doctrines', p. 19. See further his insightful conclusions concerning Pentecostal theology and exegesis in *Thinking in the Spirit*, pp. 353-64.

[80] The Evangelicals become the first group to consider the vitality of Pentecostals and invite partnership with them. An official cooperation begins with the formation of the National Association of Evangelicals in 1942. Pentecostal groups with immediate interest include Pentecostal Holiness Church, Open Bible Standard Churches, Church of God (Cleveland, TN), Assemblies of God and Pentecostal Assemblies of Canada. On the origins and impact of the Pentecostal alliance with the National Association of Evangelicals, see Cecil Robeck, 'National Association of Evangelicals', *NIDPCM*, pp. 922-25.

CHAPTER 2

STAGE 2—THE DUNN FACTOR: PENTECOSTALS ENTER THE INTELLECTUAL MARKETPLACE

> *Watch out you evangelicals—the young Pentecostal*
> *scholars are coming ...*
> *St. Luke does support a charismatic theology and religion.*
> *Some of our best people, like Dale Bruner and James Dunn, have tried*
> *to impose their reading of Paul upon Luke's writings and*
> *have distorted it.*
> *Ironically, there is greater diversity in the New Testament*
> *than even Jimmy Dunn is prepared to grant! ...*
> *The theologies of Luke and Paul are complementary to each other*
> *but must not be confused as being identified in the usual way ...*
> *Luke must not be imprisoned in one room of the Pauline house.*
> *(Clark Pinnock)*[1]

Russell Spittler captures the trajectory of early Pentecostalism by way of the following summary: 'Surely it can be argued that the term "Pentecostal studies" is a contradiction in terms ... Pentecostals have made better missionaries than theologians. They write pamphlets, not books—tracts, not treatises. When a Pentecostal book is published, it will reflect more likely personal testimony than reasoned argument'.[2] But winds of change eventually begin to blow. Given the steady growth of Pentecostalism as well as the burgeon-

---

[1] Clark Pinnock in the Foreword to *Charismatic Theology*, by Roger Stronstad (Peabody: Hendrickson, 1984), p. vii.

[2] Russell P. Spittler, 'Suggested Areas for Further Research in Pentecostal Studies', *Pneuma* 5 (Fall 1983), p. 39.

ing Charismatic movement of the 1960's, a young upstart doctoral student takes notice: 'Since 1960 Pentecostal teaching has been making a significant penetration in older denominations. Taken together, these facts make imperative a close study of the distinctive Pentecostal doctrines'.[3] James Dunn creates unforeseen possibilities for Pentecostal scholarship through the 1970 publication of his doctoral thesis entitled *Baptism in the Spirit*. Ironically, Pentecostals receive a monumental boost in spite of Dunn's critique of the classic Pentecostal view of Spirit baptism in Luke–Acts. In fact, Pentecostals continue to find no dialogue partner more provocative and stimulating than Dunn. Initial responses to Dunn significantly shape the context for the coming out of Pentecostal scholarship in the 1970's and 1980's. This dialogue remains well rehearsed for Dunn's efforts on Luke–Acts quickly become the premier voice of the non-Pentecostal Evangelical community and thereby thrust Pentecostals into the academic marketplace.[4]

Though Dunn applauds Pentecostals for drawing attention to Luke's emphasis upon Spirit baptism and rediscovery of Spirit experience, Dunn concludes that 'the gift of the Spirit is the most fundamental aspect of the event or process of becoming a Christian, the climax of conversion-initiation'.[5] Pentecostals respond with routine criticism for Dunn's reading of Luke–Acts through Pauline lenses. Ironically, Dunn, a champion of 'diversity within unity' in his own right, must listen to a constant refrain: the different emphases of different New Testament writers should not be homogenized and flattened to produce a uniform pneumatology (see Pinnock above). Several of Dunn's fundamental arguments arouse ongoing responses from Pentecostals. He claims that Jesus' baptism is not primarily an anointing of power; but rather marks Jesus' initiation into the new age. The Jordan anointing serves as the pivotal introduction of a new epoch in salvation history, the beginning of the

---

[3] James D.G. Dunn, *Baptism in the Holy Spirit*, p. 3.

[4] Surveys of the dialogue between Dunn and Pentecostals in order of appearance include: the two part response by William Atkinson, 'Pentecostal Responses to Dunn's *Baptism in the Holy Spirit*: Luke–Acts' and 'Pentecostal Responses to Dunn's *Baptism in the Holy Spirit*: Pauline Literature'; Frank Macchia, 'Salvation and Spirit Baptism: Another Look at James Dunn's Classic', *Pneuma* 24 (2002), pp. 1-6 and Kenneth J. Archer, 'Pentecostal Hermeneutics: Retrospect and Prospect', *JPT* 8 (April 1996), pp. 63-81.

[5] Dunn, *Baptism in the Holy Spirit*, p. 4.

messianic era. Similarly, the events on the day of Pentecost serve as an initiation for the disciples.[6] For Dunn, baptism in the Spirit refers to an initiatory experience, the means by which one enters into the new age. His view is deemed by many, particularly Pentecostals, as a form of illegitimate identity transfer that attempts to harmonize Lukan and Pauline pneumatology.

Dunn's reading of Luke–Acts spawns at least in part the work of five Pentecostal scholars who become constrained to respond: Gordon Fee, Roger Stronstad, Howard Ervin, James Shelton, and Robert Menzies. These critics challenge Dunn's methodology and seek to interpret Luke as a theologian in his own right, thereby highlighting Luke's distinctive contribution to a New Testament theology of the Spirit. Dunn's sympathies to Pentecostal experience continue to produce ongoing dialogue but with little movement. In 1970, he states: 'while the Pentecostal's belief in the dynamic and experiential nature of Spirit-baptism is well founded, his separation of it from conversion-initiation is wholly unjustified'.[7] In 1998, though Dunn offers the following reflection: 'I would hardly have imagined that a technical Ph.D. thesis would be of such interest to a wider Christian world, and even more astonished to learn that it could still be of such interest more than a quarter of a century later',[8] his initial position remains unchanged: 'To insist that the recognition of biblical diversity requires us to narrow Luke's concept of the Spirit to that of charismatic phenomena, or even engracing for witness, would be to transform a Lukan emphasis into a dogmatic distinction, indeed, into a differing Spirit'.[9] Though Dunn re-

---

[6] Dunn, *Baptism in the Holy Spirit*, pp. 23-32 and 40-41. See also *Jesus and the Spirit: A Study of the Religious and Charismatic Experience of Jesus and the First Christians as Reflected in the New Testament* (Philadelphia: Westminster Press, 1975).

[7] Dunn, *Baptism in the Spirit*, p. 4.

[8] Dunn, ''Baptism in the Spirit ... yet once more.' Paper presented at the European Pentecostal Theological Association Conference. Mattersey Hall, England 1998. *EPTA* 18 (1998), p. 3. Keith Hacking, a recent student of Dunn, reaches conclusions similar to his mentor in *Signs and Wonders, Then and Now: Miracle-Working, Commissioning and Discipleship* (Nottingham: Apollos/IVP, 2006). Robert Menzies suggests Hacking's critique of the Third Wave is reminiscent of Dunn's earlier critique of Pentecostal exegesis (Review of Keith Hacking, *Signs and Wonders, Then and Now: Miracle-Working Commissioning, and Discipleship, Evangelical Quarterly* 79.3 [2007], pp. 261-65).

[9] Dunn, 'Baptism in the Spirit: A Response to Pentecostal Scholarship on Luke–Acts', *JPT* 3 (1993), p. 26. See further Dunn's 'Spirit-Baptism and Pentecos-

mains resolute, the cumulative effects of his conclusions lead to the emergence of an initial scholarly awakening for Pentecostalism.[10]

2.1 RESPONSES

2.1.1 GORDON FEE

In the post-1970 era, there is no Pentecostal scholar who addresses the broader academic world more prolifically than Gordon Fee. I place Fee at this juncture not because he offers direct response to Dunn but because his exegesis serves also to stimulate a wide range of scholarship to this day. In the same way Dunn serves as a premier voice of Evangelicals to Pentecostals, Fee serves as the initial academic voice of Pentecostals to Evangelicals. The first world-class Pentecostal scholar to experience substantial acceptance within the academic world, Fee celebrates the ability of Pentecostals to recapture for the church the empowering dimension of life in the Spirit. However, Fee's scholarly relationship with his Pentecostal friends remains consistently tumultuous. On the one hand, his reading of the Acts narrative leaves him at best cautious concerning classical Pentecostal attempts to advance beyond patterns to normative Christian experience. According to Fee, Pentecostal insistence upon 'separability and subsequence' concerning conversion and Spirit baptism via tongues takes the Lukan narratives too far. In an article so titled, he states: 'Pentecostals are generally right on bibli-

---

talism.' *Scottish Journal of Theology* 23 (1970), pp. 397-407 and *Unity and Diversity in the New Testament: An Inquiry into the Character of Earliest Christianity* (3d edn; London: SCM Press, 2006).

[10] Note also that Dunn's commentary (*The Acts of the Apostles* [ECS; Valley Forge: Trinity Press International, 1996]) offers no recognition of his dialogue with Pentecostals and garners virtually no attention from Pentecostal scholars. Pentecostals in conversation with Dunn do so primarily via ongoing response to *Baptism in the Spirit*.

Also noteworthy is the work of Bruner, *A Theology of the Holy Spirit*, p. 92. While not as important in the ongoing conversation, he offers similar objections. He states: 'A principle error of Pentecostalism ... is the conviction that the gospel is sufficient for the beginning but not for the continuing of the Christian life, for bringing the Holy Spirit initially but not fully.' He cites inconclusive evidence for the subsequent nature of Spirit baptism by noting Pentecostal reliance upon four Lukan stories and warns against attempts at symmetry. See also a similar critique in the popular work of John Stott (*Baptism and Fullness*): 'Some Christians give the impression that they hold a kind of 'Jesus Plus' doctrine, namely, 'You have to come to Jesus, which is fine; but now you need something extra to complete your initiation' (p. 10).

cally as to their experience of the Spirit. Their difficulties arose from the attempt to defend it biblically at the wrong point'.[11] He states elsewhere:

If in his attempt to recapture this New Testament pattern, the Pentecostal saw the dynamic element as 'distinct from and subsequent to', he should not thereby be faulted. The fault perhaps lay with the church which no longer expected or experienced life in the Spirit in a dynamic way.[12]

In short, Fee embraces Pentecostal experience but remains cautious as to normative applications based upon the Lukan narrative. On the other hand, Pentecostal scholars owe Fee a debt of gratitude for his ability to provoke new awareness of hermeneutical issues. While many Pentecostals continue to take considerable exception to Fee's limited employment of historical precedent, Fee stands beside Dunn in forging a path that directs Pentecostals into the academic marketplace. As Pentecostals debate with Fee and garner success for larger hermeneutical possibilities, they begin to employ far more sophisticated and scholarly arguments for their cause than their predecessors.[13]

---

[11] Fee, 'Baptism in the Holy Spirit: The Issue of Separability and Subsequence', *Pneuma* 7 (1985), p. 89. Originally presented at the annual meeting of the Society for Pentecostal Studies, Boston, MA, November 1984. Fee's reference to the church implicates the global ecclesial body at the turn of the twentieth century.

[12] Fee, 'Hermeneutics and Historical Precedent: A Major Problem in Pentecostal Hermeneutics', in Russell P. Spittler (ed.), *Perspectives on the New Pentecostalism* (Grand Rapids: Baker, 1976), p. 122. Similar exegetical elements of this thesis appear in 'Acts: The Question of Historical Precedent', a chapter in the influential volume co-authored with Douglas Stuart, *How to Read the Bible for All Its Worth* (Grand Rapids: Zondervan, 1981). This work, now in its third edition, remains in print.

[13] Bradley Truman Noel, 'Gordon Fee and the Challenge to Pentecostal Hermeneutics: Thirty Years Later', *Pneuma* 26 (2004), pp. 79-80. Craig Keener's work on Luke–Acts also deserves mention in this context. He indicates his respect for and basic agreement with Fee's work on Pauline pneumatology (*God's Empowering Presence: The Holy Spirit in the Letters of Paul* [Peabody: Hendrickson, 1994]), but shifts his attention to the Gospels and Acts. Like Fee, Keener also finds Spirit empowerment subsequent to conversion, but suggests that the emphasis may rest less on the initial crisis experience than ongoing Spirit-enablement (*The Spirit in the Gospels and Acts: Divine Purity and Power* [Peabody: Hendrickson, 1997], pp. 4-5). With Pentecostal roots in the foreground, Keener recognizes not only reception of the Spirit at conversion but also sudden inspirations of the Spirit for voca-

2.1.2 ROGER STRONSTAD

Roger Stronstad produces the first work by a classical Pentecostal to be taken seriously by non-Pentecostal Lukan scholars. Stronstad builds upon methodological advances that take shape in the 1970's. By pressing for a fresh critical approach to Luke–Acts, he sets the stage not only for his scholarly career but also a generation alongside him. Stronstad suggests Luke's complex purpose includes specific interest in the life of the Spirit. A pioneer in Pentecostal scholarship, Stronstad advances Luke's purpose beyond the historical dimension to include didactic and theological dimensions. Thus, Luke writes not only 'to narrate the events relating to the origin of Christianity and its spread in a sweep northwest to Rome' but also to 'instruct Theophilus and every other reader who will subsequently make up his audience'.[14] Luke complements the historical dimension with a theological one, a narrative designed to offer instruction on matters such as christology, soteriology, missiology, and most important for Pentecostals, pneumatology.[15]

His most enduring work, *The Charismatic Theology of St. Luke*, published in 1984, remains in print to this day.[16] While not a direct response to Dunn, Stronstad challenges Dunn's conclusions. Stronstad notes Paul's singular use of the phrases 'baptism in the Spirit' (1 Cor. 12.13) and 'filled with the Spirit' (Eph. 5.18) compared with the twelve references to the same two phrases by Luke ('filled with the Holy Spirit': Lk. 1.15, 41, 67; Acts 2.4; 4.8, 31; 9.17; 13.9; 13.52 and 'baptism in the Holy Spirit': Lk. 3.16; Acts 1.5; 11.16) and concludes that this kind of identity transfer silences Luke's pneumatology.[17] Stronstad pays close attention to Luke's use of these terms

---

tional purposes (pp. 4-5). See further his *Three Crucial Questions on the Holy Spirit* (Grand Rapids: Baker, 1996) and *Gift Giver: The Holy Spirit for Today* (Grand Rapids: Baker, 2001).

[14] Roger Stronstad, 'Signs on the Earth Beneath: Interpreting Luke–Acts' (paper presented at the annual meeting of the Society for Pentecostal Studies, Lakeland, FL, 7-9 November 1991). This essay appears in 1995 as chapter 5 in *Spirit, Scripture and Theology* (Baguio City, Philippines: ATSP, 1995), esp. pp. 6-13.

[15] Stronstad, *Spirit, Scripture and Theology*, p. 11.

[16] Roger Stronstad, *The Charismatic Theology of St. Luke* (Peabody: Hendrickson, 1984).

[17] Stronstad, *The Charismatic Theology of St. Luke*, p. 9. See further "Filled with the Spirit' Terminology in Luke–Acts.' *New and Old Issues in Pentecostalism* (paper presented at the annual meeting of the Society for Pentecostal Studies, Fresno,

and equates Lukan pneumatology not with Dunn's Pauline sense as initiatory, but rather charismatic, vocational and prophetic.[18] According to Stronstad, Luke's multiplex purpose follows in the tradition of the Septuagint and resonates with the didactic methodologies of the editors and chroniclers of Israel's sacred history.[19] He roots Lukan pneumatology in the Old Testament background of the transfer of the charismatic Spirit from leader to successor(s), like Moses to his elders (Num. 11.14-17, 25) and Elijah to Elisha (2 Kgs 2.9, 15). As Luke moves to his own era, the same Spirit to rest upon Jesus (Lk. 4.18-21) and empower Jesus' entire mission is transferred from Jesus to the disciples at Pentecost.[20] This transfer of the gift of the charismatic Spirit on the day of Pentecost becomes a paradigmatic experience of the eschatological people of God. Stronstad suggests the term 'charismatic' as an experiential equipping by way of the Holy Spirit for any vocational task to which an individual or group is called.

Elsewhere, Stronstad not only emphasizes Jesus as the consummate man of the Spirit but also Jesus' teaching to his disciples concerning future promises of the Holy Spirit and Luke's ensuing narration of their fulfillment. Jesus' promise and encouragement concerning reliance upon the Holy Spirit during difficult times (Lk. 11.13; 12.12; 21.14-15; Acts 1.4-5; and 1.8) finds ongoing fulfillment through the powerful witness of the likes of the Apostles, Stephen,

---

CA, 16-18 November 1989); reprinted on pp. 1-14 in *The Holy Spirit in the Scriptures and the Church: Essays Presented to Leslie Thomas Holdcroft on his 65ᵗʰ Birthday* (ed. Roger Stronstad and Laurence M. Van Kleek. Clayburn, BC: Western Pentecostal Bible College, 1987).

[18] See further Stronstad's 'Unity and Diversity: Lucan, Johannine, and Pauline Perspectives on the Holy Spirit', *Paraclete* 23 (Summer 1989), pp. 15-28. A later revision appears in *Spirit, Scripture and Theology*, pp. 169-92.

[19] Stronstad incorporates material from his earlier work entitled: 'The Influence of the Old Testament on the Charismatic Theology of St. Luke', *Pneuma* 2 (Spring 1980), pp. 32-50.

[20] Stronstad, *Charismatic Theology*, pp. 45, 52. In so doing, Stronstad points not to pneumatology but Christology as Luke's primary focus: 'Luke portrays Jesus as a man of the Spirit, a charismatic leader who is anointed, led, and empowered by the Holy Spirit. For Luke, in a way which is unique in the New Testament, Jesus is the charismatic Christ' ('The Holy Spirit in Luke–Acts', *Spirit, Scripture and Theology*, p. 143. An earlier version of this article appeared in two parts *Paraclete* 23 (Winter 1989), pp. 8-13 and 23 (Spring 1989), pp. 18-26.

and Paul.[21] In *Charismatic Theology*, Stronstad emphasizes that Spirit enablement, available to all Christians, includes the ability to perform miracles, engage in persuasive and bold witness (Acts 2.41; 4.31), prophesy via invasive speeches of worship, witness and judgment, guidance through visions and dreams, as well as wisdom and faith (Acts 6.3, 5; 11.24). The effect of Stronstad's work for Pentecostals remains apparent. By emphasizing divine enablement, Stronstad argues that Luke's understanding of Spirit-reception is devoid of the soteriological connotations as suggested by Dunn and Bruner.[22] Instead, the church described by Luke becomes a charismatic community, called and empowered for mission through the Spirit.

In *The Prophethood of All Believers*, Stronstad expands the Reformation axiom 'priesthood of all believers' to a Pentecostal/Charismatic axiom 'prophethood of all believers'.[23] He argues for the potential of an all-embracing, pervasive category for the people of God in continuity with the prophetic life of Jesus and the new community of prophets including Stephen, Philip, Barnabas, Agabus, Peter, and Paul. In this 1999 monograph, Stronstad builds on his earlier work by arguing that Luke's vision of the eschatological people of God positions the new community as heirs to the former people of God, who were a nation of priests but now function as a permanent, though only partially restored, community of individual and collective prophets. Stronstad sees the contemporary Pentecostal/Charismatic renewal as a means by which this important Lukan reality moves toward fruition.[24]

---

[21] Roger Stronstad, *Signs on the Earth Beneath: A Commentary on Acts 2:1-21* (Springfield: Life Publishers International, 2003), p. 23.

[22] Stronstad, *Charismatic Theology*, pp. 63-69.

[23] Stronstad, *The Prophethood of All Believers: A Study in Luke's Charismatic Theology* (JPTSup 16; Sheffield: Sheffield Academic Press, 1999). Earlier articles that introduce this concept appear as the popular article 'Prophets and Pentecost', in *The Pentecostal Testimony* 57 (March 1976), p. 5; 'The Prophethood of All Believers: A Study in Luke's Charismatic Theology' in *Pentecostalism in Context: Essays in Honor of William W. Menzies* (ed. Wonsuk Ma and Robert Menzies; JPTSup 11; Sheffield: Sheffield University Press, 1997), pp. 60-79. Later revised as 'Affirming Diversity: God's People as a Community of Prophets' (presidential address at the annual meeting of the Society for Pentecostal Studies, Wheaton, IL, 10-12 November 1994) and published in *Pneuma* 17.2 (1995), pp. 145-57.

[24] Stronstad offered an early presentation of this material as a 1993 lectureship at Asia Pacific Theological Seminary in Baguio City, Philippines later pub-

Finally, Stronstad also serves as an important voice in hermeneutical dialogue. He criticizes Fee and intends to demonstrate that, for Luke, historical narrative can and does have normative didactic purpose and instructional intentionality. According to Stronstad, Luke does this by introducing key theological themes and then re-establishing, illustrating, and re-enforcing those themes through further historical episodes.[25] Concerning the pursuit of 'Pentecostal Experience and Hermeneutics', Stronstad concedes some of the inherent concern directed toward certain Pentecostals for uncritical and emotional flaunting of their experience. For example, he responds to Donald Carson's denigration of Pentecostalism as raw triumphalism. Though Carson accuses Pentecostals of exegeting their own experience, Stronstad suggests that Carson and certain Evangelical (particularly Cessationist) critics similarly exegete their non-experience.[26] Elsewhere, Stronstad emphasizes the role of 'charismatic experiential presuppositions' and 'experiential verification' in the hermeneutical process. He implores readers of Lukan narratives to utilize the complementary role of grammatico-historical exegesis and contemporary experience.[27] Finally, Stronstad continues to revisit his initial thesis outlined in *Charismatic Theology*. In a recent paperback, *Baptized and Filled with the Spirit*, Stronstad includes not only a theology of statement and a compendium of

---

lished as a series of four lectures with the foregoing title, 'The Prophethood of All Believers' in William Menzies (ed.), *Contemporary Issues in Pentecostal Theology* (Baguio City: APTS, 1993), pp. 1-50. See also the response by Max Turner, 'Does Luke Believe Reception of the 'Spirit of Prophecy' Makes all 'Prophets'? Inviting Dialogue with Roger Stronstad', *JEPTA* 20 (2000), pp. 3-24.

[25] Stronstad, 'Hermeneutics of Lucan Historiography', *Paraclete* 22 (Fall 1988), p. 16. See also 'Trends in Pentecostal Hermeneutics', *Paraclete* 3 (Summer 1988), pp. 1-12. Both essays appear later in his *Spirit, Scripture and Theology*, pp. 31-52, 11-30 respectively. See also 'The Biblical Precedent for Historical Precedent' (paper presented at the annual meeting of the Society for Pentecostal Studies, Springfield, MO, 12-14 November 1992) and 'Pentecostal Hermeneutics' (review of Gordon D. Fee, *Gospel and Spirit: Issues in New Testament Hermeneutics*), *Pneuma* 15 (1993), pp. 215-22.

[26] Roger Stronstad, 'Pentecostal Experience and Hermeneutics', *Paraclete* 26 (Winter 1992), pp. 14-30. This article appears revised and enlarged in *Spirit, Scripture and Theology*, pp. 53-78. See the critique of Pentecostals by Donald A. Carson in *Showing the Spirit: A Theological Exposition of 1 Corinthians 12-14* (Grand Rapids: Baker, 1987), p. 12.

[27] Roger Stronstad, 'Pentecostalism, Experiential Presuppositions and Hermeneutic' (paper presented at the annual meeting of the Society for Pentecostal Studies, Dallas, TX, November 1990).

previously based conclusions on Luke's distinctive theology, but also valuable insight into his personal experience of the Holy Spirit as revealed in the Lukan story.[28]

2.1.3 HOWARD ERVIN

Howard Ervin, a Charismatic scholar with Baptistic roots, publishes an important work in the same year as Stronstad. As the title (*Conversion-Initiation and the Baptism in the Holy Spirit: An Engaging Critique of James D.G. Dunn's 'Baptism in the Holy Spirit'*) suggests, Ervin offers the most direct response to Dunn, a systematic and comprehensive theological evaluation of Dunn's conclusions. Ervin states: 'I have limited myself to an examination of the inadequacies and errors in the exegesis offered in support of the conversion-initiation thesis. I have simply accepted the gauntlet wherever Dr. Dunn has thrown it down'.[29] Like Stronstad, Ervin issues a hermeneutical challenge to Dunn's metaphysical assumptions about the nature of spiritual reality, which lead to Dunn's non-Pentecostal interpretation. According to Ervin, 'both the conversion-initiation and the Pentecostal advocates appeal to Scripture and logic ... a fundamental difference, however, is the added appeal of the Pentecostal witness to a personal experience with the charisms of the Spirit subsequent to conversion'.[30] Ervin's appeal to a 'Pentecostal experience does not preempt the first two criteria but is understood as a corroborative witness to the biblical integrity of the Pentecostal thesis'.[31] In other words, experience in its broadest sense provides

---

[28] Roger Stronstad, *Baptized and Filled with the Spirit* (Springfield: Africa's Hope Publications, 2004), p. 5. See also the recent 'The Charismatic Theology of St. Luke *Revisited* (Special Emphasis Upon Being Baptized in the Holy Spirit)', in Steven Studebaker (ed.), *Defining Issues In Pentecostalism: Classical and Emergent* (McMaster Theological Studies Series; Eugene: Pickwick, 2008), pp. 101-122.

[29] Howard Ervin, *Conversion-Initiation and the Baptism in the Holy Spirit: An Engaging Critique of James D.G. Dunn's 'Baptism in the Holy Spirit'* (Peabody: Hendrickson, 1984), p. v. Dunn offers numerous references to an earlier work by Ervin in *Baptism in the Spirit*, pp. 39, 55, 57, 70, 73, 79, 83, 86, 93, 128, 171, and 180. As Ervin's earlier work entitled *These are Not Drunken as Ye Suppose* (Plainsfield, NJ: Logos, 1968) provides impetus for Dunn's first look at the Pentecostal understanding of Spirit baptism, so Dunn's *Baptism in the Spirit* provides motivation for Ervin's more meticulous *Conversion-Initiation*. Ervin's *These Are Not Drunken* undergoes revision and appears as *Spirit Baptism: A Biblical Perspective* (Peabody: Hendrickson, 1987). See also the Ervin's analysis of Pentecostal experience in *This Which Ye See and Hear: A Layman's Guide to the Holy Spirit* (Plainfield: Logos, 1972).

[30] Ervin, *Conversion-Initiation*, p. 23.

[31] *Conversion-Initiation*, p. 6.

readers a key source of pre-understanding alongside biblical inter-pretation.[32] While Stronstad notes exegetical biases based on non-experience, Ervin goes one step further. According to Ervin, Dunn's non-experience, specifically, the lack of a post-conversion Spirit baptism, hinders exegetical perceptivity. Ervin affirms Pente-costal experience of the Spirit and presents thorough exegesis of relevant texts. His exegetical defense includes a chapter-by-chapter, systematic challenge to Dunn's exegesis of Pentecost (Acts 2), Sa-maria (Acts 8), Paul's conversion (Acts 9), Cornelius' conversion (Acts 10), and the Ephesian disciples (Acts 19). In each case, Ervin argues that Luke keeps separate what Dunn has joined, namely, sal-vation and the gift of the Holy Spirit. Further, this reception of the Spirit occurs not only subsequent to conversion, but also serves to equip the believer with supernatural charisms of the Spirit as evan-gelistic signals of God's power.[33]

2.1.4 JAMES SHELTON

In the revision of his PhD thesis offered at Sterling University un-der John Drane, James Shelton also emphasizes the charismatic im-pulse of the early church: 'recipients of the Spirit are, like Moses, "mighty in ... words and deeds" (Acts 7:22), even as Jesus himself was "mighty in deed and word" (Luke 24:19)'.[34] According to Shel-

---

[32] See also his 'Hermeneutics: A Pentecostal Option', in Elbert (ed.), *Essays on Apostolic Themes*, pp. 23-35.

[33] Ervin, *Conversion-Initiation*, p. 71. See further an earlier rebuttal to Dunn (*Baptism*, p. 71): 'An Excursus on Acts 4:8, 31; 13:9' (paper presented at the an-nual meeting of the Society for Pentecostal Studies, Pasadena, CA, 1982), R1-R9. Ervin refutes Dunn's assertion that Acts 4.8 refers to 'sudden inspiration and empowering ... which would not last beyond the hour of need.' Finally, note David A. Dorman, Review of Howard M. Ervin, *Conversion-Initiation and the Bap-tism in the Holy Spirit*, *Pneuma* 8 (Spring 1986), pp. 60-64 and David Petts, Review of Howard M. Ervin, *Conversion-Initiation and the Baptism in the Holy Spirit*, *JEPTA* 6 (1987), pp. 16-17. See also the recent tribute to Ervin by Daniel D. Isgrigg, 'Pil-grimage into Pentecost: The Pneumatological Legacy of Howard M. Ervin' (pa-per presented at the annual meeting of the Society for Pentecostal Studies, Tulsa, OK, 2008). Isgrigg provides a valuable review of Ervin's contributions to Lukan pneumatology.

[34] James Shelton, *Mighty in Word and Deed: The Role of the Holy Spirit in Luke–Acts* (Peabody: Hendrickson, 1991), p. 6. See reviews by Robert P. Menzies, James Shelton's *Mighty in Word and Deed: A Review Article*, *JPT* 2 (1993), pp. 105-115 and John Christopher Thomas, 'Review of James Shelton *Mighty in Word and Deed: The Role of the Holy Spirit in Luke–Acts*', *Pneuma* 15 (Spring 1993), pp. 125-28. Like, Stronstad and Ervin above, Shelton also enters into direct dialogue with Dunn, 'A

ton, the same Spirit initiates and directs every step of Christian mission equipping believers to preach boldly, perform miracles, and supply whatever strengths, skills or qualities may be necessary for the tasks to which witnesses are called.[35] Once again, the post-conversion role of the Spirit remains central to his argument. When discussing the disciples in the upper room on the day of Pentecost, he doubts that Luke would present the disciples as witnesses of Jesus' death, resurrection, and ascension, as recipients of his commission and blessing, as joyful, united, and devoted to prayer, and yet not see them as converted.[36] Like Stronstad and Ervin, Shelton charges Dunn with reading Luke through Pauline lenses and proffers a Pentecostal response: reception of the Spirit according to Luke does not make one a Christian but produces bold witness.[37]

Shelton also notes continuity between the Third Gospel and Acts. Whether referring to the Spirit-inspired witness of John the Baptist, Jesus, or early Christians, Luke accents continuity in salvation history. This continuity becomes especially apparent via Luke's narration of Jesus' anointing with the Spirit. Shelton links the anointing of the Lukan Jesus at the Jordan with the disciples at Pentecost and proposes Jesus' experience serve as an archetype for believers.[38] Shelton states: 'In Luke–Acts, the most frequent function of the Holy Spirit is to witness to Jesus by empowering believers to speak authoritatively concerning Jesus … This special function of the Holy Spirit in Acts serves the overall purpose of Acts. To be filled with the Holy Spirit means primarily to be a witness to Jesus and his works'.[39]

Reply to James D.G. Dunn's 'Baptism in the Spirit: A Response to Pentecostal Scholarship on Luke–Acts',' *JPT* 4 (1994), pp. 139-43. See finally 'Epistemology and Authority in the Acts of the Apostles: An Analysis and Test Case Study of Acts 15.1-19' (paper presented at the annual meeting of the Society for Pentecostal Studies, Springfield, MO, 1999).

[35] Shelton, *Mighty in Word and Deed*.

[36] Shelton, *Mighty in Word and Deed*, pp. 126-30.

[37] While Shelton does not submit to Dunn's position of Spirit baptism as conversion-initiation, neither does he believe that Luke expects every Spirit-filled believer to speak in tongues as in the initial evidence doctrine of classical Pentecostals.

[38] Shelton, *Mighty in Word and Deed*, p. 157.

[39] Shelton, *Mighty in Word and Deed*, p. 12. See further '"Filled with the Holy Spirit" and "Full of the Holy Spirit": Lucan Redactional Phrases', in Paul Elbert (ed.), *Faces of Renewal: Studies in Honor of Stanley M. Horton* (Peabody, MA: Hendrickson, 1988), pp. 80-107.

Shelton also emphasizes the overarching role of the Spirit in Luke–Acts even when specific references to the Spirit are not included. He argues that Luke's readers should recognize implicit references to the Spirit. Initial references to the Spirit upon an individual or a community often remain adequate unless Luke wishes to emphasize activity of the Spirit in a special circumstance. Given Luke's already frequent references to the activity of the Spirit, Shelton's conclusions prove critical. Luke not only establishes the central role of the Holy Spirit, but also varies the language, thereby enlarging further the prominence of the Spirit.[40]

2.1.5 ROBERT MENZIES

Robert Menzies comes into view as the final Pentecostal scholar of this period to engage in serious conversation with Dunn. Menzies' most important work to date, *Empowered for Witness: The Spirit in Luke–Acts*, appears as an updated revision of his PhD thesis under I. Howard Marshall.[41] While the title suggests a study limited to Luke–Acts, it is in fact a comprehensive survey of the development of pneumatology from pre-Christian Judaism to the post-Pauline church with special emphasis on Luke–Acts. His conclusions resonate with the work of the previous scholars under observation:

> … the disciples receive the Spirit, not as the source of cleansing and a new ability to keep the law, nor as the essential bond by which they (each individual) are linked to God, not even as a foretaste of the salvation to come; rather, the disciples receive the Spirit as a prophetic *donum superadditum* which enables them to participate effectively in the missionary enterprise of the church.[42]

---

[40] Shelton, 'Filled with the Holy Spirit', p. 84.

[41] Robert P. Menzies, *Empowered for Witness: The Spirit in Luke–Acts* (JPTSup 6; Sheffield: Sheffield Academic Press, 1994) and the original PhD thesis entitled: *The Development of Early Christian Pneumatology with Special Reference to Luke–Acts* (JSNTSS 54; Sheffield: Sheffield University Press, 1991). For further responses to Dunn, see Menzies, 'Hermeneutics: Luke's Distinctive Contribution', and 'Exegesis: A Reply to James Dunn', in *Spirit and Power: Foundations of Pentecostal Experience* (ed. William and Robert Menzies; Grand Rapids: Zondervan, 2000), pp. 47-62; 63-68 and Stronstad. 'Review of Robert Menzies Empowered for Witness: The Spirit in Luke–Acts', *Pneuma* 20 (Spring 1998), pp. 116-19.

[42] *Empowered for Witness*, p. 279.

However, in contrast to Stronstad and Shelton, Menzies argues that Luke does not link the activity of the Spirit with both empowerment for witness and performance of miracles, but singularly the Spirit of prophecy, which Luke interprets exclusively in terms of prophetic vocation for witness to Christ.[43] Menzies then affirms the classical Pentecostal position of evidential tongues as the most notable example of inspired speech in Acts. According to Menzies, while Paul is the first Christian to attribute soteriological and ethical functions to the Spirit (1 Cor. 6.11; Rom. 2.29; 8.14-17; 14.17; 15.16; Gal. 4.6; 5.5, 16-26), Luke (as well as Matthew, Mark, and Q) remains consistent with the Septuagintal tradition that locates the role of Spirit as the supplementary gift of inspired speech.

In an essay on the prophecy of John the Baptist in Lk. 3.16, Menzies argues that baptism with 'the Holy Spirit and fire' need not refer to cleansing or transformation.[44] On the contrary, the contextual winnowing metaphor suggests that the deluge of the Spirit initiated by Messiah sifts the people of Israel not in terms of purification but as prophetic separation of the righteous remnant from the chaff (see also Lk. 2:34).[45] Menzies reaches forward to Jesus' preaching at Nazareth in Luke 4 as the prophetic Spirit of Isa. 61.1-2 and Pentecost as the prophetic nature of the gift envisaged by Joel (2.28-32). For Menzies, the consistent anticipation for experience of the Spirit is one of revelation, visionary phenomena, and inspired speech. The Spirit is granted on these occasions to aid missionary expansion of the kingdom/church, and as such is a prophetic anointing for the benefit of those as yet untouched.[46]

---

[43] *Empowered for Witness*, p. 124.

[44] Robert P. Menzies, 'The Baptist's Prophecy in Lukan Perspective: A Redactional Analysis of Luke 3:16' (paper presented at the annual meeting of the Society for Pentecostal Studies Dallas, TX, 1990).

[45] *Empowered for Witness*, pp. 12-14.

[46] See Menzies' further work including 'The Distinctive Character of Luke's Pneumatology', *Paraclete* 25 (1991), pp. 17-30; 'Complete Evangelism' (Review of Pedrito U. Maynard-Reid, *Complete Evangelism: The Luke–Acts Model*). *JPT* 13 (1998), pp. 133-42; 'Evidential Tongues: An Essay on Theological Method', *AJPS* 1 (1998), pp. 1-9 and 'Jumping off the Postmodern Bandwagon', *Pneuma* 16 (1994), pp. 115-20. Repr. William W. Menzies and Robert Menzies (eds.), *Spirit and Power* (Grand Rapids: Zondervan, 2000), pp. 63-68.

2.1.6 MAX TURNER

Before I conclude the inaugural Dunn era, Max Turner deserves recognition as another critical dialogue partner for Pentecostals. Turner begins his academic journey as a young Pentecostal student and embarks on a thesis on Lukan pneumatology. Following on the heels of Dunn, Turner seeks a middle ground. The Pentecostal gift of the Spirit in Acts functions not only as a Christianized version of the Jewish 'Spirit of prophecy', but also as an ecclesiological and soteriological agent. The Lukan 'Spirit of prophecy' serves as the source of the whole charismatic dimension of Christian life, providing wisdom, guidance, revelation, prophecy and doxological speech (including tongues) in order to fuel not only the Church's witness to outsiders, but also vigorously shape its own dynamic life of worship and discipleship.[47] Today, while Turner admittedly stands outside of classical Pentecostalism, he maintains robust conversation with several Pentecostals, including his former doctoral student, Robert Menzies.[48] As Menzies pushes significant aspects of Turner's thesis in the direction of classical Pentecostalism, Turner re-enters the foray, and thirty years after Dunn, begins to serve as a new and Dunn-like dialogue partner.

Turner challenges Menzies' contracted understanding of the Spirit as a *donum superadditum*, but also declines to reduce the work of the Spirit to soteriological agency as in Paul.[49] While Turner re-

---

[47] See Max Turner, *Power from On High: The Spirit in Israel's Restoration and Witness in Luke–Acts* (JPTSup 9. Sheffield: Sheffield Academic Press, 1996) and a number of earlier articles as a result of his doctoral thesis ('Luke and the Spirit: Studies in the Significance of Receiving the Spirit in Luke–Acts' PhD Thesis. Cambridge University, 1980) including: 'Jesus and the Spirit in Lucan Perspective', *TynB* 32 (1981), pp. 3-42; 'The Significance of Receiving the Spirit in Luke–Acts: A Survey of Modern Scholarship', *TrinJ* 2 (1981), pp. 131-58; 'Spirit Endowment in Luke–Acts: Some Linguistic Considerations', *VoxEv* 12 (1981), pp. 45-63; 'Spiritual Gifts: Then and Now', *VoxEv* 15 (1985), pp. 7-64; *The Holy Spirit and Spiritual Gifts in the New Testament Church* (Peabody: Hendrickson, 1998).

[48] Turner's *Power from on High*, pp. 11-12, 14.

[49] Turner's *Power From on High* is the culminating effort of a series of articles first published in the early 1990's including: 'The Spirit and the Power of Jesus' Miracles in the Lucan Conception', *NovT* 33 (1991), pp. 124-52; 'The Spirit of Prophecy and the Power of Authoritative Preaching in Luke–Acts: A Question of Origins', *NTS* 38 (1992), pp. 66-88; '"Empowerment for Mission"? The Pneumatology of Luke–Acts' (An Appreciation and Critique of James B. Shelton's *Mighty in Word and Deed*), *VoxEv* 24 (1994), pp. 103-122. Note also that Turner and Menzies continue their dialogue. See Menzies 'Spirit and Power in

mains true to his earlier work, he cites the benefits of Pentecostal and Charismatic theology and praxis pointing Luke's readers to anticipate reception of the charismata to make different contributions, both spontaneously, and in more long-term ministries in the Church and in her mission.[50] But he does not support the classical Pentecostal view of 'subsequence' for the primary purpose of mission. For Turner, Luke is much closer to Paul in 1 Corinthians 12-14 where the charismatic 'Spirit of prophecy' serving the church and empowering its pastoral ministries is complementary to table service in Acts 6.3-5, the ministry of the prophets in Acts 9.31; 11.24; 15.32 and of elders/overseers in Acts 20.28, as well as evangelism: 'The Pentecostal Spirit is thus not simply "the gift of power upon the sanctified life", but the charismatic Spirit of prophecy as a "power from on high" which both transforms and shapes ("sanctifies") the community and drives and empowers her mission'.[51] Similarly, Turner neither denies that Jesus' disciples experience the beginnings of salvation before Pentecost, nor that Samaria tastes salvation before the arrival of the apostles in Acts 8.14. But he does contend that the Spirit is not absent but working through the charismata of Jesus and Philip respectively and, thus, Luke could not visualize how the experience of salvation and discipleship could be maintained, deepened, and extended without the gift of the Spirit granted to the disciples.[52] Finally, Turner does not side with classical Pentecostalism on evidential tongues. He states:

> To avoid misunderstanding, I should clarify that I am not claiming the evidence of Acts 'absolutely refutes' the majority traditional Pentecostal view on initial tongues (even less am I attempting to distinguish the theological significance of glossolalia, when and where it occurs). I am merely saying the evidence to support it is weak and fragmentary, and so the case for the

Luke–Acts: A Response to Max Turner', *JSNT* 49 (1993), pp. 11-20 and 'Exegesis: A Reply to Max Turner', in *Spirit and Power*, pp. 87-109. See further William P. Atkinson, 'The Prior Work of the Spirit in Luke', *Australasian Pentecostal Studies* 5/6 (2002): http://aps.webjournals.org/articles/1/04/2002/2991.htm?id={ED4 C92 D8-DC69-4076-AE07-4F678C173FC0}.

[50] Turner, *Power From on High*, p. 443.

[51] Turner, *Power from on High*, pp. 443-46.

[52] Turner, *Power from on High*, p. 446. See also his 'Interpreting the Samaritan of Acts 8: The Waterloo of Pentecostal Soteriology and Pneumatology?' *Pneuma* 23 (2001), pp. 265-86.

view is very largely inferential. The alternative reading (that tongues is merely one of several charismata that might attest initial reception of the Spirit) is more plausible because it accounts for slightly more evidence and reads it more contextually … Luke–Acts does not provide adequate support to make such a rigid 'rule' a 'safe' verdict.[53]

Turner warns that it is not the doctrines of subsequence and initial evidence that will safeguard the spiritual dynamic of the church, but 'ongoing evidence', namely continuous and appropriate teaching, exhortation and pastoral leadership on the implementation of gifts and pneumatological emphases as portrayed through Luke and Paul.[54] Turner's sharp yet sympathetic analysis perpetuates the Dunn-like dialogue and alongside Dunn remains symbolic of the enduring centrality of this discussion both inside and outside of Pentecostalism.

Before summarizing these responses, the recent effort of Youngmo Cho symbolizes the ongoing quest to reconcile Lukan and Pauline pneumatologies.[55] Cho sets a foundation for his thesis with a review of Robert Menzies' discontinuity, James Dunn's continuity, and the mediating position of Max Turner. Cho links the role of the kingdom of God in relation to Pauline and Lukan pneumatologies. Cho likens Jesus' limited reference to the Spirit and strong emphasis on the kingdom to Paul's heavy use of Spirit. He then distinguishes between Paul's innovative soteriological use of the Spirit and Luke's traditional use of the Spirit as prophetic and inspirational. Finally, Cho links the Spirit in Luke–Acts with the source of kingdom proclamation.[56] Cho advances further the diver-

---

[53] Turner, *Power from on High*, p. 447.

[54] Turner, *Power from on High*, pp. 450-51.

[55] Youngmo Cho, *Spirit and Kingdom in the Writings of Luke and Paul: An Attempt to Reconcile these Concepts* (Paternoster Biblical Monographs; Waynesboro, GA: Paternoster, 2005).

[56] See also Cho's earlier essay: 'Spirit and Kingdom in Luke–Acts: Proclamation as the Primary Role of the Spirit in Relation to the Kingdom of God in Luke–Acts', *AJPS* 6:2 (2003), pp. 173-97. See also Cynthia L. Westfall, 'Paul's Experience and a Pauline Theology of the Spirit' in *Defining Issues in Pentecostalism: Classical and Emergent* (Eugene, OR: Pickwick Publications, 2007), pp. 123-43. She undertakes to connect Paul's experience of the Spirit in Acts with Pauline pneumatology. Although the language of baptism in the Holy Spirit does not feature prominently in Pauline literature, Westfall links the themes of new creation, the

sity of New Testament pneumatologies by signaling the role of kingdom language as a bridge between Pauline and Lukan pneumatologies. While Pentecostals continue to reap the dividends of literary analysis, Cho provides possibilities for a new way; he calls for Pentecostals not to abandon literary analysis but to look for a more synchronic approach to pneumatology.[57]

2.1.7 SUMMARY

While the work of these scholars is by no means uniform, a number of their general conclusions continue to gain recognition in the larger world of Lukan scholarship. First, these Pentecostals serve as a pioneering generation of scholars more inclined to view Luke as a theologian with distinct contributions to biblical theology. This marks a significant methodological victory for Pentecostalism since they root historical and theological defense of distinctive Spirit baptism in the Lukan narratives. Second, the conclusions of these Pentecostal scholars, in contrast to Dunn, bring to light a distinction in Luke's thought between entrance to the new covenant through forgiveness of sins and reception of the gift of the Spirit, which Luke presents rather as divine empowering for various enterprises of the church. Third, Pentecostal scholars begin to highlight continuity between the Spirit's empowering of the life of Jesus and the divine enablement granted to the disciples. For Pentecostals, this merits pursuit of the Spirit, in order to experience the same enablement as Jesus and those of the emerging community in Acts. Finally, these scholars set the stage not only for further Pentecostal examination of the Lukan narratives, but also give the first signal to the broader academic arena that Pentecostal scholars will offer formidable contributions to Lukan studies.

---

church as the temple of the Holy Spirit, and the filling, gifts, and fruits of the Spirit as broader metaphors for Spirit baptism. Westfall and Cho demonstrate the growing search for points of continuity in place of the discontinuity presupposed in traditional Pentecostal biblical studies.

[57] For a response to Cho, see Mittelstadt, 'Review of Youngmo Cho, *Spirit and Kingdom in the Writings of Luke and Paul: An Attempt to Reconcile these Concepts*', *JPT* 16.2 (2008), pp. 103-112.

2.2 PRESSING ISSUES

[Charismatic Exegesis] includes a playful interaction
between the text of the Bible and the present situation,
in which the story of scripture is interwoven with that of the community.
Conversely, the believers recognize themselves in the text.
The story is best suited for expressing communal experiences in a way
which not only encourages the building up of the community
but also makes these experiences accessible to newcomers
(Jean-Jacques Suurmond)[1]

In the previous section, I argue that the monumental work of James Dunn catapults Pentecostals into the academic arena. In this section, I propose that the primary development of this inaugural academic awakening, namely, scholarly awareness of Luke as a theologian in his own right, brings at least three concurrent controversies into further focus. Pentecostals must wrestle with questions concerning: 1) cessationism; 2) enduring defense of Spirit baptism; and 3) ongoing hermeneutical questions. I turn first to Pentecostal defense of their theology and experience against still prevalent cessationist theology. As they read Luke–Acts, Pentecostal passion for experience equivalent to the original apostolic community proves to be a common thread. Pentecostals of this inaugural academic era undertake no greater challenge than the belief that charismatic life in the Spirit ceases with the close of the apostolic age.

2.2.1 CESSATIONISM
In order to continue in the direction of positive scholarly credibility, emerging Pentecostal scholars necessarily enter into serious discussion with proponents of cessationism. Given Pentecostal emphasis

---

[1] Jean-Jacques Suurmond, *Word & Spirit at Play: Towards a Charismatic Theology* (Grand Rapids: Eerdmans, 1994), pp. 22-23.

upon Spirit baptism, tongues, healing, and prophetic revelation, tension mounts as North American Christianity finds itself steeped in modernity. Of the Pentecostal scholars to address this subject, no one offers a more sustained argument than Jon Ruthven.[2] Ruthven begins with Jesus' central mission to inaugurate the kingdom 'in power' and 'in word and deed' (Lk. 4.23-27; 24.19). Signs and wonders manifest the core activity of Jesus' mission and thereby begin displacement of the physical and spiritual ruin of the demonic kingdom. Miraculous *charismata* such as prophecies, exorcisms and healings, not only continue through Jesus' earthly ministry, but are also bestowed through his followers as a result of his exaltation.[3] These *charismata* reflect the pattern of Peter's earliest sermon: 'In the last days, before the day of the Lord, You will receive the gift of the Holy Spirit ... This promise is for you, your children and for all who are far off—for all whom the Lord our God will call' (Acts 2.17, 20, 39). According to Ruthven, Lukan emphasis upon the Holy Spirit offers significant implications for the post-apostolic church. First century believers seek to be 'filled', repeatedly and constantly, in order to participate in and continue Jesus' charismatic ministry.[4] Ruthven concludes that miracles provide more than mere 'accreditation' for proclamation; instead, preaching articulates miracles and illicits implications for onlookers. In short, Luke locates the miraculous in a proper christological setting, whereby the consistent combination of preaching and miracles demands a believing and repentant response. In the current day, Ruthven argues that the work of the exalted Christ is not complete as some cessationists might suggest, but remains active in the church through Jesus' presence and distribution of the whole variety of spiritual gifts.[5]

An early effort by Cecil Robeck draws attention to Luke's use of the gift of prophecy. Robeck examines five passages in Acts: 1) Acts 11.27-30; 2) Acts 21.8-14; 3) Acts 2.14-21 and 19.6; 4) Acts 13.1-3; and 5) Acts 15.32-35.[6] He emphasizes the importance of the prophetic tradition in the Church during the formative years by high-

---

[2] Jon Ruthven, *On the Cessation of the Charismata: The Protestant Polemic on Postbiblical Miracles* (JPTSup 3; Sheffield: Sheffield University Press, 1993).

[3] Ruthven, *On the Cessation of the Charismata*, pp. 115-18.

[4] Ruthven, *On the Cessation of the Charismata*, p. 212.

[5] Ruthven, *On the Cessation of the Charismata*, pp. 187-88.

[6] Cecil M. Robeck, 'The Gift of Prophecy in Acts and Paul, Part I', *Studia Biblica et Theologica* 5.1 (1975), pp. 15-38.

lighting Luke's use of a prophetic office as the gift of prophecy seemingly resident in people like Agabus, Judas, Silas, and some of the five men in Acts 13.1-3. These individuals engage in prophetic activity under a broad range of subjects including not only prediction of future events (Acts 11.28; 20.23; 21.11), but also directives for church-related action (Acts 13.2) and distillation of vital information to the church (Acts 20.23; 21.11; and probably 21.4). According to Robeck, the role of the prophetic element in Acts generally concerns the welfare of the church and functions in concert with Paul's scheme of edification, encouragement and consolation in 1 Corinthians 14.3.[7] John Michel Penney argues in a similar vein that the Spirit of prophecy proves critical for participation in a community where missionary proclamation becomes paramount.[8] He cites at least seven Lukan scenes with exemplary implications: (1) direct revelation of the Spirit (Acts 10.10-43); (2) charismatic wisdom (Lk. 21.14; Acts 6.3,5,10); (3) boldness and assurance (Acts 4.8-12,31); (4) revelatory speech accompanied by the miraculous (Acts 13.9-12); (5) complementary manifestations (Acts 2.1-4; 13.51-14.3); (6) guidance and direction (Acts 13.2-4; 16.6,9); and (7) prediction of future events (Acts 11.28; 21.10-11). According to Penney, these scenes are paradigmatic and therefore confront a cessationist hermeneutic. Robert Wadholm points to miracles performed by Jesus (and the disciples) as signs of Christ's ministry, role, and identity. Wadholm compiles a comprehensive list of signs and wonders in Luke–Acts (Lk. 2.8–12, 34–35; 11.14–20, 29–32; 21.5–36; 23.8–11; Acts 2.1–41, 42–47; 4.1–22, 23–31; 5.12–16; 6.8–10; 7.35–39; 8.5–13; 14.1–3; 15.12) and attests to Luke's intentional establishment of their ability to prove the ongoing validity and veracity of the kerygma.[9]

---

[7] Robeck, 'The Gift of Prophecy in Acts and Paul, Part I', pp. 34-35, 37-38. On the similarity of prophetic function between Luke and Paul, see further his 'The Gift of Prophecy in Acts and Paul, Part II', *Studia Biblica et Theologica* 5.2 (1975), pp. 37-54.

[8] John Michel Penney, 'The Testing of New Testament Prophecy', *JPT* 10 (1997), p. 57.

[9] Robert Wadholm, 'The Role of Experience in the Interpretation of Miracles Narratives in Lucan Literature' (paper presented at the annual meeting of the Society for Pentecostal Studies, Cleveland, TN, March 2007), p. 6. See also his 'An Apologetic of Signs and Wonders in Luke–Acts' (M.A. Thesis, Global University, 2005).

Charismatic Catholics Kilian McDonnell and George Montague emphasize the integral role of charisms in the early church and to-day. In a joint effort, Montague surveys the New Testament and McDonnell examines post-biblical texts. Though they find it impossible to separate the gift of the Spirit from initiation, they agree, in contrast to cessationists, that charisms of the Spirit as found in Luke–Acts and the history of the church belong to the church to-day and must be constantly rediscovered and accepted.[10] Whereas classical Pentecostals typically defend their experiences of Acts-like ministry through their restorationist lenses, Catholics look for continuity throughout church history.[11] Thus Pentecostal Galen Hertwerk locates the events of the early church in Acts as the 'Early Rain' and the twentieth century recovery of the *charismata* as the 'Latter Rain'. He suggests that the presence of miracles place the church in eschatological tension. The reemergence of miraculous powers fits into a restorational framework and provides a taste of the age to come.[12] Note, however, the influential monograph by classical Pentecostal scholar Ron Kydd; in his *Charismatic Gifts in the Early Church*, Kydd draws similar conclusions to McDonnell and Montague.[13] Kydd challenges cessationism not through restoration-ist lenses but by way of apostolic continuity. After thorough analysis of primary literature, Kydd concludes that the early church remains strongly charismatic through the end of the second century and maintains sporadic Charismatic impulses into the third century and

---

[10] Killian McDonnell and George Montague, *Christian Initiation and Baptism in the Holy Spirit: Evidence from the First Eight Centuries* (Collegeville: The Liturgical Press, 1991). A pastoral summary of this work appears as *Fanning the Flame: What Does Baptism in the Holy Spirit Have to Do with Christian Initiation* (Collegeville: The Liturgical Press, 1991).

[11] See the invaluable collection of official documents compiled by McDonnell, *Presence, Power, Praise: Documents on the Charismatic Renewal* (3 vols.; Collegeville: The Liturgical Press, 1980).

[12] Galen Hertweck, 'The Holy Spirit in the Eschatology of Acts', *Paraclete* 16 (Summer 1982), pp. 26-28.

[13] Ronald Kydd, *Charismatic Gifts in the Early Church* (Peabody: Hendrickson, 1984). Kydd has since moved into the Anglican tradition. See also *Are Miraculous Gifts for Today? Four Views* (Grand Rapids: Zondervan, 1996) edited by Wayne Grudem. Four representative perspectives include 'Cessationist' (Richard Gaffin); 'Open But Cautious' (Robert Saucy); 'Third Wave' (C. Samuel Storms); and 'Pentecostal/Charismatic' (Doug Oss). On a more popular level, see also Ralph W. Harris, *Acts Today: Signs and Wonders of the Holy Spirit* (Springfield: Gospel Publishing House, 1995).

beyond. Kydd shares similar sympathies with Charismatic Catholics, who emerge in the mid-twentieth century and generally lament a decline and then seek to celebrate a revival of the spiritual gifts. Kydd, like these Charismatics, tends not to read history via 'Early/Latter Rain', but calls upon Christians to reemphasize the Church's unbroken link to first century apostolic Christianity.

Finally, in a passionate plea to members of the Evangelical Theological Society, Paul Elbert maintains that in spite of great exegetical and theological strides dialogue remains critical. In a stern challenge directed at scholars in the Evangelical Theological Society, Elbert bemoans marginalization of Luke's narrative cohesion by diminishing Lukan examples and precedents concerning the likes of Spirit-reception and fulfillment of prophecy themes.[14] Elbert's sympathies resonate with all Pentecostals; the challenge to cessationist hermeneutics proves central to Pentecostal theology and praxis.

2.2.2 SPIRIT BAPTISM

The central role of Spirit baptism in a Pentecostal worldview brings scholars consistently to the Lukan narratives to provide answers for seemingly endless questions. Because of the vast literature on Spirit baptism in Luke–Acts, I note only a few examples from the bibliography according to the helpful categorical questions provided by Cecil Robeck: 1) 'When does baptism in the Spirit occur?'; 2) 'How does one verify, or is it possible to verify that one has indeed been baptized in the Holy Spirit?'; and 3) 'For what purpose is this baptism given?'[15]

Throughout their brief history, Pentecostals continue to defend and debate post-conversion experience of Spirit baptism. Since I have already singled out for consideration the implications introduced by Dunn, Fee, Turner, and respondents, I turn now to other angles from important but less voluminous contributors.[16] Stanley

---

[14] Paul Elbert, 'Pentecostal/Charismatic Themes in Luke–Acts at the Evangelical Theological Society: The Battle of Interpretive Method', *JPT* 12 (2004), p. 181.

[15] Cecil M. Robeck, 'Baptism in the Holy Spirit: Its Purpose(s)', *Pneuma* 7 (Fall 1985), p. 83.

[16] See the impressive compilation of sources on the initial evidence debate by Gerald Flokstra, 'Sources for the Initial Evidence Discussion: A Bibliographic

Horton's *What the Bible Says about the Holy Spirit* may be the most influential defense of the Spirit baptism toward the close of the twentieth century; in it, he examines key passages in Acts and defends the classical Pentecostal position in succinct fashion.[17] As Horton serves the Assemblies of God, so also French Arrington serves the Church of God (Cleveland, TN); Arrington defends the classic distinction between the indwelling of the Spirit at regeneration and Spirit baptism; he also provides thorough analysis of the assorted terms associated with the Spirit in Luke–Acts.[18] Less known scholars walk a different path. Tak-Ming Cheung supplements a constructive review of representative Pentecostal, Evangelical and Catholic understandings of Spirit baptism and then underscores the eschatological fulfillment of Spirit baptism within broader salvation-history.[19] Mark Lee attempts to build a bridge between Pentecostals and Evangelicals by targeting baptismal language within a first century context.[20] Since baptism typically signifies entrance into community, Lee believes the basic Pentecostal message often remains lost on Evangelicals. Whereas terms like *poured out, clothed, filled, come upon, received*, or *fell upon* share similar connotations to *baptism*, they function descriptively, that is, as language for manifestation of the Spirit. Lee argues that Evangelicals have difficulty grasping the heart of the Pentecostal insistence on praying to re-

---

Essay', *AJPS* 2/2 (1999), pp. 243-59. Flokstra documents over 140 books and articles by scholars and pastors alike from the first hundred years of the movement.

[17] Stanley Horton, *What The Bible Says About The Holy Spirit* (Springfield: Gospel Publishing House, 1976), specifically chapter 7: 'The Spirit in the Book of Acts', pp. 135-66. See further the earlier works (in order of publication): Harold Horton, *The Baptism in the Holy Spirit: A Challenge to Whole-Hearted Seekers After God* (Nottingham: Assemblies of God Publishing House, 1961); L. Thomas Holdcroft, *The Holy Spirit: A Pentecostal Interpretation* (Springfield: Gospel Publishing House, 1962); William G. MacDonald, *Glossolalia in the New Testament* (Springfield: Gospel Publishing House, 1964). These writers representative of the Assemblies of God defend the classical Pentecostal position on Spirit baptism with significant reliance upon Acts.

[18] French Arrington, 'The Indwelling, Baptism, and Infilling with the Holy Spirit: A Differentiation of Terms', *Pneuma* 3.2 (Fall 1981), pp. 1-10.

[19] Tak-Ming Cheung, 'Understandings of Spirit-Baptism', *JPT* 8 (1996), pp. 115-28.

[20] Mark Lee, 'An Evangelical Dialogue on Luke, Salvation and Spirit Baptism', *Pneuma* 26 (2004), pp. 81-98.

ceive the Holy Spirit due to Pentecostal use /'misuse' of baptismal language.[21]

Others focus specifically on crucial Lukan passages. Lawrence Grimes offers defense of the post-conversion Spirit baptism of the Ephesian Disciples in Acts 19. He argues that proper translation of Paul's question concerning the nature of Spirit baptism at Ephesus solves the problem. Grimes favors a translation of Acts 19.2 as 'Have you received the Holy Spirit *since/after* you believed?' over 'Did you receive the Holy Spirit *when* you believed'.[22] Ben Aker argues that Luke patterns the post-conversion anointing of the disciples on the Day of Pentecost after the experience of Jesus at Jordan.[23] According to Aker, Jesus' anointing at Jordan is not an enduement based upon Jesus' need but anticipates Jesus' release of the Spirit upon his disciples. The inaugural anointing provides the foundation for Acts 2.33b where Jesus, the Lord of the church, pours out the Spirit.[24] In a later work, Aker continues this discussion; he focuses on Acts 2 as paradigmatic by way of fresh insights founded upon narrative and social science criticism.[25]

Charles Holman opts for a synchronic approach to the Dunn-induced debate by suggesting greater harmony between Lukan and Pauline pneumatology than typically acknowledged by Pentecostals.[26] Though Paul does not speak clearly of a dual reception of the Spirit (Rom. 8.15; 1 Cor. 2.12; 2 Cor. 1.21; 5.5; 11.4; Eph. 1.13), Holman finds possible continuity with Luke via Paul's affirmation and expectation of subsequent experiences and manifestations of the Spirit (as in Eph. 5.18). Similarly, David Petts, a seldom-cited respondent to Dunn, warrants consideration. In an attempt to find

---

[21] Lee, 'An Evangelical Dialogue on Luke, Salvation and Spirit Baptism', pp. 96-97.

[22] Lawrence R. Grimes, 'When or After?' *Paraclete* 20 (Summer 1986), p. 29. Emphases original.

[23] Ben Aker, 'New Directions in Lucan Theology: Reflections on Luke 3:21-22 and Some Implications', in Elbert (ed.), *Faces of Renewal*, pp. 108-127.

[24] Aker, 'New Directions in Lucan Theology: Reflections on Luke 3:21-22 and Some Implications', p. 123.

[25] Ben Aker, 'Acts 2 as Paradigmatic Narrative for Luke's Theology of the Spirit' (paper presented at the annual meeting of the Evangelical Theological Society, 1998), Online: http://www.agts.edu/faculty/faculty_publications/ articles/aker_acts2.pdf.

[26] Charles Holman, 'Spirit Reception in Acts and Paul', in *Memory & Hope: The Society for Pentecostal Studies at 25 Years* (paper presented at the annual meeting of the Society for Pentecostal Studies, Toronto, ON, March 1996), p. 2.

middle ground between classic Pentecostal Spirit baptism and Dunn, Petts concludes:

> His [Dunn's] chief strength is that he has rightly drawn attention to the centrality of the gift of the Spirit in conversion-initiation. I believe Ervin is wrong to limit Christian initiation to repentance/faith and water baptism. We must with Dunn (and Acts 2:38) add the gift of the Spirit. But that is not to make the gift of the Spirit salvation itself. It is distinct from salvation as it is distinct from water-baptism. Yet it is intimately connected to both, and in a sense, without it, salvation, in the full New Testament use of the term, is incomplete.[27]

The second and no less controversial question concerns the role of tongues as evidence for Spirit baptism. Passionate debate continues into the present day, both within and outside the tradition. A number of essays focus upon specific exegetical issues as in two papers by Robert Graves. In the first, Graves argues that Luke's use of *gar* in Acts 10.46 provides the ground, reason, or proof that the Gentiles receive the Holy Spirit: 'for they heard them speaking in tongues'.[28] In the second, Graves compares this same initial outpouring on the Gentiles with the initial outpouring upon the apostolic Jewish community in Jerusalem. In both events, tongues serve as precedents and archetypes. Luke intends for both Jew and Gentile to hark back to these events and long for a similar outpouring with the ensuing tongues.[29] Like Graves, Lim Yeu Chuen finds didactic commonalities between the pivotal Jewish and Gentile Pentecosts.[30] As part of a larger Jewish-Gentile framework, Luke intends to show the approval of God toward all people by way of similar

---

[27] David Petts, *The Baptism in the Holy Spirit in Relation to Christian Initiation* (MTh Thesis. Nottingham University, 1984), p. 87. I do not include Petts among the earlier respondents to Dunn simply because of the minimal response to his work. Only Atkinson refers to Petts in 'Pentecostal Responses to Baptism in the Holy Spirit: Luke–Acts', p. 105.

[28] Robert W. Graves, 'Use of *gar* in Acts 10:46', *Paraclete* 22 (Spring 1988), pp. 15-18.

[29] Robert W. Graves, 'The Jerusalem Council and the Gentile Pentecost', *Paraclete* 18 (1984), p. 6.

[30] Lim Yeu Chuen, 'Acts 10: A Gentile Model for Pentecostal Experience', *AJPS* 2 (pp. 195-211). Originally presented and published in *Contemporary Issues in Pentecostal Theology* (First Annual Pentecostal Lectureship Series. Baguio City: APTS, 1993), pp. 73-84.

encounters with the Spirit. Luke intends validation of Jews and the inclusion of Gentiles through a normative Spirit baptism with glossolalia as initial evidence. Verna Linzey's subtitle 'The Reception of the Holy Spirit as Confirmed by Speaking in Tongues' states clearly her motivation. Linzey's ironic defense of tongues at Samaria proves most interesting.[31] She compares the Samaritan Pentecost to the events on the Day of Pentecost; in both narratives, new converts are baptized in water and then filled with the Spirit. Following her presentation of post-conversion Spirit baptism, she assembles a lengthy catalogue of non-Pentecostal commentators, who agree that the Samaritans experienced a post-regeneration, visible, outward, and miraculous manifestation of the Spirit; she notes further that nearly all of these same commentators mention 'speaking in tongues as almost certainly the manifestation or one of the manifestations'.[32]

James Edwards defends initial evidence through literary analysis of six Pentecostal scenes (Acts 2, 4, 8, 9, 10, 19) and analyzes various literary patterns. He suggests that Luke's use of type scenes could posit answers for those puzzled by Luke's silence on tongues in Acts 4, 8, and 9. Since tongues play a central role in the events on the Day of Pentecost, the type scene pattern, Edwards suggests that Luke views tongues as important to all of the subsequent scenes.[33] In other words, though Luke does not specifically reference tongues in each scene, Edwards maintains that it is reasonable to conclude that the symbolic importance of tongues in the anchor archetype-scene serves as implied evidence for the baptism in the Holy Spirit. An argument to the contrary comes from Larry Hurtado. In a response to a collection of essays on the initial evidence, Hurtado proposes that tongues are 'normal, but not a norm'.[34] Accordingly,

---

[31] Verna M. Linzey, *The Baptism with the Holy Spirit: The Reception of the Holy Spirit as Confirmed by Speaking in Tongues* (Longwood, FL: Xulon Press, 2004).

[32] Linzey, *The Baptism with the Holy Spirit*, p. 99. Linzey collects the views of more than twenty-five commentators, including such popular commentators as Matthew Henry, Adam Clarke, William Burkitt, Philip Schaff, Albert Barnes, Alexander Mclaren, Arthur S. Peake, and John Wesley (pp. 94-99).

[33] James Edwards, 'Initial Evidence of Holy Spirit Baptism and Pentecostal Type-Scenes in Acts' (paper presented at the annual meeting of the Society for Pentecostal Studies. South Hamilton, MA, November 1984), p. 20.

[34] Larry Hurtado, 'Normal, But Not a Norm: 'Initial Evidence' and the New Testament' in Gary McGee (ed.), *Initial Evidence: Historical and Biblical Perspectives on the Pentecostal Doctrine of Spirit Baptism* (Peabody: Hendrickson, 1991), pp. 189-201.

the Pentecostal doctrine of initial evidence rests upon three references to tongues in Acts (2.1-4; 10.44-47; 19.1-7). Instead of inferring a connection between tongues and Spirit-reception upon other scenes, Hurtado notes that each of the above scenes provides a basis not for how the Spirit is received but that the Spirit prompts and accompanies the progress of the gospel to new ethnic and cultural groups (Acts 2—the beginning of proclamation; Acts 10—the gospel to the Gentiles; and Acts 19—the gospel fulfills and eclipses the ministry of John the Baptist).[35] Edwards argues that Luke's inclusion of tongues in these three scenes emphasizes their importance at critical junctures of the mission. Still another proposal comes from Jenny Everts, who argues that the NRSV translation of Acts 2:4—'to speak in other languages' (λαλεῖν ἑτέραις γλώσσαις) creates contextual inconsistency. The translation is misleading because the NRSV translators choose to retain 'tongues' in two other references to 'γλώσσαις' (Acts 10.46, 19.6) thereby diminishing an authorial connection between the events of Pentecost and the subsequent events of Caesarea and Ephesus. According to Everts, this undermines Pentecostal belief that the tongues of Acts 2 establish a normative pattern for the life of the believer.[36]

The final question concerns development surrounding the purposes of Spirit baptism. Just as the earliest Pentecostals quickly reject and reform the failed attempt to ground their experience in 'Missionary Tongues', so also contemporary Pentecostals wrestle with purposeful relevance. For many Pentecostals, the primary purpose of Spirit baptism converges upon Jesus' words in Acts 1.8 correlating anticipated reception of the Spirit and divine enablement for witness. For example, Anthony Palma articulates the classic position. He speaks briefly to hermeneutical matters including cessationism and defense of subsequence and separability before addressing initial physical evidence. In his final chapter, Palma links purposes of Spirit baptism with fulfillment of prophecy and the exemplary life of Jesus. Results include not only power for procla-

---

[35] Hurtado, 'Normal, But Not a Norm, p. 194.
[36] Jenny Everts, 'Tongues or Languages? Contextual Consistency in the Translation of Acts 2', *JPT* 4 (April 1994), pp. 71-80.

mation and performance, but also personal transformation and ministry to the Christian community.[37]

While the notion of a baptism of power remains central to Pentecostal identity, the newfound engagement of Pentecostals in the academic marketplace spurs discussion beyond self-preservation. Scholars seek fresh approaches within broader ecclesial, canonical, pastoral, ecumenical, and dramatic purposes. For example, Robeck places life in the Spirit within an ecclesial context. Robeck implores Pentecostals to enlarge their pneumatology to include not only individual empowerment for witness, but also to view the church as a community of the Spirit; for example, a 'Spirit movement' that receives guidance for collective decision-making.[38]

At a canonical level, Pentecostals begin to pay closer attention to Luke's notion of Spirit enablement in relation to the broader Scriptures. Wonsuk Ma examines Spirit baptism based upon pneumatological motifs in the Old Testament. According to Ma, Luke applies two pneumatological impulses found in the Hebrew Scriptures, namely, Spirit-directed leadership and prophetic speech. Both impulses provide a charismatic context for Luke; as leaders fulfill God's divine calling, they receive prophetic wisdom to carry out God-given tasks.[39] Roger Cotton and Gregory Leeper explore independently the specific literary relationship between Numbers 11 and Acts 2. According to Cotton, if Acts 2 serves as the key text in understanding Pentecostal pneumatology in the New Testament, Numbers 11 serves as a key anticipatory text in the Old Testament.[40] Similarly, Leeper proposes that Numbers 11 informs Luke's pneumatology; descent of the Spirit on the seventy elders for voca-

---

[37] Anthony D. Palma, *Baptism in the Holy Spirit* (Springfield: Gospel Publishing House, 1999). For another summary of the classical Pentecostal position, see William Menzies' 'The Initial Evidence Issue: A Pentecostal Response', *AJPS* 2.2 (1999), pp. 261-78. Menzies produces brief summaries and critiques of Robert Menzies, Roli G. dela Cruz, Frank Macchia, Tan May Ling, Harold D. Hunter, Mathew S. Clark, David Lim, and Max Turner.

[38] Cecil M. Robeck, 'The Church: A Unique Movement of the Spirit', *Paraclete* 16 (1982), pp. 1-4.

[39] Wonsuk Ma, 'The Empowerment of the Spirit of God in Luke–Acts: An Old Testament Perspective', in *The Spirit and Spirituality: Essays in Honor of Russell P. Spittler* (JPTSup 24; ed. Wonsuk Ma and Robert P. Menzies; London: T & T Clark, 2004), p. 40.

[40] Roger Cotton, 'The Pentecostal Significance of Numbers 11', *JPT* 8 (1996), pp. 195-211.

tional empowerment foreshadows fulfillment of Moses' prophetic wish that 'all the Lord's people were prophets!'[41] When viewed in conjunction with Peter's quotation of Joel 2.28-32 in the Pentecost sermon, Luke infers complex expression concerning the fulfillment of a broader canonical anticipation for contemporary life of the Spirit. Glen Menzies explores 'Pre-Lucan Occurrences of the Phrase 'Tongues of Fire" as in Acts 2.3 and links its function to that of an inverted *Merkabah* text. He states: 'a visionary does not take a trip to heaven in order to experience a taste of divine glory. Instead, a bit of heaven comes down to earth'.[42] According to Menzies, Acts 2.3 should be translated 'tongues as of fire' thereby connecting Luke's rendering of this phrase with Semitic origins. Menzies then concludes that the 'tongues as of fire' provide divine accreditation to the ensuing glossolalia. Robert Menzies pursues theological and pastoral connections between Lukan and Pauline literature as suggested by a work entitled 'Spirit Baptism and Spiritual Gifts'. Menzies looks to Paul's understanding of spiritual gifts as complementary to Spirit-empowerment found in Luke.[43] So also Melvin Ho offers a comparison of glossolalia in Acts and 1 Corinthians 12-14. Ho argues for complementary purposes: 'the former is the initiation of the latter resulting in growing edification of the body and the expansion of the kingdom of God'.[44]

According to Paul Elbert, Luke writes to assist Theophilus in further pursuit and enlargement of a supernatural encounter of the Holy Spirit.[45] Luke directs Theophilus to pray for the gift of the

---

[41] Gregory J. Leeper, 'The Nature of the Pentecostal Gift with Special Reference to Numbers 11 and Acts 2', *AJPS* 6 (2003), pp. 23-38. See also James Hamill's ('The Pentecostal Experience: Acts 2.37-41', *Paraclete* 14 [1980], pp. 1-3) links between the events of Acts 2 with the Day of Pentecost, an annual Jewish harvest festival. I also recommend Wilf Hildebrandt's *An Old Testament Theology of the Spirit of God* (Peabody: Hendrickson, 1995). Hildebrandt makes fine connections between Old Testament and Lukan pneumatology.

[42] Glen Menzies, 'Pre-Lucan Occurrences of the Phrase 'Tongues of Fire',' *Pneuma* 22 (2000), p. 59.

[43] Robert P. Menzies, 'Spirit Baptism and Spiritual Gifts', in *Pentecostalism in Context: Essays in Honor of William W. Menzies* (ed. Wonsuk Ma and Robert Menzies; JPTSup 11; Sheffield: Sheffield Academic Press, 1997), pp. 48-59.

[44] Melvin Ho, 'A Comparison of Glossolalia in Acts and Corinthians', *Paraclete* 20 (Spring 1986), pp. 15-19.

Spirit (Lk. 11.13) and follows this train of thought via anticipatory texts (Lk. 24.47, 49; Acts 1.8) and initial fulfillment on the day of Pentecost (Acts 2.38). Elbert's unique contribution consists of his exegesis of events surrounding Apollos and the Ephesian community (Acts 18.23-19.7). Elbert demonstrates that this community has not yet heard and therefore not received the gift of the Spirit as in the Jerusalem/Petrine tradition. As the Lukan Paul brings the Ephesian community into this tradition, so also 'if a disciple like Theophilus prays for the gift of the Spirit as Jesus taught, then it will be given by the spiritual Jesus'.[46]

The emergence of the Roman Catholic-Pentecostal Dialogue produces valuable ecumenical discussion often centering on interpretation of Acts. For example, numerous contributors to a 1974 edition of *One in Christ*, a Catholic ecumenical journal, address various aspects of Pentecostal theology, history and exegesis. Canon Jean Giblet focuses directly upon the baptism in the Spirit in Acts; he concludes that Christian initiation is a single act consisting of conversion, baptism, and the gift of the Holy Spirit. Giblet acknowledges a 'certain spacing-out in time' (as in Samaria and Ephesus) yet does not favor an interpretation of Spirit baptism as 'a stage which only those who prepare themselves fervently will attain'.[47] However, in fine ecumenical fashion a later essay in this same volume by J. Rodman Williams argues for the classical Pentecostal position on Spirit baptism.[48]

According to Frank Macchia, tongues speech breaks barriers, protests racism and models a culturally diverse yet common witness to the gospel. In contrast to many provincial approaches to charismatic empowerment, he strives to create a liberating vision for a Pentecostal pneumatology. Macchia draws upon Moltmann's ecumenical metaphor of the Spirit inhaling to draw people together,

---

[45] Paul Elbert, 'Towards an Understanding of Luke's Expectations for Theophilus Regarding the Lukan Gift of the Holy Spirit' (paper presented at the annual meeting of the Society for Pentecostal Studies Kirkland, WA, 2000), pp. 1-50.

[46] Elbert, 'Towards an Understanding of Luke's Expectations for Theophilus Regarding the Lukan Gift of the Holy Spirit', p. 48.

[47] Jean Giblet, 'Baptism in the Spirit in the Acts of the Apostles', *One in Christ: A Catholic Ecumenical Review* 10 (1974), p. 171.

[48] J. Rodman Williams, 'Pentecostal Spirituality', *One in Christ: A Catholic Ecumenical Review* 10 (1974), pp. 180-92.

and exhaling as the missional drive into the world.[49] Richard Baer places Pentecostal tongues in a similar ecumenical context. Whereas Pentecostals link spiritual receptivity to glossolalia, Quakers and Catholics experience functional equivalence via their respective emphases upon silence and liturgy. All reveal the limits of human rationality and in their own way utilize these rituals as evidence of the presence of God.[50] Finally, Simon Chan compares the effect of Pentecostal tongues to tears with sadness. For Chan, the tears of Teresa of Avila align well with glossolalia: the 'yielded human vessel is controlled entirely by the divine Spirit—hence unlimited and unrestrained' and 'when by the Spirit Himself, using their yielded, enraptured faculties, they [the believers in Acts 2] began to magnify God … in divers languages'. Chan connects the logic of Pentecostal experience to a divine drama where participants step out of the ordinary world into a different world; such encounter might be described as 'the willing suspension of unbelief'.[51] In short, Macchia, Baer and Chan take the purpose of Spirit baptism beyond empowerment to a transformative experience.[52] As Pentecostals continue to wrestle with the relevance of Spirit baptism, scholars continue to seek not only fresh articulation of the Lukan narratives by drawing on their historical investment in a theology of divine enablement, but also the transforming nature of encounter with the living God.

2.2.3 HERMENEUTICS

A close link to any conversation of Spirit baptism obviously includes questions and concerns surrounding the hermeneutical enterprise. Since Pentecostals remain intent on sustaining and developing various interpretive identities, debate focuses regularly upon Luke–Acts. The sectional bibliography consists of an extensive compilation of essays that may not focus exclusively on Luke–Acts,

---

[49] Frank Macchia, 'Sighs Too Deep for Words: Toward a Theology of Glossolalia', *JPT* 1 (1992), pp. 47-72 and 'Groans Too Deep for Words: Toward a Theology of Tongues as Initial Evidence', *AJPS* 1.2 (1998), pp. 149-73.

[50] Richard Baer, 'Quaker Silence, Catholic Liturgy, and the Pentecostal Glossolalia—Some Functional Similarities', in Russell P. Spittler (ed.), *Perspectives on the New Pentecostalism* (Grand Rapids: Baker, 1976), pp. 152-54.

[51] Simon Chan, 'Evidential Glossolalia and the Doctrine of Subsequence', *AJPS* 2 (1999), p. 207.

[52] Chan, 'Evidential Glossolalia and the Doctrine of Subsequence', pp. 195-211. See also the brief work of Raymond Cox, 'Is Acts 2:4 Divisive?' *Paraclete* 7 (Winter 1973), pp. 11-14.

but speak to issues pertaining to biblical interpretation. Pentecostal proponents often posit their hermeneutical arguments via similar strategies to the aforementioned Dunn-like debate; they defend the adequacy of their Pentecostal theologies and practices via conversation with those of different persuasions and/or current hermeneutical models. Of these, several scholars provide influential and categorical contributions to the ongoing dialogue: Paul Elbert, Robert K. Johnston, William and Robert Menzies, French Arrington, and Russell Spittler regularly deal with the Pentecostal relationship to Evangelicals; Gerald Sheppard addresses the 'uneasy relationship' between Pentecostals and Dispensationalists; Veli-Matti Kärkkäinen considers Pentecostals in conversation with Catholic sacramentalism; and finally, Jerry Camery-Hoggatt, Timothy Cargal, Murray Dempster, Paul Lewis, and Douglas Jacobsen examine possibilities for Pentecostal theology and praxis in a postmodern world.[53]

---

[53] Concerning Evangelical issues see Paul Elbert, 'Pentecostal/Charismatic Themes' and 'Possible Literary Links Between Luke–Acts and Pauline Letters Regarding Spirit-Language', in *Intertextuality in the New Testament: Explorations of Theory and Practice* (ed. T.L. Brodie, D.R. MacDonald and S.E. Porter; NT Monographs 16; Sheffield: Sheffield University Press, 2006), pp. 226-54. See further Robert K. Johnston, 'Pentecostalism and Theological Hermeneutics: Evangelical Options', *Pneuma* 6 (Spring 1984), pp. 51-66; William Menzies, 'The Methodology of Pentecostal Theology: An Essay on Hermeneutics', in Elbert (ed.), *Essays on Apostolic Themes*, pp. 1-14. ; Robert Menzies, 'Hermeneutics: Luke's Distinctive Contribution', in William Menzies and Robert Menzies (eds.), *Spirit and Power: Foundations of Pentecostal Experience* (Grand Rapids: Zondervan, 2000), pp. 37-46; French Arrington, 'The Use of the Bible by Pentecostals', *Pneuma* 16 (1994), pp. 101-107; Russell Spittler, 'Scriptures and the Theological Enterprise: View from a Big Canoe', in Robert K. Johnston (ed.), *The Use of the Bible in Theology: Evangelical Options* (Atlanta: John Knox Press, 1985), pp. 56-77, 223-26 and Ronald Kydd, 'A Prolegomenon to Pentecostal Theologizing' (paper presented at the annual meeting of the Society for Pentecostal Studies; Wilmore, KY, 1988), p. 131. Concerning dispensationalism, see Gerald Sheppard, 'Pentecostals and the Hermeneutics of Dispensationalism: The Anatomy of an Uneasy Relationship', *Pneuma* 6 (1984), pp. 5-33 and 'Biblical Interpretation after Gadamer', *Pneuma* 16 (1994), pp. 121-41. Concerning sacramental methodologies, see Veli-Matti Kärkkäinen, 'Reading in the Spirit in Which It was Written: Pentecostal Bible Reading in Dialogue with Catholic Interpretation' (paper presented at the annual meeting of the Society for Pentecostal Studies, Cleveland, TN, March 1998). And concerning postmodern methodologies, see Jerry Camery-Hoggatt, *Speaking of God: Reading and Preaching the Word of God* (Peabody: Hendrickson, 1995); Timothy Cargal, 'Beyond the Fundamentalist-Modernist Controversy: Pentecostals and Hermeneutics in a Postmodern Age', *Pneuma* 15 (1993), pp. 163-87; Murray Dempster, 'Paradigm Shifts and Hermeneutics: Confronting Issues Old and New', *Pneuma* 15 (1993), pp. 129-35; Paul W. Lewis, 'Toward a Pentecostal Epistemology: The Role

The approaches of Camery-Hoggatt and Jacobsen warrant closer analysis. First, Camery-Hoggatt dedicates an entire volume to hermeneutics. He offers a theoretical and practical guide for preachers interested in reader response criticism. While his target audience extends beyond Pentecostals, Camery-Hoggatt addresses technical terms highly relevant for Pentecostal exegetes such as gaps, ambiguity, polyvalence, aural textures and sequence. He is also practical. He supplies two test cases, specifically his own sermons with exegesis and application on the anointing of Jesus (Lk. 7.36-50) and the parable of the Good Samaritan (Lk. 10.25-37).[54] Second, the analysis of Anabaptist Douglas Jacobsen provides a fine synopsis of current Pentecostal goals for biblical study. His conclusions connect early Pentecostal methodologies to postmodernism. Jacobsen suggests that Pentecostals employ at least ten distinguishable components in the hermeneutical process beyond the basic and standard exegetical interest in authorial intent. These include: experience, inherited interpretive schemes, intuition, systematic analysis, communal corroboration, reader response 'expansion' of the text, ritual response, desired result, academic analysis and a second naïveté. Jacobsen captures Pentecostal interest in the convergence of historical, literary, and experiential elements for biblical interpretation. Students and scholars of the Lukan narrative will benefit from his cogent summation of the interpretative process.[55]

2.2.4 SUMMARY

The first wave of Pentecostal scholarship on Luke–Acts produces respondents to the watershed work of James Dunn. While Pentecostals remain committed to their primary impulses concerning the Lukan story, they work hard to widen their vision. As they do, new concerns and ideas come into focus. While questions concerning cessationism/dispensationalism, Spirit baptism, and hermeneutics

---

of Experience in Pentecostal Hermeneutics', *The Spirit and Church* 2 (2000), pp. 95-125 and 'Reflections for Pentecostal Charismatic Research', *Cyberjournal for Pentecostal-Charismatic Research* 12 (February, 2003): www.pctii.org/cyberj/index. html.

[54] Camery-Hoggatt, *Speaking of God.*

[55] Douglas Jacobsen, 'Pentecostal Hermeneutics in Comparative Perspective' (paper presented at the annual meeting of the Society for Pentecostal Studies, Cleveland, TN, March 1998). See also the review essay by Ben Aker entitled: 'Streams in the Desert: Sources on the Spirit for Pentecostal Preachers', *Encounter: Journal for Pentecostal Ministry* 1 (2004), pp. 1-5.

remain in view, lively debate brings fresh color to the Lukan story. The above mentioned topics continue to generate significant discussion within and beyond Pentecostal studies, but these same groundbreaking efforts prepare Pentecostals well for their first full generation in the academic marketplace. For Pentecostal scholars, particularly those interested in Luke–Acts, the emergence of new paradigms and the postmodern shift provides just the right kind of methodological milieu for a Pentecostal coming of age.

CHAPTER 3

STAGE 3—OUT OF THE SHADOWS

Historicity, not narrative theology and pneumatology,
has dominated Evangelical scholarship in Acts.
And this is, of course a proper and important enterprise.
But if it becomes an exclusive vision, the interpretation of Paul (dis-
pensational and otherwise) can unduly overshadow the Christian tradi-
tion, description, and practice as portrayed by Luke.
(Paul Elbert)[1]

Pentecostals have been doing narrative theology for years although with-
out the added dimension of critical self-reflection. Hence there is a criti-
cal need for hermeneutical theorizing along these lines. And narrative
theology as it is developing outside of Pentecostalism may often provide
helpful vocabulary and criteria of evaluation as we become self-conscious
about what we have for so long done naturally …
With the discovery of narrative theology we are suddenly on the cutting
edge of the contemporary theological scene.
(Jerry Camery-Hoggatt)[2]

In this chapter I propose a third stage of Pentecostal scholarship on
the Lukan story. Following the pre-critical and Dunn-influenced
eras, Pentecostal scholars though relatively new to the academic
arena delve into new territory. With battles concerning Cessation-

---

[1] Elbert, 'Pentecostal/Charismatic Themes', p. 207.
[2] Personal correspondence between Jerry Camery-Hoggatt (July 23, 1985) and
Michael Dowd cited in 'Contours of a Narrative Pentecostal Theology and Practice' (paper presented at the annual meeting of the Society for Pentecostal Studies, Gaithersburg, MD, November 1985).

ism, post-conversion experience of the Spirit and certain hermeneutical questions in check, fresh areas of research take shape. In
the chapter at hand, I begin with concerns long central to Pentecostal understanding and utilization of Luke–Acts. Whether relying on
the Lukan narrative for theology and praxis surrounding missions
and evangelism, healing and exorcism, or controversial issues such
as Oneness or women, Pentecostal scholars bring their history—
literally their stories—into their scholarship. While the categories in
the next two chapters share certain similarities with general surveys
of Luke–Acts, it is important to note how unique questions and
concerns guide the emergence of Pentecostal scholarship.[3] With
this in mind I begin with the emergence of literary criticism. It
would be hard to imagine a more timely methodological shift for
Pentecostals. In fact, growing interest in literary criticism brings the
above mentioned categories not only to the fringe of Lukan scholarship but also creates possibilities for cutting edge contributions.

3.1 THE TRIUMPH OF NARRATIVE THEOLOGY

Any survey of the history of Christian doctrine regularly points to
the importance of creeds and propositional statements as the basis
for belief and praxis. However, as John Goldingay notes:

> Narrative, story, dominates scripture ... At one level, Christian
> tradition has indeed always recognized the importance of story,
> but you would not guess this from the nature of Christian theol-
> ogy, or from the nature of most writing on spirituality ... It is a
> natural and biblical way to do theology; it takes up the discourse
> methods of Paul. Yet narrative is scripture's more dominant way
> of doing theology.[4]

This statement certainly resonates with the emergence of Pentecostal scholarship. Recent hermeneutical and theological advances

---

[3] For example, see Bovon (*Luke The Theologian*). He presents a survey of
Luke–Acts research according to (1) Theology, History, Literature, the History of
Salvation, and Eschatology; (2) the Holy Scriptures; (3) Christology; (4) the Holy
Spirit; (5) Conversion; (6) Ethics; (7) Ecclesiology, Church, Mission, Baptism,
Meals and Eucharist, Ministry, Worship and Prayer (504).

[4] John Goldingay, 'Biblical Story and the Way It Shapes Our Story', (paper
presented as a Wesley Gilpin Lecture; Regents Theological College, Nantwich,
England, 1997). Later published in *EPTA* 17 (1997), pp. 5-6.

gained through narrative theology give Pentecostals fresh opportunities to voice ideas previously either out of bounds or otherwise difficult to convey. For example, in 1977, Ronald Kydd penned a popular pamphlet for the Pentecostal Assemblies of Canada. In *I'm Still There!*, Kydd defends classic Spirit baptism and initial evidence by way of narrative application, yet offers minimal reference to narrative terminology.[5] Only a few years later, the rapid development of narrative criticism provides the necessary language. The recent migration of the literary/narrative critical methodologies from the humanities into biblical studies provides Pentecostals, possibly more than any other contemporary tradition, opportunity in an ever-changing academic arena. The exegetical impulses of the early Pentecostals find in narrative analysis the technical language necessary for their emergence in the academic marketplace.[6]

In a seldom-cited essay, Michael Dowd discusses the likes of Hans Frei, Robert Alter, Northrop Frye and Walter Ong. Using Ong-like discourse, Dowd argues Pentecostals have long been aware that the power of the Holy Spirit is unleashed through orality—in witnessing, telling and hearing stories of God's mighty love and actions—otherwise not possible through mere theological argument.[7] Dowd explains that Pentecostals have long proclaimed that propositional truth cannot report the whole truth. To the contrary, narrative theology aids Pentecostals by counterbalancing undemanding, propositional theologies and hermeneutics with one that is more experiential, imaginative, story-based and Spirit-led. While he recognizes the value of methodological advances from source criticism, form criticism, redaction criticism and other 'historical-critical' approaches, he maintains that for Pentecostals these tools

---

[5] Ronald Kydd, *I'm Still There! A Reaffirmation of Tongues as the Initial Evidence of the Baptism in the Holy Spirit* (Toronto: Pentecostal Assemblies of Canada, 1977).

[6] Methodological transitions begin to occur in the 1970s. For example, R. Hollis Gause (Church of God [Cleveland, TN]) completed a PhD dissertation at Emory University under the supervision of William Beardslee. In *The Lukan Transfiguration Account: Luke's Pre-Crucifixion Presentation of the Exalted Lord in the Glory of the Kingdom of God* (PhD diss., Emory University, 1975) Gause produces what may well be the first doctoral project on Luke–Acts by a Pentecostal. Gause utilizes form and redaction criticism to argue that the Transfiguration and Ascension narratives furnish the early Christians with a proleptical experience of the consummated kingdom of God and the Parousia respectively.

[7] Michael B. Dowd, 'Contours of a Narrative Pentecostal Theology and Practice', p. 3.

offer only pre-interpretive work.[8] Another important essay on narrative methodology comes by way of William Menzies' challenge to Fee (see 2.1.1 above) and Evangelicals steeped in historical criticism. Menzies argues that narrative analysis offers readers fresh possibilities for the doctrine of subsequence not available via earlier methodologies.[9] In short, the power of the Christian story and of individual biblical stories shines forth not only via dissection, but also through its ability to grab attention, capture the imagination, draw in, and change the reader.[10]

Scott Ellington argues that Pentecostal students of the Bible find value not simply in the historicity of ancient stories, but in how these stories are best remembered in order to create, impact, shape, and re-create community identity. Such expectation means that the historical critical approach, while providing an indispensable foundation for biblical interpretation, cannot fully articulate Pentecostal approaches to hermeneutics because of a foundation in and restriction to a rationalist worldview.[11] Similarly, John Goldingay builds upon Paul Ricoeur's 'hermeneutics of testimony' and argues that narratives create expectations for future encounters with God helping the believing community transform 'the story' into 'our story'.[12] Given the dominant use of narrative in the Scriptures, Goldingay calls for a better understanding of the Christian faith as a narrative statement built upon 'biblical story and the way it shapes our story'.[13]

John Christopher Thomas views the Jerusalem Council (Acts 15) as a model for contemporary biblical application. Thomas sets up Acts 15 as a test case where the apostolic community finds a resolution to thorny issues surrounding Gentile inclusion into the early Jewish Christian community. The decision comes not only through the use of the Hebrew Scriptures, but also the Holy Spirit's inter-

---

[8] Dowd, 'Contours of a Narrative Pentecostal Theology and Practice', p. 24.

[9] William Menzies, 'Coming to Terms with an Evangelical Heritage: Pentecostals and the Issue of Subsequence' in *Contemporary Issues in Pentecostal Theology* (First Annual Pentecostal Lectureship Series; Baguio City: APTS, 1993), pp. 97-108.

[10] Dowd, 'Contours', p. 25.

[11] Scott Ellington, 'History, Story and Testimony: Locating Truth in a Pentecostal Hermeneutic' (paper presented at the annual meeting of the Society for Pentecostal Studies, Kirkland, WA, March 2000), p. 1.

[12] Goldingay, 'Biblical Story and the Way It Shapes Our Story', p. 6.

[13] Goldingay, 'Biblical Story and the Way It Shapes Our Story', p. 5.

pretative involvement during a lively discussion period. According to Thomas, the ensuing tridactic method might serve as a worthy contemporary hermeneutic; biblical interpretation ought to be discerned in the context of vibrant Pentecostal communities, who follow the leading of the Spirit via rigorous reading of the Scriptures.[14] Kenneth Archer builds on Thomas' work and suggests a similar interdependent dialogical relationship between Scripture, Spirit and community.[15]   For Archer, biblical narrative, properly understood, moves a reader beyond individualization to the place of one reader among many. This 'reader in community' finds an interpretative method already rooted in the Scriptures.[16] According to Archer (and Thomas), the apostolic community, when faced with diverse and even contradictory information concerning a particular practice or concern, receives guidance and fresh insights from the Holy Spirit through experience, visions, gifts, testimonies, and the Scriptures. Such understanding makes for fresh meaning and relevance in ever-new contexts. James Shelton also echoes employment of Luke–Acts for the defining of faith and practice. Shelton finds paradigmatic patterns in the Lukan narrative. Like Thomas and Archer, Shelton examines the proceedings at the Jerusalem Council in Acts 15 and proposes a normative pneumatic epistemology. The resolution concerning the conversion of the Gentiles comes not merely via *sola scriptura*, but as a pneumatic response, namely, the affirmation of God's action on behalf of Gentiles as interpreted by Spirit-led

---

[14] John Christopher Thomas, 'Women, Pentecostals and the Bible: An Experiment in Pentecostal Hermeneutics', *JPT* 5 (1994), pp. 41-56; See also his 'Reading the Bible from Our Tradition: A Pentecostal Test Case', in *Between Two Horizons: Spanning New Testament Studies and Systematic Theology* (ed. Joel Green and Max Turner; Grand Rapids: Eerdmans, 2000), pp. 108-122.

[15] Kenneth Archer, *A Pentecostal Hermeneutic for the Twentieth Century: Spirit, Scripture and Community* (JPTSup 6. London: T & T Clark International, 2004), 2. See also his earlier works: 'A Pentecostal Hermeneutical Strategy: Spirit, Community and Scripture' (paper presented at the annual meeting of the Society for Pentecostal Studies; Wilmore, KY, March 2003); 'Early Pentecostal Biblical Interpretation' (Revision of 'Early Pentecostal Biblical Interpretation: Blurring the Boundaries'); and 'Pentecostal Story: The Hermeneutical Filter for the Making of Meaning', *Pneuma* 26 (Spring 2004), pp. 36-59.

[16] Archer, *A Pentecostal Hermeneutic*, pp. 12-13. See the response to Archer by Paul Elbert, 'Toward a Pentecostal Hermeneutic: Observations on Archer's Progressive Proposal', *AJPS* 9.2 (2006), pp. 320-28.

apostles.[17] In short, the interpretative methods of the early church provide a model for contemporary readers in their current communities.[18]

Paul Elbert serves as another influential pioneer for narrative interpretation of Luke–Acts. In a number of independent essays, Elbert looks specifically at the use of narrative in ancient contexts. In 'An Observation on Luke's Composition and Narrative Style of Questions', Elbert builds upon the earlier work of Cadbury and compares Luke's narrative style to that of the epic poet Homer.[19] Elbert concludes that Luke's extensive use of questions (152 in Luke; 70 in Acts) often directs the flow of the narrative thereby leading readers to possibilities of clarity, plausibility and persuasiveness.[20] Luke and Homer share stylistic tendencies; both make use of analytical questions in order to move readers toward narrative comprehension (e.g., Lk. 12.51; 17.18; Acts 8.30; 8.36; 19.2). Elbert also examines the work of Theon of Alexandria, a contemporary of Luke. Elbert mines Theon's *Progymnasmata*, a treatise on narrative composition, and discusses Theon's rhetorical devices, particularly questions designed to get at the interior life of characters.[21] In a similar vein, Luke makes use of pithy questions such as 'What does this mean?' (Acts 2.12) or 'Brethren, what shall we do?' (Acts 2.37). Such questions serve as rhetorical devices to anticipate intended (or at least implied) responses from characters and in turn appropriate responses by subsequent readers. These questions also provide further information befitting the narrative-rhetorical categories of amplification/elaboration; they enhance vividness, stimulate cognitive

---

[17] Shelton, 'Epistemology and Authority in the Acts of the Apostles: An Analysis and Test Case Study of Acts 15:1-29' (paper presented at the annual meeting of the Society for Pentecostal Studies, Springfield, MO, March 1999).

[18] See also French L. Arrington, *The Acts of the Apostles: Introduction, Translation and Commentary* (Peabody, MA: Hendrickson, 1988), p. 118.

[19] Paul Elbert, 'An Observation on Luke's Composition and Narrative Style of Questions', *CBQ* 66 (2003), pp. 98-109.

[20] Elbert, 'An Observation on Luke's Composition and Narrative Style of Questions', pp. 100, 102.

[21] See the most recent critical edition by Michael Patillon, *Aelius Théon Progymnasmata: Texte établi et traduit* (Collection des Universités de France; Paris: Les Belles Lettres, 1997).

reactions, encourage new ideas, review previous material, and/or call for reevaluation of current conditions.[22]

In a second paper, Elbert suggests 'Luke's Fulfillment of Prophecy Theme' be understood as prophetic historiography. Luke writes as an apologist by providing examples and precedents for use in defense and definition of Christian experience and tradition. For example, prophecies concerning Jesus as a heavenly and previously earthly character find their fulfillment both within the Lukan story and also beyond narrative time.[23] This realization and awareness produces a certain excitement and a mood of expectancy for Theophilus and other Christian readers temporally 'afar off'. Readers continue to participate amidst prophetic fulfillment into the current day.[24] In a later article, Elbert critiques the limiting historiographical methodology of Pentecostal historian Vinson Synan. In 'Acts of the Holy Spirit', Elbert builds upon the previous essay and argues that Pentecostals do not simply overturn a dominant cessationist paradigm by reversing the categories for spiritual gifts and supernatural intervention. Instead, Pentecostals venture to apply Luke's long idle narrative expectations for the work of the Holy Spirit as prophetic fulfillment. Elbert advises Pentecostal scholars to embrace the global magnitude of renewal/revival experiences and celebrate the ongoing prophetic fulfillment anticipated in the Lukan story.[25] In these studies, Elbert not only emphasizes the didactic value that both Luke and the ancients would have expected for their readers, but also extends meaning to include ongoing didactic benefit for contemporary readers.

In still another previously cited essay focused on 'Pentecostal/Charismatic Themes', it comes as no surprise that Elbert challenges members of Evangelical Theological Society for their limited approach to narrative texts. He chides Evangelicals for statements such as 'We believe the events of Acts happened, we just don't want

---

[22] Elbert, 'An Observation on Luke's Composition and Narrative Style of Questions', p. 105.

[23] Elbert, 'Luke's Fulfillment of Prophecy Theme: Introductory Exploration of Joel and the Last Days' (paper presented at the annual meeting of the Society for Pentecostal Studies, Milwaukee, WI, March 2004), p. 24.

[24] Elbert, 'Luke's Fulfillment of Prophecy Theme', p. 24.

[25] Elbert, 'Acts of the Holy Spirit: Hermeneutical and Historiographical Reflections', *Refleks: Med Karismatisk Kristendom i Focus* 4/1 (2005), pp. 48-97.

them to happen to us'.[26] Ironically, though conservative Evangelicals fight alongside Pentecostals to defend the historical reliability of the Lukan narratives, Pentecostals employ a narrative methodology and expect that the Lukan story 'happens to them'.

In two final papers, Elbert considers the implications of literary links between Luke–Acts and the Pauline literature. In an exegetical review entitled 'Paul of the Miletus Speech' (Acts 20.18-35), Elbert offers an appreciative critique of Steve Walton.[27] Elbert affirms Walton's narrative-critical conclusion that the speech of the Lukan Paul at Miletus seeks to pass on and commend Pauline tradition, specifically verbal parallels in vocabulary and thought from 1 Thessalonians, as well as themes from Jesus' life and teaching in the Third Gospel (Lk. 12.1-53; 22.14-38). Elbert echoes Walton's suggestion of four primary speech themes (faithful fulfillment of leadership responsibility, past and future suffering, attitudes to wealth and work, and Jesus' death) and illustrates Luke's intent for Paul's speech to serve as a concrete example of an evangelist/pastor communicating revelatory details to those under his ministry. In 'Possible Literary Links', Elbert argues that Luke clarifies for his readers Paul's treatment on the activity of the Spirit. Luke produces for Theophilus a progymnastically-suited narrative that provides

---

[26] Elbert, 'Pentecostal/Charismatic Themes', p. 207. See also Gary McGee's '"More Than Evangelical": The Challenge of the Evolving Identity of the Assemblies of God', in David Roozen & James Nieman (eds.), *Church, Identity and Change: Theology and Denominational Structures in Unsettled Times* (Grand Rapids: Eerdmans, 2005), pp. 35-45. McGee points to the turn from a sympathetic hermeneutic between early Pentecostals with Wesleyan Holiness and Higher Life teachings to a less sympathetic one now held by Evangelicals revealing the influence of classical Reformed theology (p. 41). D.A. Carson (*Showing the Spirit: A Theological Exposition of 1 Cor 12-14*) gives such a caricature:

> The charismatics, they (non-charismatics) think, have succumbed to the modern love of 'experience', even at the expense of truth. Charismatics are thought to be profoundly unbiblical, especially when they evaluate their experience of tongues to the level of theological and spiritual shibboleth. If they are growing, no small part of their strength can be ascribed to their raw triumphalism, their populist elitism, their promise of short cuts to holiness and power ... (they are) devoid of any real grasp of the Bible that goes beyond mere prooftexting (p. 12; it should be noted that Carson distances himself from this position).

[27] Elbert ('Paul of the Miletus Speech and 1 Thessalonians: Critique and Considerations', *ZNW* 95/2 [2004], pp. 258-64) responds to Steve Walton, *Leadership and Lifestyle: The Portrait of Paul in the Miletus Speech and 1 Thessalonians* (SNTSMS 108; Cambridge: Cambridge University Press, 2000).

both clarifying examples and resultant precedents for life in the Spirit.[28]

Just as classical Pentecostals benefit from narrative analysis, so also members of the Charismatic community begin to practice narrative analysis. Unfortunately, while Charismatic Catholic William Kurz ranks among the most prolific Lukan scholars of this generation, he receives little attention from the Pentecostal/Charismatic community. Though due in part to Kurz's intentional relationship to the broader academic community, he remains an occasional visitor to the Society for Pentecostal Studies. His work certainly deserves further attention in the Pentecostal community. As for his affinity to the Charismatic community, Kurz states in an early discipleship guide: 'as a teacher, scripture scholar, and priest, I am convinced that the messages in Luke and Acts are meant for today'. [29] He offers autobiographical commentary to highlight Luke's emphasis upon Spirit empowerment as the way of the Christian. He states: '... just as the charismatic movement of God's Spirit provided the occasion for my turning point, so the Baptist's movement at the Jordan did for Jesus. At the beginning of his mission, Jesus experienced the Father's love and Spirit's power, in a way I can appreciate more because of my own experience'.[30] This experience surely sets Kurz on a prolific journey into Lukan scholarship. It is also noteworthy that this discipleship booklet represents one of the earliest concerted efforts at a reading of Luke–Acts as a two-volume work.

---

[28] Elbert, 'Possible Literary Links', pp. 252-54. As to Luke's awareness of the Pauline letters, Elbert writes: '"If Luke knows Pauline letters, why doesn't he quote them?" My response is that to do so directly does not suit his purpose, just like quoting probable prophetic speech by Phillip's daughters (Acts 21:8-9) did not suit his purpose' (p. 254). A modified version of this essay appears as 'Probable Literary Connections Between Luke–Acts and Pauline Letters Regarding Spirit-Language' (paper presented at the annual meeting of the Society for Pentecostal Studies, Pasadena, CA, March 2006).

[29] William Kurz, *Following Jesus: A Disciple's Guide to Luke and Acts* (Ann Arbor, MI: Servant Books, 1984). A revised edition appeared in 2003. See his similarly popular and reflective commentaries *The Acts of the Apostles* (Collegeville Bible Commentary 5; Collegeville, MN: Liturgical Press, 1983); *The Acts of the Apostles* (The Collegeville Bible Commentary; ed. Diane Bergant & Robert Karris; Collegeville, MN: Liturgical, 1989), pp. 1031-68; 'Journey with Jesus (in Luke)', *God's Word Today* 3/12 (1981), pp. 37-43; parts reprinted in *The Sooner Catholic* 10/26 (December 18, 1983), p. 9. Note also that Kurz began his journey into Luke–Acts with his dissertation entitled 'The Function of Christological Proof from Prophecy for Luke and Justin' (PhD diss., Yale University, 1976).

[30] Kurz, *Following Jesus*, p. 15.

In *Reading Luke–Acts: Dynamics of Biblical Narrative*, Kurz, now a seasoned scholar, provides students and scholars alike a thorough methodological guide to narrative criticism. He explores questions concerning authors, narrators, and readers as well as literary conventions such as prologues, point of view, narrative speed, narrator sympathies, *prosopopoeia* (narrative mouthpieces), positive and negative *exempla*, comparison between characters (individuals and groups), gaps, plotting, sequence, foreshadowing and flashbacks, repetition, and irony all through a Lukan lens.[31] Though devoid of classical Pentecostal language and no conspicuous support for Pentecostal distinctives, Kurz strives to read Luke–Acts as a narrative model for imitation and thereby reveals exegetical sympathies comparable to Pentecostals on the nature of Luke's charismatic theology.

Kurz contributes to Lukan scholarship not only by way of critical methodologies but also through specific exegetical efforts. For example, Kurz situates the Lukan story in the tradition of Hellenistic and Septuagintal models for imitation. Luke employs overt *exempla* as well as implicit paradigmatic elements, both familiar to an informed first century reader. According to Kurz, since all writers compose in the absence of would-be readers, they must imagine the concerns of their readers.[32] Therefore, farewell addresses by Jesus (Lk. 22.14-38) and Paul (Acts 20.17-30) serve as authoritative guides for Christian leadership. As Jesus reclines for a final meal with his disciples, he implies that they too would take, bless, and give bread to future followers. Jesus also exhorts his disciples to imitate his reversal of authority. The disciples should not 'lord' over the kingdom, but serve in the same manner as their master. Following the Last Supper, the Lukan Jesus prays on the Mount of Olives and then implores his disciples not to fall into temptation (Lk. 22.39). In

---

[31] Kurz, *Reading Luke–Acts: Dynamics of Biblical Narrative* (Louisville: Westminster/John Knox, 1993). See further earlier articles that introduce Kurz's methodological development: 'Narrative Approaches to Luke–Acts', *Biblica* 68.2 (1987), pp. 195-222; 'Luke–Acts' in *New Catholic Encyclopedia: Volume XVIII Supplement 1978-1989* (2nd ed; New Catholic Dictionary Supplemental Series 3; Palatine, IL: Jack Heraty & Associates with the Catholic University of America, 1989), pp. 268-71. Kurz includes sections entitled 'New Approaches', 'Shifts in Scholarship', and 'Narrative Criticism'.

[32] Kurz, 'Narrative Models for Imitation in Luke–Acts', in *Greeks, Romans, and Christians: Essays in Honor of Abraham J. Malherbe* (ed. David L. Balch, Wayne A. Meeks, and Everett Ferguson; Minneapolis: Fortress, 1990), pp. 171-89.

the narrative context, Luke utilizes this scene of the praying Jesus as an implicit model for failing disciples. In Paul's farewell address, the Lukan Paul admonishes Ephesian leaders (and future leaders) to remember and imitate his oversight as a guardian of the people of God.[33]

Though Kurz remains a virtual unknown in many Pentecostal/Charismatic circles, he demonstrates significant affinity with Pentecostal exegesis and application of the Lukan story. He states: 'the Hellenistic rhetorical paradigmatic use of narratives provides a grounding in the text for typical ethical, homiletic, and other church uses of Lukan stories as models for contemporary Christian behavior'.[34] By way of summary, Elbert, Kurz and other literary specialists provide technical language complementary to Pentecostal intuition. Pentecostals undoubtedly locate their literary perceptivity alongside any syntactical and lexical data or historical-critical proclivities.

---

[33] Kurz devotes considerable attention to the farewell addresses in Luke 22 and Acts 20 in the following works: 'Luke 22.14-38 and Greco-Roman and Biblical Farewell Addresses', *JBL* 104 (1985), pp. 251-68 and the ensuing monograph *Farewell Addresses in the New Testament* (Zacchaeus Studies: New Testament; Collegeville: Liturgical Press [A Michael Glazier Book], 1990).

[34] Kurz, 'Narrative Models', pp. 188-89. Readers should consult further works (in order of appearance): 'Acts 3:19-26 as a Test of the Role of Eschatology in Lukan Christology', *SBLSP* 16 (1977), pp. 309-23; 'Hellenistic Rhetoric in the Christological Proof of Luke–Acts', *CBQ* 42 (1980), pp. 171-95; 'Luke–Acts and Historiography in the Greek Bible', *SBLSP* 19 (1980), pp. 283-300; 'Luke 3.23-38 and Greco-Roman and Biblical Genealogies' in Charles H. Talbert (ed.), *Luke-Acts: New Perspectives from the Society of Biblical Literature Seminar* (New York: Crossroad, 1984), pp. 169-87; 'Luke the Artist', *Continuum* 1 (Autumn 1990), pp. 180-182; 'The Problem with Prophecy—Part I', *New Covenant* 23.2 (September 1993), pp. 11-13; 'The Problem with Prophecy—Part II: Every Prophecy Must Be Discerned', *New Covenant* 23.3 (October 1993), pp. 23-26; 'Intertextual Use of Sirach 48.1-16 in Plotting Luke–Acts' in Craig A. Evans and W. Richard Stegne (eds.), *The Gospels and Scriptures of Israel* (JSNTSS 104; Sheffield, England: Sheffield Academic Press, 1994), pp. 308-24; 'Effects of Variant Narrators in Acts 10-11', *New Testament Studies* 43 (1997), pp. 570-86; 'The Open-Ended Nature of Luke and Acts as Inviting Canonical Actualization', *Neotestamentica* 31.2 (1997), pp. 289-308; 'Promise and Fulfillment in Hellenistic Jewish Narratives and in Luke and Acts' in David P. Moessner (ed.), *Jesus and the Heritage of Israel: Luke's Narrative Claim upon Israel's Legacy* (*Luke the Interpreter of Israel*, vol. 1; Harrisburg, PA: Trinity Press International, 1999); Co-authored volume with Luke Timothy Johnson, *The Future of Catholic Biblical Scholarship: A Constructive Conversation* (Grand Rapids: Eerdmans, 2002); *Reading the Bible as God's Own Story: A Catholic Approach for Bringing Scripture to Life* (Ijamsville, MD: Word Among Us Press, 2007). On a personal note, Father Kurz served as my dissertation mentor; he played a crucial role not only in my passion for Lukan studies, but also in helping to locate my theology and worldview firmly in the Pentecostal tradition.

3.2 MISSIOLOGY

Any informed reader of Luke–Acts with reasonable longevity in the Pentecostal tradition knows well the importance of missions. Pentecostals easily recall innumerable homiletical and pastoral references to Luke's story as a standard for evangelism. For this reason, it comes as no surprise that as Pentecostals move into the academic marketplace, they focus squarely on Luke's keen interest in evangelism. For the sake of structure, I offer the following general categories: 1) the relationship between Spirit and missions; 2) the relationship between ecclesiology and missions; and 3) the intersection of ethics and missions.

First, given Pentecostal interest in Spirit baptism and the *charismata*, Pentecostals feast on the meeting point between Spirit and missions. Straightforward examples include David Chee Wai Cheum's identification of the early Christian community as Spirit-filled, Spirit-led, and Spirit-directed in their evangelistic endeavors. The early church ever filled and disciplined in prayer provides a paradigm for effective contemporary mission.[35] Roli G. dela Cruz examines Luke's use of Joel 2.28-32 and its fulfillment in Acts 2. He concludes that Luke strategically places a faithful abstract of Peter's real speech at this critical juncture to exhort the young apostolic mission toward similar Spirit enablement.[36]

Paul Brooks suggests the '*when*' and '*where*' questions of mission find answers by way of the Holy Spirit. Followers of Jesus experience the convergence of Spirit and power, Spirit and timing, Spirit and guidance, and Spirit and impartation for the purpose of witness.[37] Like Brooks, Mark Wilson examines four passages that deal specifically with missiological direction given by the Spirit: the prediction of a famine by Agabus (11.27-30), the commissioning and sending of Paul and Barnabas from Antioch (13.1-4), Paul's bypassing of Asia and Bithynia (16.6-7), and Paul's Spirit-driven march to

---

[35] David Chee Wai Cheum, 'The Spirit and Mission in the Book of Acts', *Journal of Asian Mission* 6.1 (2004), pp. 3-15. Murray W. Dempster, 'Pentecostal Social Concern and the Biblical Mandate of Social Justice', *Pneuma* 9 (Fall 1987), pp. 129-53.

[36] Roli G. dela Cruz, 'Luke's Application of Joel 2:28-32 in Peter's Sermon in Acts 2', *CPCR* 4 (1998): http://www.pctii.org/cyberj/cyberj4/cruz.html.

[37] Paul Brooks, 'The Spirit and Mission in Acts', *Paraclete* 25 (Winter 1991), pp. 14, 22.

Jerusalem (20.22-24).[38] Jerry Roberts produces a similar outline and examines five decision-making episodes in Acts, namely, the selection of Matthias (Acts 1.15-26); the decision to continue ministry in the midst of persecution (Acts 4.23-31); the selection of the Seven (Acts 6.1-7); a defense of Gentile conversion (Acts 11.1-18) and the Jerusalem Council (Acts 15.1-35), in light of the apostolic mission. Roberts analyzes Luke's integrative use of Scripture, prayer, Christology, storytelling, and pneumatology to conclude that these pivotal events provide a paradigm for missiological discernment linked to Jesus' promise in Acts 1.8.[39] Mark Barclift reviews Luke's use of 'negative guidance' whereby Paul and his companions receive instruction from the Spirit not to preach in Asia (Acts 16.6) and to stay out of Bithynia by the Spirit of Jesus (Acts 16.7).[40]

Youngmo Cho affirms that the Spirit in Luke–Acts inspires proclamation of the gospel; like others before him, Cho contrasts Luke's pneumatological missiology with that of Paul, who views the Spirit as the source of kingdom living.[41] Assemblies of God missiologist Melvin Hodges looks to Acts 1 as a missiological bridge that takes the ministry of Jesus to unchartered territory. Luke transfers responsibility for preaching of the kingdom to the disciples. When the earthly Jesus ascends, the disciples do not fail but forge ahead. According to Hodges, the new mission succeeds not simply because the disciples receive adequate preparation and experience the risen Lord, but by way of their Pentecost experience and the accompanying power of the Holy Spirit. Once equipped with necessary understanding and experience, the disciples set out and fulfill their mission.[42]

---

[38] Mark Wilson, 'The Role of the Holy Spirit in Paul's Ministry Journeys' (paper presented at the annual meeting of the Society for Pentecostal Studies. Wilmore, KY, March 2003). Concerning Paul's vision of the man of Macedonia, see also M.A. Barclift, 'Supernatural Guidance in Acts 16:6-10', *Paraclete* 18 (Fall 1984), pp. 8-10.

[39] Jerry Roberts, *Discerning God's Will: Spiritual Guidance from an Acts-Luke Perspective* (Kearney, NE: Morris Publishing, 2005).

[40] Mark Barclift, 'Supernatural Guidance', pp. 8-10.

[41] Youngmo Cho, 'Spirit and Kingdom in Luke–Acts: Proclamation as the Primary Role of the Spirit in Relation to the Kingdom of God in Luke–Acts', *AJPS* 6 (2003), pp. 173-97.

[42] Melvin L. Hodges, 'Acts 1—Bridge to an Apostolic Ministry', *Paraclete* 12 (Summer 1978), pp. 29-31.

John Michael Penney investigates the eschatological presence of the Spirit as the inaugurating fulfillment of the Abrahamic promise to reverse the fall and restore blessing to the ends of the earth.[43] The Spirit serves not merely as a force to compensate for the ascended Christ, but the power of Christ to bring God's promises to fruition. For Luke, incorporation into the community of the faithful means sharing in its pneumatic mission.[44] C. Peter Wagner reads Acts as a missiological theorist and church growth specialist.[45] In a chapter entitled 'Should Foreigners Run the Church? Acts 6', Wagner surveys cross-cultural and paradigmatic elements of the selection of Spirit-led ordained leaders from within the ranks of the Gentile community thereby moving the church from a monocultural to bi-cultural movement.[46] Finally, Manual Bagalawis connects Luke's emphasis on the power of the Holy Spirit to miracles and evangelism. According to Bagalawis, Luke associates twenty of twenty-five references to power with miraculous acts.[47] Just as signs and wonders greatly enhance the disciples' witness in Acts, so also miracles and supernatural manifestations today make evangelistic efforts more effective.[48]

Second, numerous scholars find a Lukan link between missions and ecclesiology. In an analysis of Acts 1-8, Tim Munyon links Luke's use of the adverb *homothumadon* (10/11 times in Acts—for example, 1.14; 2.46; 4.24; 5.12; 8.6) and the verb *proskartereo* (6/10 times in Acts—1.14; 2.42; 2.46; 6.4; 8.13) as parallel criteria for revival. As the early Christians 'continued steadfastly' in 'one accord',

---

[43] John Michael Penney, *The Missionary Emphasis of Lukan Pneumatology* (JPTSup 12; Sheffield: Sheffield Academic Press, 1997), p. 121.

[44] Penney, *The Missionary Emphasis of Lukan Pneumatology*, p. 122.

[45] C. Peter Wagner, *Spreading the Fire: A New Look at Acts—God's Training Manual For Every Christian* (vol. 1 of Acts of the Holy Spirit; Ventura, CA: Regal Books, 1994).

[46] Wagner, *Spreading the Fire*, pp. 167-92.

[47] Manuel A. Bagalawis, '"Power" in Acts 1:8; Effective Witnessing Through Signs and Wonders', *Asian Journal of Mission* 3 (2001), pp. 3-4. References to power and the miraculous include: Lk. 1.35; 4.36; 5.17; 6.19; 8.46; 9.1; 10.13, 19; 19.37; 21.26, 27; Acts 2.22; 3.12; 4.7, 33; 6.8; 8.10, 13; 10.38; 19.11. Bagalawis also notes the five references to power apart from miraculous acts: Lk. 1.17 (power causing people to repent); 4.14-15 (power for proclamation); and three ambiguous acts (Lk. 22.69; 24.49; Acts 1.8).

[48] Bagalawis, '"Power" in Acts 1:8', p. 1.

the church grows.[49] In classic Pentecostal fashion Larry Williams and John Amstutz utilize Acts as a model for church growth.[50] Amstutz specifically highlights components of the newly formed and developing ecclesiological community: visible expressions to the love of God, conducive structure, priesthood of all believers, expanding base of leadership, indigenization, cultural sensitivity, strategic focus on receptive people, and a focus upon the multiplication of disciples. Jeff Stacey finds correlation between revivals in Northampton under Jonathan Edwards in 1734-35 and 1740-42 and the various sequences, frequencies, and distribution of events and activities in Acts 2-19. Stacey charts similarities such as movement of preachers, the geographical scope of the movement, proclamation, miracles, positive and negative responses as well as short and long term impact.[51] John Tipei examines Luke's employment of the laying on of hands and finds at least three purposes. Whether by way of healing (Lk. 4.40; 13.13; Acts 5.12, 9.17; 14.3; 19.11; 28.8), reception of the Spirit (Acts 8.17; 19.6), or commissioning (Acts 6.6; 13.2), hands of the leaders signal the transference of God's power and anointing.[52]

F.J. May proposes six major church growth principles employed by Luke and still relevant for today, namely, the role of the Holy Spirit, the ministry of prayer, the primacy of apostolic preaching, signs and wonders, cross-cultural contextualization, and church planting. May also emphasizes the critical role of pastoral leadership and a well trained laity.[53] Norman Scheffer insists that Acts emphasizes not only the call to faithful proclamation for spiritual and nu-

---

[49] Tim Munyon, 'Two Criteria for Revival in Acts 1-8', *Paraclete* 25 (Winter 1991), pp. 10-13.

[50] John Amstutz, 'Beyond Pentecost: A Study of Some Sociological Dimensions of New Testament Growth From the Book of Acts', in Elbert (ed.), *Essays on Apostolic Themes*, pp. 208-25 and Larry Williams, 'The Basic Pattern for Church Growth', *Paraclete* 22 (Spring 1988), pp. 27-30.

[51] Jeff Stacey, 'Does the Historical Phenomenon of Revival Have a Recognizable 'Pattern' of Characteristic, Observable Features?' *Australasian Pentecostal Studies* 8 (2004): http://aps.webjournals.org/Issues.asp?index=216&id={040F588 A-17ED-484A-93CD-51C5827AB5D9}

[52] John F. Tipei, 'The Function of Laying on of Hands in the New Testament', *JEPTA* 20 (2000), pp. 93-115. Tipei later produces the full length monograph entitled: *The Laying on of Hands in the New Testament: Its Significance, Techniques, and Effects* (Lanham, MD: University Press of America, 2008).

[53] F.J. May, *The Book of Acts and Church Growth* (Cleveland, TN: Pathway Press, 1990).

merical growth but also church planting.[54] Scheffer notes that the church at Antioch is planted due to the scattering of new Christians connected with Stephen (11.19-21). Then just as the church at Jerusalem sends Barnabas to Antioch (11.25-26), so also the church at Antioch becomes a planting church by ordaining Saul and Barnabas as foreign missionaries to plant churches throughout Asia Minor. According to Scheffer, Luke establishes a pattern of producing and reproducing/multiplying churches. Still in the ecclesial vein, Charles Holman examines Isaiah's Servant of Yahweh (Isa. 42.1-4; 49.1-6; 50.4-9; 52.13-53.12) in a missional context.[55] The Servant in Isaiah refers to collective Israel—Spirit-anointed, suffering, and a light to the nations (Isa. 42.6; 49.6). According to Holman, Luke relocates these Isaianic texts in light of the mission of Jesus and the church. As Jesus witnesses through the anointing of the Spirit, lives and dies as the suffering servant, and provides light to the lost, so also the church extends the servant ministry of collective Israel and Jesus.[56]

A third category includes scholars weighing in on the relationship between mission, morality and/or judgment. Trevor Grizzle argues that Luke utilizes several scenes to highlight purity such as the symbol of fiery tongues in Acts 2.3, the deaths of Ananias and Sapphira (5.1-11) and the conversion of Simon Magus (8.13-24). Grizzle maintains that the same Spirit vital to the believing community for missionary endeavors also emboldens the community to preserve its integrity against corruption and seduction. The same Spirit that empowers also impels purging and cleansing so that the agents reflect the integrity of the message.[57] So also Blaine Charette locates the presence of the Spirit and fire at Pentecost as a reminder to readers that God's activity is double-edged. Luke corrects any thought that the blessing of Pentecost is one-sided as a misrepresentation of the work of the Spirit. Charette links the appearance

---

[54] Norman Scheffer, 'The Biblical Imperative for Church Planting', *African Journal of Pentecostal Studies* 2 (2004), pp. 23-34.

[55] Charles L. Holman, 'Isaiah's Servant of Yahweh and Christian Mission in Luke–Acts' (paper presented at the annual meeting of the Society for Pentecostal Studies. Kirkland, WA, 2000), M1-6.

[56] Holman, 'Isaiah's Servant of Yahweh and Christian Mission in Luke–Acts', M2, M6.

[57] Trevor Grizzle, 'Purity and Power According to the Acts of the Apostles' (paper presented at the annual meeting for the Society for Pentecostal Studies. Cleveland, TN, March 1998).

of fire to Luke's interest to the integrity of God's people. Charette suggests that the gift of the Spirit, available to all people from every nation, brings people to a point of decision with judgment as the result for those who refuse God and his messengers. The outpouring of the Spirit testifies both to the potential inclusivity of the gospel and possible exclusivity of a narrow nationalistic understanding of God's redemptive activity.[58] In a later and related work, Charette addresses Luke's dual interest in the opening scene in Acts, namely the coming of the Spirit and the restoration of Israel. Charette argues that for Luke the coming of God's rule benefits the afflicted of Israel; the very people who for so long appear outside of God's provision and often overlooked by those exercising earthly power become the beneficiaries of God's rule. Through the power of the Spirit, the kingdom of God is restored to Israel through good news to the poor and in the ensuing fulfillment of Israel's covenant obligation to the nations (Lk. 4.18; Acts 13.47).[59] Finally, John Poirier also links kerygmatic mission with its ecclesial origin on the Day of Pentecost. According to Poirier, Peter's sermon on the day of Pentecost represents the debut of the church and stands in continuity with Eph. 2.20. If *kerygma* proper provides the foundation of the Church, then the events of Pentecost provide the inaugural paradigm for the establishment of the early church.[60] In the future, Pentecostal scholars will undoubtedly continue to mine the Lukan narratives in further pursuit of Luke's interest in mission.

---

[58] Blaine Charette, ''Tongues as of Fire': Judgment as a Function of Glossolalia in Luke's Thought' (paper presented at the annual meeting of the Society for Pentecostal Studies, Tulsa, OK, March 2001).

[59] Blaine Charette, 'Restoring the Kingdom to Israel: Kingdom and Spirit in Luke's Thought' (paper presented at the annual meeting of the Society for Pentecostal Studies, Cleveland, TN, March 2007), pp. 7-8. See also David Parker, 'Situating the Spirit in the Preface of the Acts Narrative', *Australasian Pentecostal Studies* 5/6 (2006): http://aps.webjournals.org/articles/1/03/2006/6664. htm?id={040 F588A-17ED-484A-93CD-51C5827AB5D9}.

[60] John Poirier, 'The Day of Pentecost as the Birthday of the Church' (paper presented at the annual meeting of the Society for Pentecostal Studies, Cleveland, TN, March 2007).

3.3 HEALING/EXORCISM

On January 1, 1923, Aimee Semple McPherson establishes the (International) Church of the Foursquare Gospel. Historians trace the name of the organization to July 1922, when in a moment of 'divine inspiration', McPherson preaches on Ezekiel's vision of the four cherubim with four faces and concludes that they typify Christ's fourfold ministry. Henceforth, she declares the 'Foursquare Gospel' of Jesus the 'Savior', 'Baptizer with the Holy Ghost', 'Physician and Healer', and 'Soon Coming King'.[61] Her emphasis upon divine healing resonates well with the Pentecostal tradition and proves symbolic of belief, proclamation, and experience. The early Pentecostals locate contemporary healing ministry in continuity with the life of Jesus and the apostles; believers in concert with the early church heal in a way reminiscent of Jesus and as a continuation of his healing activity.[62] While it is difficult to bring together all exegesis on Luke–Acts dealing with this subject, specific works reflect ongoing interest and pursuit.[63]

Tim Powell produces a straightforward interpretation of the healing of the lame man at the Temple gate (Acts 3.1-10) as a paradigmatic story by highlighting 'Request, Requirement, Remedy, Responsibility'.[64] John Wilson produces a catalogue of 38 miracles in Acts and notes the consistent role of God's agents; they speak to the problem, pray, and act. Like Powell, Wilson finds patterns and principles for contemporary pursuit of healing.[65]

Howard Ervin (see earlier section) parallels the ministry of Jesus to Israel and the ministry of the apostles to the world. Their respec-

---

[61] In the late nineteenth century, popular preacher and theologian A.B. Simpson proclaims and pens an earlier yet similar 'fourfold gospel' with Jesus as Savior, Sanctifier, Healer, and Coming King (*The Fourfold Gospel* [Harrisburg, PA: Christian Publications, 1887]). McPherson 'pentecostalized' these themes with emphasis upon Spirit baptism and dismissal of sanctification as a second blessing.

[62] Keith Warrington, 'Healing Then: Healing Now', *Pentecostalism and the Body* (paper presented at the Society for Pentecostal Studies. Marquette University: WI, March 2004), p. 16.

[63] Note also a number of pre-scholarly booklets/pamphlets in sermonic form. For example, evangelist W.V. Grant, *Luke was a Physician and Six Other Deliverance Sermons* (Dallas: the Author, n.d.).

[64] Tim M. Powell, 'The Spirit of Healing', *Paraclete* 18 (Winter 1984), pp. 9-11.

[65] John A. Wilson, 'Ministry to the Sick as Described in the Acts of the Apostles' (paper presented at the annual meeting of the Society for Pentecostal Studies, Virginia Beach, VA, November 1987).

tive ministries share three things in common: 1) an invitation to discipleship via preaching the gospel of the kingdom of God; 2) teaching on the nature of the kingdom of God; and 3) performing of messianic signs of the kingdom.[66] Ervin maintains that the messianic sign of healing includes dual aspects of God's salvific activity. Messengers of the kingdom not only seek to 'save or preserve from eternal death' but also proclaim a 'faith that heals is the faith that saves, and the faith that saves is the faith that heals'.[67] Ervin does not shy away from contemporary examples of healing as well as the challenging situations where people are not healed.[68]

Raymond Gen also connects healing with mission; he produces an innovative yet sobering analysis of divine affliction in Luke–Acts. After offering impressive tables charting the positive impact of healings, deliverance and an assortment of miracles in Luke–Acts, Gen wrestles with the phenomenon of divine infliction.[69] He cites the following five examples: 1) the muting of Zechariah (Lk. 1.5-25); 2) Death of Ananias and Sapphira (Acts 5.1-14); 3) Death of Herod Agrippa I (Acts 12.20-23); 4) Blinding of Bar Jesus (Acts 13.4-12); and 5) blinding of Saul (Acts 9.1-21; 22.6-16; 26.12-18). Gen concludes that malevolent miracles function similar to benevolent ones educing any one of or a combination of amazement, fear and growth of the word of God.[70]

In *The Devil, Disease and Deliverance*, John Christopher Thomas provides a thorough analysis of illness in the New Testament and identifies three primary causes: God, the devil or demons, and neutral or natural causes.[71] Thomas surveys Luke's diversity concerning infirmity. In the Third Gospel, infirmity may be linked to any of the

---

[66] Howard M. Ervin, *Healing: Sign of the Kingdom* (Peabody: Hendrickson, 2002).

[67] Ervin, *Healing: Sign of the Kingdom*, p. 12.

[68] Ervin, *Healing: Sign of the Kingdom*, p. 12. In chapters 10-12 ('Faith and Healing'; 'All Are Healed—Or Are They?'; ' Some Are Healed'), Ervin's chapter titles reveal his willingness to deal not only with success but also disappointment in the Charismatic healing movement.

[69] Raymond M. Gen, 'The Phenomena of Miracles and Divine Infliction in Luke–Acts: Their Theological Significance' *Pneuma* 11 (Fall 1989): Table 1: 4-5; Table 2: 6.

[70] Gen, 'Phenomena', pp. 16-18.

[71] John Christopher Thomas, *The Devil Disease and Deliverance: Origins of Illness in New Testament Thought* (JPTSup 13; Sheffield: Sheffield Academic Press, 1998), p. 304.

above with the added aside that Luke attributes Zechariah's loss of speech to an angel of the Lord (Lk. 1.20).[72] In a chapter on Acts, Thomas also adds Luke's unique willingness to attribute sickness as in the blindness of Saul (Acts 9.8-9) or death, as in the case of Herod (Acts 12) or Ananias and Sapphira (Acts 5.1-11), who are from the believing community, to the hand of God. Like Gen, Thomas makes a sobering contribution to a topic often avoided by scholars.

Closely related to the ministry of healing, Pentecostals also take interest in Luke's employment of exorcism or deliverance ministry. The most prolific Pentecostal scholar on this subject, Graham Twelftree, devotes numerous works to exorcism in the Lukan narratives.[73] According to Twelftree, Luke not only narrates the importance of exorcism in Jesus' ministry (Lk. 7.20; 13.32), but also recasts healing as exorcism. A crippled woman suffers from the bondage of Satan with a 'spirit of sickness' (Lk. 13.11; 13.16) and the healing of Peter's mother-in-law finds Jesus standing over her and rebuking the fever (Lk. 4.38-41/Mk 1.29-34).[74] Exorcism serves first as a primary means by which the Lukan Jesus brings in the powerful presence of the kingdom of God and the respective defeat of Satan (Lk. 11.20), but also displays Jesus' compassion (for example, Jesus' response to a homeless and poverty stricken demoniac [Lk. 8.27] and to the cries of a pleading father concerning his 'only' epileptic son [Lk. 9.38]).[75] Twelftree locates Luke's ascription of miracles including exorcisms to Jesus' power (*dunamis*) versus Luke's employment of the Spirit as the source of inspiration for proclamation (Lk. 5.17; 8.46).[76] Twelftree stresses continuity between the Lukan Jesus and his apprentices. Jesus sends out the Twelve and Seventy-two with the command to preach and heal as well as pronounce authority over demons (Lk. 9.1-6; 10.1-12, 17-

---

[72] Thomas, *The Devil Disease and Deliverance*, p. 225.

[73] In order of publication, a pastoral work entitled: *Christ Triumphant: Exorcism Then and Now* (London: Hodder and Stoughton, 1984); a revision of his PhD thesis under the direction of James Dunn: *Jesus the Exorcist: A Contribution to the Study of the Historical Jesus* (Peabody: Hendrickson, 1993); *Jesus the Miracle Worker: A Historical and Theological Study* (Downers Grove: InterVarsity, 1999); and *In The Name of Jesus: Exorcism Among Early Christians* (Grand Rapids: Baker Academic, 2007).

[74] Twelftree, *In the Name of Jesus*, p. 132.

[75] Twelftree, *In the Name of Jesus*, p. 136.

[76] Twelftree, *In the Name of Jesus*, p. 136. See also *Jesus: The Miracle Worker*.

20). In so doing, Luke enlarges the mission of Jesus in a manner comparable to Moses and the Seventy (Num. 11.16). In Acts, Luke includes specific exorcisms by Peter (Acts 5.12-16), Philip in Samaria (Acts 8.4-8), and Paul (Acts 16.16-18) thereby continuing a balanced approach to Jesus' ongoing ministry.[77] Twelftree also downplays fewer stories of deliverance in Acts by locating Luke's emphasis upon undefined 'signs and wonders' under the umbrella of the miraculous. Taking a more pragmatic angle, the ever-popular theologian Jack Hayford offers a study on the pastoral demands of deliverance ministry. He launches his essay with Jesus' words in Lk. 11.20 ('but if I cast out demons with the finger of God, surely the kingdom of God has come upon you'). According to Hayford, the range of this ministry in the life of the Lukan Jesus includes: 1) saving (*sodzo*) as in the case of the Gaderene demoniac (Lk. 8.26-34); 2)

---

[77] Twelftree, *In the Name of Jesus*, 154. The majority of the articles and essays below serve as the foundation for the full length monographs cited above: 'Demon Possession and Exorcism in the New Testament', *Churchman* 94 (1980), pp. 10-25 and 'La possession démoniaque et l'exorcisme dans le Nouveau Testament', *Hokhma* 51 (1992), pp. 34-52; 'Demon-Possession and Exorcism in the New Testament', with James D.G. Dunn, in *The Christ and the Spirit, collected essays of James D.G. Dunn* (2 vols.; Edinburgh: T & T Clark, 1998), 2, pp. 170-86 coauthored with Dunn; 'If I Cast Out Demons?' in *The Miracles of Jesus* (ed. David Wenham and Craig Blomberg; Gospel Perspectives 6; Sheffield: Sheffield Academic Press, 1986), pp. 361-400; 'The Place of Exorcism in Contemporary Ministry', *St Mark's Review* 127 (September 1986), pp. 25-39; 'Exorcism in the New Testament and in Contemporary Ministry: A Reader's Guide', *Christian Book Newsletter* 5 (8 November 1987), pp. 7-11; 'Jesus as an Exorcist', *New Times* (May 1987), pp. 9-10; 'Devil and Demons', and 'Exorcism', in *New Dictionary of Theology*, pp. 196-98 and 244-46; 'Church Agenda: The Lucan Perspective', in R. Dean Drayton (ed.), *Evangelism and Preaching in Secular Australia: Essays in Honour of Arthur Jackson* (Melbourne: JBCE, 1989), pp. 59-73; 'Blasphemy', 'Demon, Devil, Satan', and 'Temptation of Jesus', *Dictionary of Jesus and the Gospels*, pp. 75-77, 163-72, 821-27; 'But What is Exorcism?' *New Times* (March 1993), p. 14; 'The Demonic', *New Dictionary of Christian Ethics and Pastoral Theology*, pp. 296-97; 'The Place of Exorcism in Contemporary Ministry', *Anvil* 5 (1988), pp. 133-50; 'Signs and Wonders', 'Spiritual Powers', 'Testing', *New Dictionary of Biblical Theology*, pp. 775-81, 796-802, 814-15; 'The Miracles of Jesus: Marginal or Mainstream'? *Journal for the Study of the Historical Jesus* 1 (2003), pp. 104-124; 'The History of Miracles in the Jesus of History', in *The Face of New Testament Studies: A Survey of Recent Research* (ed. Scot McKnight and Grant R. Osborne; Grand Rapids: Baker Academic and Leicester, UK: Apollos/IVP, 2004), pp. 191-208; 'Prayer and the Coming of the Spirit in Acts', *ExpTim* 117 (2006), pp. 271–76; 'Beelzebub', *New Interpreter's Dictionary of the Bible*, 1, pp. 417-18; 'Jesus the Exorcist and Ancient Magic', *A Kind of Magic. Understanding Magic in the New Testament and its Religious Environment* (ed. Michael Labahn and Bert Jan Lietaert Peerbolte; Library of New Testament Studies 306; London, New York: T & T Clark, 2007), pp. 57-86.

therapeutic treatment, caring and healing (*therapeuo*) of Mary Magdalene (Lk. 8.1-3); 3) the curative deliverance of suffering (*iaomai*) of the boy near Caesarea-Philippi (Lk. 9.37-42); and 4) confrontational conflict with satanic beings that torment, invade, or manipulate human beings (*apolou*) as in the apparent adherent in the synagogue at Capernaum and the woman crippled with a deformity (Lk. 4.31-37; 13.10-17).[78]

A final essay by Amos Yong brings Pentecostal interest in healing to the science and religion conversation. By building on the work of John Pilch, Yong calls upon Pentecostals to consider the cognitive sciences in order to understand better the various experiences of the Spirit as recorded in Acts.[79] Pilch links biblical research with cultural and medical anthropology in order to illuminate Luke's understanding of experience.[80] Pilch studies ecstatic or trance experiences in light of the neurosciences and according to Yong suggests 'the neurological "hardware" of human brains are the means of receiving healing or divining answers to existential and concrete problems of life'.[81] Pilch connects various experiences of first century Christians to alternate states of consciousness (ASC)—in terms of God, angels, miracles, and the larger supernatural world. He produces the following examples: 1) 'looking intently' or 'staring' as a means of precipitating ASCs and accessing the supernatural (Acts 1.10; 3.4; 7.55; 13.9-10; 14.9); 2) fasting as entry to trances and visionary experiences (Acts 9.9-12; 10.10; 13.1-3); visionary experiences induced by concentration and meditation (Acts 9); and bright lights as trance-like experiences (Acts 6.15; 9.3-6 [22.4-11; 26.9-18]; 12.7).[82] Though Yong (and Pilch) refuses to reduce supernatural experience to neurological activity, he invites Pentecostals to utilize neuroscience and encourages Pentecostals to renew their commitment to the Lukan faith tradition: a world of dreams, visions, healings, exorcisms, and a host of other signs and wonders.

---

[78] Hayford, 'The Finger of God', *A Reader on the Holy Spirit: Anointing, Equipping and Empowering for Service* (ed. Eloise Clarno; Los Angeles: International Church of the Foursquare Gospel, 1993), 220-21.

[79] Amos Yong, 'Academic Glossolalia? Pentecostal Scholarship, Multidisciplinarity, and the Science-Religion Conversation', *JPT* 14.1 (2005), pp. 63-82.

[80] John J. Pilch, *Visions and Healing in the Acts of the Apostles: How the Early Believers Experienced God* (Collegeville, MN: Liturgical Press, 2004).

[81] Yong, 'Academic Glossolalia', p. 66.

[82] Yong, 'Academic Glossolalia', pp. 68-69.

Given the historic commitment of Pentecostals to the supernatural, Pentecostal scholarship on this subject will surely intensify.

3.4 WOMEN

'God Almighty is no fool ...' shouts Eleanor Frey. 'Would He fill a woman with the Holy Spirit—endow her with ability—give her a vision for souls and then tell her to shut her mouth?'[83] Though early Pentecostals demonstrate general empowerment of women in ministry, these polemic words from an early female evangelist prove ironic. As the years go by, Pentecostals hold women and the gifts they bring in high regard, but also continue to send mixed signals to many women (and men) attempting to enact God's call.[84]

Assemblies of God scholars Deborah Gill and Barbara Caveness produce a valuable biblical theology of women in ministry with significant reliance upon Luke–Acts. In sections on the Third Gospel, they note Jesus' affirmation of women in a male dominated society, his inclusion of women in the larger group of disciples, and their role in the ensuing mission.[85] Concerning Acts, Gill and Caveness point to the role of women in fulfillment of Acts 2.17-18. Women participate in the events of Pentecost (Acts 2.7, 15) and embrace the gospel message (Acts 5.14; 8.12; 17.4, 34). A woman suffers the consequences of lying to the Holy Spirit (Acts 5.7-10), Saul drags men and women off to prison (Acts 8.3; 9.2), and Lydia and Philip's four daughters impact respective missions (Acts 16.3-5; 21.9).[86]

Paul Elbert comes to similar conclusions via a fictive and personal 'Letter to Theo'. Elbert laments the dismissal or stifling of 'half the potential workforce' due to worldviews often committed

---

[83] This statement dated 1928 from the personal letters of Canadian Pentecostal Evangelist Eleanor Frey cited by Grant Wacker in *Heaven Below: Early Pentecostals an American Culture* (Cambridge: Harvard University Press, 2001), p. 169.

[84] See for example the strong endorsement by way of the Assemblies of God position paper entitled: 'The Role of Women in Ministry as Described in Holy Scripture' (http://ag.org/top/Beliefs/Position_Papers/pp_downloads/pp_4191_women_ministry.pdf). Note, however, that this paper carries no official authority.

[85] Deborah Gill and Barbara Caveness, *God's Women: Then and Now* (Springfield: Grace & Truth, 2004), pp. 73-81.

[86] Gill and Caveness, *God's Women*, pp. 84-86. On a more popular level, see Loren Cunningham and David Joel Hamilton, *Why Not Women? A Fresh Look at Scripture on Women in Missions, Ministry, and Leadership* (Seattle: YWAM Publishing, 2000).

to cessationist tendencies that strike against charismatic enablement. Like Gill and Cavaness, Elbert also concludes that Luke's affirmative voice on women as equal partners in ministry and spiritual gifts in the church finds complementary affirmation throughout the New Testament.[87]

In a number of exegetical articles, Pentecostal scholars insist on Luke's high regard for the role of women in kingdom exploits. Nelson Estrada begins with the Lukan Birth narrative. He argues that the classic view of a hymn pattern based upon a trajectory of promise-fulfillment-praise by Mary (*Magnificat*), Zechariah (*Benedictus*), and Simeon (*Nunc Dimittis*) leaves little room for Luke's emphasis upon Anna the prophetess and Elizabeth. Instead, Estrada produces a revised structure, whereby Elizabeth, Mary, Zechariah, Simeon, and Anna form a continuous strand with each character participating in the salvific songs of God's current activity.[88] Rick Williamson suggests Luke's employment of male/female pairs. He recognizes repetitious examples, statements, arguments and characters in the narrative paired by gender.[89] His list, though not exhaustive, includes the following characters in Jesus' teaching: the Widow of Zarephath and Naaman the Syrian (4.23-30), the woman and the lost coin alongside the man and the lost sheep (15.1-10), and the Persistent Widow and the Tax Collector (18.1-14). Other paired characters to appear in the narrative consist of Zechariah/Elizabeth and Zechariah/Mary (1.5-79), Simeon and Anna (2.25-38), the Pharisee and the sinful woman (7.36-50), and the women at the tomb alongside the two men on the Emmaus road (23.55-24.35).[90] According to Williamson, gendered pairs prove deliberate; Luke emphasizes proclamation must not restricted by gender conventions but on God's gracious and free bestowal upon 'sons and daughters' alike (Acts 2.17). Both men and women receive the Holy Spirit as the single most important qualification for anointed speech. Such

---

[87] Paul Elbert, *Pastoral Letter to Theo: An Introduction to Interpretation and Women's Ministries* (Eugene, OR: Wipf & Stock, 2008).

[88] Nelson P. Estrada, 'Peace for Promise Fulfilled: A Study on the Significance of the Anna the Prophet Pericope', *AJPS* 2 (1999), pp. 5-18.

[89] Rick L. Williamson, 'Female/Male Pairs in Luke: Gender Balance in Proclaiming the Word of God' (paper presented at the annual meeting of the Society for Pentecostal Studies, Cleveland, TN, March 1998), pp. 1-3.

[90] Williamson, 'Female/Male Pairs in Luke', pp. 1-3.

enablement makes women and men equally competent to minister with prophetic authority.[91]

Other writers move forcefully to invite contemporary leaders and believers to live out a Lukan approach to women. According to James Arlandson, women, often associated with slaves, the unclean and degraded (sick, demonized, prostitutes, ethnic outcasts), and expendables (widows and persecuted), find their fortunes reversed in the Lukan narrative.[92] Arlandson examines social hierarchy in first century culture in conjunction with Luke's use of the teachings of Jesus and the apostles in order to flesh out Luke's theological concerns for the Christian community. Arlandson links Luke's reversal of the fortunes of women with Simeon's prophecy of falling and rising; women from the lowest levels of Greco-Roman culture often rise from their troubled circumstances, while men fall out of favor. Arlandson suggests Luke employs women as test cases for 'the rise of many' while men serve as foils and represent 'the falling of many' (Lk. 2.34).[93]

Janet Everts Powers points to Acts 2.16-17 (in fulfillment of Joel 2.28) as a crucial text used by early Pentecostals to empower women for proclamation of the gospel. While she cites the Spirit as the great equalizer who plays no favorites and breaks down all barriers for ministry, she also laments that the exegetical intrusion of Reformed and Evangelical theology fosters marginalization of women's ministries in many Pentecostal churches.[94] In a related work, John Christopher Thomas utilizes Acts 15 as a model for decision-making based upon Scripture, the prompting of the Spirit,

---

[91] Williamson, 'Female/Male Pairs in Luke', p. 12.

[92] James Malcolm Arlandson, *Women, Class, and Society in Early Christianity: Models from Luke–Acts* (Peabody: Hendrickson, 1997). Arlandson compiles an impressive list of women and their role in order of appearance in Luke–Acts. He begins with women receptive to or favored on account of the gospel followed by those resistant and therefore not favored by the kingdom of God (pp. 121-23). Note, however, that Arlandson also challenges the often uncritical attempts at portrayal of women as uniformly underclass. Positions and/or roles among first century women include landowners, merchants, traders, and artisans (pp. 67-119).

[93] Arlandson, *Women, Class, and Society in Early Christianity*, p. 5.

[94] Janet Everts Powers, '"Your Daughters Shall Prophesy": Pentecostal Hermeneutics and the Empowerment of Women', *The Globalization of Pentecostalism: A Religion Made to Travel* (ed. Murray Dempster, Byron Klaus, and Douglas Petersen; Irvine, CA: Regnum Press, 1999), pp. 313-37.

and the role of the community.[95] He applies this case study to contemporary Pentecostal churches by suggesting that women often remain undermined on the basis of one or two texts instead of the broader scriptural witness, sensitivity to the Spirit's witness, and the cultural dynamics of the contemporary community.[96] The cumulative effect of these writers should compel Pentecostal scholars and practitioners to adhere to Luke's desire for general and specific ministerial enablement of women.

3.5 SPIRITUAL FORMATION

As Pentecostals embark on examination of the Lukan narratives beyond missiological impulses, new themes begin to surface. The previous categories demonstrate the significance of narrative analysis in propelling Pentecostals to new heights regarding patterns for evangelism, healing, and the participation of women in ministry. Though Pentecostals remain fervent on these topics, recent interests include Luke's concern for the formation of believers and believing communities. A number of themes materialize in the literature thus far.

First, the Lukan Jesus functions as paradigmatic example for life, conduct, and ministry. For example, Jon Ruthven develops a Spirit Christology and argues that Jesus' life and ministry goes beyond a unique sacrifice for sin to an example for piety and ethics, to a normative exemplar of charismatic ministry worthy of replication. Luke's narrative not only shows Jesus' ministry replete with mira-

---

[95] John Christopher Thomas, 'Women, Pentecostals and the Bible: An Experiment in Pentecostal Hermeneutics', *JPT* 5 (1994), pp. 41-56.

[96] At the same time, as Pentecostalism emerges in the global south, it will be interesting to follow the trajectory of interpretation from strong patriarchal cultures. Women in the global north, undoubtedly, benefit from a worldview more conducive to egalitarian models. A valuable piece on the importance of cultural values upon interpretation is William Webb's *Slaves, Women & Homosexuals: Exploring the Hermeneutics of Cultural Analysis* (Downers Grove: IVP: 2000). Pentecostal readers should also consult Gill and Cavaness. Though they do not include a specific section on women in Luke–Acts, they provide a background chapter on women in 'Greco-Roman, Jewish and Christian Contexts' followed by a specific chapter on 'Jesus' treatment of women' (*God's Women*, pp. 59-82). Along similar lines, see Estrelda Alexander and Amos Yong, eds., *Philip's Daughters: Women in Pentecostal-Charismatic Leadership* (Princeton Theological Monograph Series 104; Eugene, OR: Pickwick Publications, 2009). See particularly the article by Janet Everts Powers, 'Pentecostalism 101: Your Daughters Shall Prophesy', pp. 133-51.

cles, healings, and exorcisms (Lk. 4.15; 4.40-41; 6.19; 9.11; 13.33), but this same Jesus sends out the disciples to echo his mission (Lk. 9.1-2; 10.9). In Acts, the disciples follow Jesus' pattern of healing, exorcism and miraculous power as well as the transformational characteristics of a Christ follower (see especially Acts 1.1).[97] Like Ruthven, M.H. Choi agrees with the classic Pentecostal emphasis upon the Spirit as 'empowering for witness' but also emphasizes the Spirit's 'personality' in guidance, speech and teaching.[98] As descent of the Spirit places Jesus in close connection to the Father, so also the disciples find close fellowship with the Spirit as Spirit-guided agents for God's plan of salvation. Choi concludes. 'The more deeply one share [*sic*] an intimate fellowship with the Spirit, the more mightily the power of the Spirit emerges through his (or her) life and witness (mission)'.[99]

Second, John Christopher Thomas focuses on 'discipleship in the Synoptic Gospels'. In an essay focused primarily upon Mark's gospel, Thomas finds the title 'Rabbi' inadequate, preferring to label Jesus as charismatic leader with charismatic followers.[100] In a later essay, Thomas moves to Acts and explores connections between literary markers and charismatic anointing. He discovers eight panels that include a description of charismatic anointing, a reference to someone so anointed or an account of the Spirit's charismatic activity.[101] Accordingly, after Luke's prologue (Acts 1.1-5), Thomas proposes the following outline based upon the experience and leadership of the charismatic disciples:

---

[97] Jon Ruthven, 'Jesus as Rabbi: A Mimesis Christology: The Charismatic Pattern of Discipleship in the New Testament' (paper presented at the annual meeting of the Society for Pentecostal Studies, Cleveland, TN, March 1998). Reprinted as '"The Imitation of Christ" in Christian Tradition: Its Missing Charismatic Emphasis', *JPT* 16 (2000), pp. 60-77.

[98] M.H. Choi, 'An Examination of the Existing Paradigm for the 21st Century Pentecostal Spirituality and Movement' (paper presented at the annual meeting of the Society for Pentecostal Studies, Tulsa, OK, 8-10 March 2001), pp. 841-57.

[99] Choi, 'An Examination of the Existing Paradigm', p. 856.

[100] John Christopher Thomas, 'Discipleship in the Synoptic Gospels' (paper presented at the annual meeting of the Society for Pentecostal Studies. Cleveland, TN, November 1998). Later renamed and published as 'Discipleship in Mark's Gospel' in Elbert (ed.), *Faces of Renewal*, pp. 64-79 and again in *The Spirit of the New Testament* (Leiden: Deo Publishing, 2005), pp. 62-76.

[101] John Christopher Thomas, (paper presented at the annual meeting of the Society for Pentecostal Studies. Wilmore, KY, March 2003); reprinted as 'The Charismatic Structure of Acts', *JPT* 13 (2004), pp. 11-12.

1) 1.6-2.47—The Anointing of the Charismatic Community in Jerusalem
    [2.14—The Outpouring of the Holy Spirit on the Day of Pentecost]

2) 3.1-6.7—The Acts of the Charismatic Leader Peter and the Charismatic Community in Jerusalem
    [4.30-31—Jerusalem Believers Are All Filled with the Holy Spirit]

3) 6.8-9.31—The Acts of Certain Charismatic Leaders in Jerusalem, Judea, and Samaria: Stephen and Philip
    [8.14-17—The Samaritans Receive the Holy Spirit]

4) 9.32-11.21—The Acts of a Certain Charismatic Leader in Lydda, Caesarea, and Jerusalem: Peter
    [10.44-48—Cornelius and his household Are Filled with the Holy Spirit]

5) 11.22-12.24—The Acts of Charismatic Leaders in Antioch and Jerusalem: Barnabas, Agabus, and Peter
    [11.24-28—Barnabas, Full of the Holy Spirit and Faith]

6) 12.25-16.5—The Acts of a Certain Charismatic Leader. Paul—From Antioch to Derbe and Back Again, and From Antioch to Jerusalem and Back Again
    [13.9—Saul/Paul, Full of the Holy Spirit]

7) 16.6-19.20—The Acts of a Certain Charismatic Leader: Paul—The Call and Journey to Macedonia
    [19.1-7—The Disciples at Ephesus Are Filled with the Holy Spirit]

8) 19.21-28.31—The Acts of a Certain Charismatic Leader: Paul—To Macedonia, Jerusalem and Rome
    [20.22-21.11—Spirit/Prophetic Activity in Paul and Agabus]

Charismatic Catholic scholar J. Massyngberde Ford concentrates on the convergence of charismatic character and leadership. She argues that Luke carefully complements miraculous exploits with moral attributes. She notes specific points in the narrative where Luke parallels manifestations of the Holy Spirit with false use of supernatural power.[102]

	Spirit of Truth	*Spirit of Perversity*
1.	Jerusalem Pentecost	The lying spirit in Ananias and Sapphira
2.	Samaritan Pentecost	The refutation of Simon Magus
3.	Gentile Pentecost	The death of Herod due to blasphemy
4.	Cure at Lystra	Repudiation of *theios aner*

Ford demonstrates that the new community must steer clear of lying to the Spirit, simony, blasphemy, false prophecy, idolatry, ventriloquism, false exorcism, and magic. Luke carefully structures Acts

---

[102] J. Massyngberde Ford, 'The Social and Political Implications of the Miraculous in Acts', in Elbert (ed.), *Faces of Renewal*, p. 151.

to juxtapose—both from a literary and a theological point of view—enthusiastic ministry and ethics. For Ford, Luke exhibits his worrisome concern for the moral evolution of the charismatic Christian community; followers of Jesus must not overemphasize enthusiasm and the miraculous at the expense of character.[103]

James Shelton takes up Acts 15.1-29 as a test case to demonstrate that acts of God interpreted by charismatic apostles play a crucial role in conflict resolution. Shelton finds no evidence for decision-making by democratic majority in Acts; instead, God provides leaders with charismatic oversight.[104] Luke employs various events as patterns for normative epistemology and authority structure. When making decisions, mature disciples (then and now) must function according to apostolic, prophetic, and scriptural norms. By way of application, Shelton suggests: 'if Acts is normative for the gifts of the Holy Spirit, then it must also be for pneumatic epistemology ... It is not the text of Scripture that is our normative authority but the Holy Spirit-filled Church living in the now in connection with the apostolic Tradition'.[105]

Two final slants on the spiritual formation of the believer concern praise and prayer in Luke–Acts. First, Peter Cullen submits that Luke emphasizes 'the authenticity of those charismatic forms of worship which give priority to praise and thanksgiving'.[106] According to Cullen, joy expressed under the shadow of the cross serves to encourage and support early Christian communities living in desolation. And second, given Luke's attention to prayer in the life of the believer, it comes as no surprise that Pentecostals would consider this practice in everyday living. Dongsoo Kim reviews the parable of the friend at midnight (Lk. 11.5-8) within the broader context of Lukan prayer (Lk. 11.1-4, 5-8, 9-13) and finds in it an attempt to establish a biblical foundation for persistent prayer in Pentecostal contexts (specifically Korean). Jesus' teaching serves as

---

[103] Massyngberde Ford, 'The Social and Political Implications of the Miraculous in Acts', pp. 155-156.

[104] James Shelton, 'Epistemology and Authority in the Acts of the Apostles: An Analysis and Test Case Study of Acts 15:1-29' (paper presented at the annual meeting of the Society for Pentecostal Studies, Springfield, MO, March 1999), p. 10.

[105] Shelton, 'Epistemology and Authority in the Acts of the Apostles', p. 11.

[106] Peter Cullen, 'Euphoria, Praise and Thanksgiving: Rejoicing in the Spirit in Luke–Acts', *JPT* 6 (1995), pp. 13-24.

an instructional guide for prayer—especially the positive nature of persistence in prayer.[107] In stark contrast to Kim, Graham Twelftree views Luke as 'l'évangéliste de la prière'. Twelftree finds strong connections between prayer and *heilsgeschichte* and concludes that Luke roots redemptive history in the sovereignty of God and not in response to prayer. As for prayer, Luke employs prayer primarily to portray the followers as faithful and devout.[108]

3.6 ONENESS THEOLOGY

In recent years, representation of Lukan scholarship from the Oneness tradition comes by way of two proponents, one a seasoned scholar, the other an up and coming doctoral student.[109] First, David Bernard remains the most respected Oneness scholar with a number of works that focus upon issues raised in Luke–Acts. In the most pertinent work entitled *In the Name of Jesus*, Bernard devotes a chapter to the baptismal pattern in Acts.[110] Bernard addresses slight variations in the wording of four passages, namely, 'Jesus Christ' (Acts 2.38); 'Lord Jesus' (Acts 8.16; 19.5); 'name of the Lord' (Acts 10.48) and goes on to assert: 'The Oneness movement understands these passages as descriptive of the baptismal formula'.[111] Bernard

---

[107] Dongsoo Kim, 'Lukan Pentecostal Theology of Prayer: Is Persistent Prayer Not Biblical?' *AJPS* 7 (2004), p. 216.

[108] Citing A. Hamman see Graham Twelftree, 'Prayer and *Heilsgeschichte* in Acts: A Reassessment' (paper presented at the annual meeting of the Society for Pentecostal Studies, Wilmore, KY, March 2003).

[109] This does not include various tracts and popular pieces put out by both sides of the Oneness debate. For example, from the Oneness traditions see *Acts 2:38: The Original New Testament Plan of Salvation* (Hazelwood, MO: Word Aflame Press, 1983); Jonathan Ellsworth Perkins, *An Honest Effort to Harmonize Matthew 28:19 With Acts 2:38 in Relation to Water Baptism* (Los Angeles: The Author, n.d). On the other side, see the self-published booklet by former UPCI minister, Bernie Gillespie, *Faith is the Essential Response to Acts 2:38* (Bernie Gillespie, 2002). See also Marvin M. Arnold *Pentecost [Acts 2:38] Before Azusa: 2000 Years of Revival in All Nations* (Jackson, MS: Arno Publications, 1991). Arnold traces personal accounts of Oneness leanings in American religious history from 1650 through to Azusa. The stories offer frequent references to Acts.

[110] David Bernard, *In the Name of Jesus* (Hazelwood, MO: Word Aflame Press, 1992), pp. 41-54.

[111] Bernard, *In the Name of Jesus*, p. 71. Concerning the reference to 'the name of the Lord' in Acts 10.48, Bernard notes early confession of Jesus as Lord (Rom. 10.9; 1 Cor. 12.3; Phil. 2.11). Bernard also indicates that this designation is found in the KJV, yet the textual evidence supports the use of 'in the name of Jesus Christ' as in all subsequent translations except NKJV (pp. 78-79).

insists that the formulaic key should not be located in the exact description of Jesus, but rather the actual invoking or uttering of 'the name of Jesus' in baptism. Bernard also defends baptism in the name of Jesus against questions arising from the potential Trinitarian formula in Mt. 28.19 and concludes that Jesus commands baptism in singular name of the Father, Son, and Holy Spirit.[112] In *The New Birth,* Bernard offers three interpretative options: 1) the Matthean and Acts formulae are contradictory—but this would render Peter's statement in Acts 2.38 and his apostolic witness unreliable; 2) only Matthew or Acts is formulaic—but both contain the problematic phrase 'in the name of'; or 3) neither the Matthean or Acts account offers a formulaic statement—a view he finds unlikely.[113] Bernard decides on the Acts formula. He sees the Matthean statement as a less direct passage that points forward to the Acts formula 'in the name of Jesus'.[114]

Given the early separation between Trinitarian and Oneness Pentecostals, it comes as somewhat of a surprise to find only three Society for Pentecostal Studies essays devoted exclusively to the Oneness debate in Luke–Acts. In a 2005 paper, Baylor University PhD candidate Kenneth Bass begins by aligning himself with classical Pentecostal interpreters by emphasizing not only the crucial role of Acts in the formation of Pentecostal doctrine but also by identifying himself as a narrative theologian. He demonstrates a commitment to reading Acts with an eye to normative implications for the believer. Bass then proceeds boldly to encourage readers to follow the apostolic and formulaic pattern of baptism in the name of Jesus (Acts 2.38; 8.14-16; 10.44-48; 19.1-7)—since Luke's account in Acts is normative for the Church.[115] In the following year, David Zampino offers a direct response. Zampino not only challenges the emphasis Oneness proponents place on the Acts of the Apostles seemingly over and against the rest of the New Testament, but also

---

[112] Bernard, *In the Name of Jesus*, pp. 60-61. See also *The Oneness of God* (Series in Pentecostal Theology 1; Hazelwood, MO: Word Aflame Press, 1983) and *The Oneness View of Jesus Christ* (Hazelwood, MO: Word Aflame Press, 1994), pp. 124-125.

[113] Bernard, *The New Birth* (Hazelwood, MO: Pentecostal Publishing House, 1993), pp. 170-71.

[114] Bernard, *The New Birth*, pp. 172-78.

[115] Kenneth Bass, 'The Normativity of Acts' (paper presented at the annual meeting of the Society for Pentecostal Studies, Virginia Beach, VA, March 2005).

raises concerns about Acts as a normative text with doctrinal import.[116] He argues that the baptismal accounts found in Acts ought to be interpreted not as formulaic but descriptive. Zampino then provides a general historical examination of early baptismal practices in order to demonstrate early church dependence on the Trinitarian formula of Mt. 28.19. Zampino employs early and geographically extensive Trinitarian examples from the likes of the *Didache*, Ignatius, and Justin Martyr.[117] In a second paper, Bass suggests Oneness scholars consider a canonical approach to baptism. Given Matthew's place as the dominant gospel in early church tradition and by moving beyond the idea of 'Matthew as a problem to be solved', Bass calls upon Oneness colleagues to recognize use of a Trinitarian formula and thereby search for canonical integrity.[118]

Undoubtedly, the continuing presence of Bernard and the emergence of Oneness scholars like Bass will continue to foster lively dialogue with Trinitarians in the years to come. Indeed, the recent report of the Society for Pentecostal Studies commissioned Oneness-Trinitarian Pentecostal Dialogue provides a synopsis of a six-

---

[116] David Zampino, 'Normative, Descriptive, or Formulaic?: A Critique of Kenneth Bass' Theology of Jesus' Name Baptism in the Acts of the Apostles' (paper presented at the annual meeting of the Society for Pentecostal Studies, Pasadena, CA, March 2006), p. 441.

[117] Zampino, 'Normative, Descriptive, or Formulaic?', p. 448. See the *Didache*: 'Regarding baptism. Baptize as follows: after first explaining all these points, *baptize in the name of the Father and of the Son and of the Holy Spirit*, in running water. But if you have no running water, baptize in other water; and if you cannot in cold, then in warm. But if you have neither, pour water on the head three times in the name of the Father and of the Son and of the Holy Spirit' (7:1-3). Ignatius of Antioch (d. AD 117) in his letter to the Philippians writes: 'Wherefore also the Lord, when He sent forth the apostles to make disciples of all nations, commanded them to "baptize in the name of the Father, and of the Son, and of the Holy Ghost" (2:20). Justin Martyr (d. circa AD 165) in his first apology writes: 'And for this [rite] we have learned from the apostles... there is pronounced over him who chooses to be born again, and has repented of his sins, the name of God the Father and Lord of the universe;...And in the name of Jesus Christ, who was crucified under Pontius Pilate, and in the name of the Holy Ghost, who through the prophets foretold all things about Jesus, he who is illuminated is washed' (LXI).

[118] Bass, 'Baptism in the Canon: Can/Should We Still Harmonize the Baptismal Formulae in Matthew and Acts' (paper presented at the annual meeting of the Society for Pentecostal Studies, Cleveland, TN, March 2007).

year study. The report considers historic divisions on baptism, Christology, the Godhead, salvation, and holiness.[119]

---

[119] Editor Frank Macchia devotes the entire issue of *Pneuma* 30:2 (2008) to the dialogue with the official report entitled 'The Oneness-Trinitarian Pentecostal Final Report, 2002-2007', pp. 203-24 . Oneness respondents include James A. Johnson, Kenneth Haney, Daniel Seagraves, and Richard Shaka; Trinitarians George Wood and William Menzies; and respective Catholic and Anglican respondents Ralph Del Colle and David Reed.

CHAPTER 4

OLD STORY, ENDURING MESSAGE: LUKE–ACTS FOR THE TWENTY-FIRST CENTURY

After I have emptied out
my store of words, depleted
all usuable sounds,
in praising God's unsayable
glory,

wasted the Oxford Dictionary,
pauperized the Coptic Lexicon,
have no breath between my teeth,
wordless beauty I give back to
God.
(Kilian McDonnell, OSB)[1]

Whereas many scholars work hard to produce boundaries for theology and praxis, new situations call for fresh insights and new practices. The beginning of a new millennium marks a major shift in human history. As Christians move into their third millennium, they face new questions in need of creative answers. Pentecostals embark on their second century. Though young in comparison to the historic Christian traditions, Pentecostals demonstrate ongoing adaptability to survive. Indeed, contemporary global Christianity with its strong Pentecostal/Charismatic impulses demonstrates the pragmatic adjustments made by Pentecostals everywhere; so also Pentecostal scholars must search for fresh insight from the biblical text in order to speak life to a growing movement. The Lukan narratives remain critical for Christians in a global community. In this

---

[1] Kilian McDonnell, *Swift, Lord, You Are Not* (Collegeville, MN: St. John's University Press, 2003).

vein, Kilian McDonnell captures well the human struggle for words in the presence of a majestic God; Pentecost calls for ever fresh encounters with the living God and his mission. Given the categories discussed below, Pentecostal scholars are indeed up to the challenge.

4.1 SOCIAL JUSTICE/ETHICS

As Pentecostal scholars press forward in the academic marketplace, it seems difficult to imagine a more sensitive topic than a sustainable theology of social justice. Many critics of early Pentecostalism chastise Pentecostals for apparent lack of social concern; since early Pentecostals focus on the soon coming return of Jesus, they tend to relativize social concerns in comparison to soul-winning. In other words, for heaven-bound believers, short-lived social concern pales in comparison to evangelism. However, Pentecostals do not ignore social concern. In fact, Pentecostals take great pride in missionary success stories that include the establishment of orphanages, leper colonies, medical outposts, and educational facilities. Moreover, recent studies demonstrate that the supposed involvement gap between historic social gospel traditions and Pentecostals no longer exist. Current day Pentecostals display active participation in social justice.[2] The disconnect appears not so much between practice versus non-practice of social justice, but lack of a theological foundation. Once again, it comes as no surprise that Pentecostal scholars mine the Lukan story for answers.

Roger Stronstad looks to the Pentecost narrative as a point of entry. He not only emphasizes the forward-looking utilization of Joel 2.28-32 in Peter's sermon, but also its retroactive implications.[3] Joel's vision of an inclusive outpouring of the Spirit finds its first fulfillment in the Lukan birth narrative. Therefore, Peter's use of Joel's prophecy not only anticipates the apostolic ministry, but also speaks to already visible fulfillment concerning the ministry of Je-

---

[2] Donald E. Miller, *Global Pentecostalism: The New Face of Christian Social Engagement* (Los Angeles: University of California Press, 2007). See further discussion via an interview by Timothy Sato, 'The S Factor: A Conversation about Pentecostalism with Donald E. Miller', *Book and Culture: A Christian Review* (Posted 7/10/2009). Online: http://www.christianitytoday.com/bc/2009/julaug/thesfactor.html.

[3] Stronstad, *Signs on the Earth Beneath*, pp. 21-22.

sus. Components of inclusivity begin in the birth narrative: John is a *son* with a prophetic ministry (Lk. 1.15-17); Mary is a *daughter* given a prophetic song (Lk. 1.46-55); John the prophet is a *young man* (Lk. 1.76); Zechariah and Simeon are *old men* given prophetic oracles (Lk. 1.22, 67; 2.25-32); Simeon is a prophetic *male bondslave* (Lk. 2.29); and Mary, a prophetic *female bondslave* (Lk. 1.38).[4] According to Stronstad, Luke situates gender equality and the breaking of social barriers in the Third Gospel as pneumatic fulfillment.

Beginning in the late 1980s, Murray Dempster becomes the first Pentecostal voice to link Lukan exegesis with social justice. By way of a number of articles he writes between 1987-2003, Dempster highlights Luke's interest in the 'already' present kingdom of God expressed through the power of the Holy Spirit. The coming of the kingdom offers not only a powerful incentive for evangelization, but also concern for economic *koinonia* and the establishment of a new redemptive order.[5] Dempster perceives the Pentecostal community as sorely in need of a social ethic to inspire, direct and validate a more holistic ministry paradigm with larger social justice agendas and programs. He cites mixed signals primarily from anxious Pentecostal leaders, who fear potential dangers of social ministry 'side-tracking' the church from its proclamation-oriented evangelistic mandate. Thus, in an attempt to secure a hearing, Dempster begins in the narratives of Luke–Acts; he formulates rudimentary principles for a biblically based theology of church mission that integrates evangelism and social concern. Using the language and insights of Stronstad, Dempster notes that the transfer of the charismatic Spirit from Jesus to the disciples includes expectation that the disciples continue to do and teach those things which Jesus began to do and teach (Lk. 4.16-21 and Acts 1.1).[6] Dempster notes

---

    [4] Stronstad, *Signs on the Earth Beneath*, pp. 21-22.
    [5] Murray W. Dempster, 'Pentecostal Social Concern and the Biblical Mandate of Social Justice', *Pneuma* 9 (Fall 1987), pp. 129-153; 'The Church's Moral Witness', *Paraclete* 23 (Winter 1989), pp. 1-7; 'Christian Social Concern in Pentecostal Perspective: Reformulating Pentecostal Eschatology', *JPT* 2 (1993), pp. 51-64; 'Holistic Mission in the Pentecostal Kingdom Paradigm' (paper presented at the annual meeting of the Society for Pentecostal Studies, Wilmore, KY, March 2003); 'The Structure of a Christian Ethic Informed by Pentecostal Experience: Soundings in the Moral Significance of Glossolalia', *The Spirit and Spirituality: Essays in Honor of Russell P. Spittler* (ed. Wonsuk Ma and Robert P. Menzies; JPTSup 24; London: T & T Clark, 2004), pp. 108-141.
    [6] Dempster, 'Pentecostal Social Concern', p. 43.

further that the Lukan Jesus exemplifies social concern as he encounters the burning moral issues of his day—the treatment of aliens, the exploitation of women, the economic exploitation of the oppressed, underemployment and unemployment, and the dignity of children. Similarly, Spirit baptism enables the charismatic community to break down walls of partition between men and women, rich and poor, Jew and Gentile, and even demarcations of religious backgrounds within the Christian community itself (Acts 2.33; 4.32-37; 10.34-48). Through Luke's story, the charismatic community proclaims a renewed social structure with visible signposts of the future kingdom age. Luke–Acts provides a biblical framework for theological reflection on church mission and ministry by linking the God who empowers for witness with the God who liberates and reigns in justice. Richard Mouw also echoes Dempster's conclusions. Mouw calls upon the Christian community to strive for holistic mission with recognition not only of the personal presence of the Spirit to convict of sin, but also to anoint ministers of justice in service of the full gospel (Lk. 4.18-19). For Mouw, this must include a call to political and economic spheres sustained through deep, pious, and prayerful reliance on the Spirit of God.[7]

The more recent and emerging scholar Matthias Wenk follows in the footsteps of his doctoral advisor, Max Turner. Wenk writes *Community–Forming Power* in contraposition to those, like Robert Menzies, who stress that the Spirit functions unilaterally as a prophetic missionary force.[8] Instead, Wenk develops specifically one component of Lukan pneumatology, namely the Spirit's influence on the ethical transformation of the believers. According to Wenk, Luke anticipates and expects the Spirit to be instrumental through charismatic leaders in order to restore covenant faithfulness. Luke builds upon the premise that the prophetic word transforms realities by bringing about not only a spiritual cleansing of God's people, but also ethical renewal. As such, Luke provides a three-pronged pneumatic dialogue between the prophet and God, the

---

[7] Richard Mouw, 'Life in the Spirit in an Unjust World', *Pneuma* 9 (Fall 1987), p. 127.

[8] Matthias Wenk, *Community-Forming Power: The Socio-Ethical Role of the Spirit in Luke–Acts* (JPTSup 19; Sheffield: Sheffield Academic Press, 2000). See also his earlier article 'Community-Forming Power: Reconciliation and the Spirit in Acts', *EPTA* 19 (1999), pp. 17-33.

prophet and the people, and the response of the people to God's message. Wenk focuses not upon passages emphasizing Spirit-led witness, but those centering attention on the preservation of unity during periods of transition and conflict. Since Wenk does not see in Acts an idealized picture of the earliest church, he proposes a Lukan model for resolving conflict and preserving ecclesial unity in times of ethnic transition and tension. Wenk considers ethnic tension surrounding the conflict between the Hebraic and the Hellenistic believers (Acts 6.1-7), the new mission in Samaria (Acts 8.4-25), the Ethiopian Eunuch (Acts 8.26-40), Jewish-Gentile Table Fellowship (Acts 10), and community identity markers at the Council of Jerusalem (Acts 15). As new groups of people experience the generous and inclusive hospitality of God, the Spirit enables leaders to navigate through and overcome potential social schisms.[9]

Wenk follows up his doctoral monograph with further essays on Luke's special concern for inter-personal reconciliation.[10] Wenk accents the programmatic care of the Lukan Jesus for those marginalized by exclusion, impurity and/or sin (Lk. 4.16-30). In turning to Acts, Wenk examines the reconciling ministry of Barnabas, a man full of Spirit and of faith (Acts 11.24), who brings Saul together with the church (Acts 9.26-28), helps connect the Jewish church in Jerusalem with the Hellenistic church in Antioch (Acts 15.22), and mediates between Paul and Mark (Acts 15.36-41).[11]

A recent work by Amos Yong does not focus primarily on Luke–Acts and precludes easy classification. Nonetheless, Yong's *Theology and Down Syndrome* deserves attention for readers of Luke–Acts. Yong calls for intentional extension of the inclusivity represented at

---

[9] Wenk, 'Community-Forming Power: Reconciliation and the Spirit in Acts', pp. 27-28.

[10] Wenk, 'The Holy Spirit as Transforming Power Within a Society: Pneumatological Spirituality and Its Political/Social Relevance for Western Europe', *JPT* 11 (2002), p. 134.

[11] Wenk, 'The Holy Spirit as Transforming Power Within a Society: Pneumatological Spirituality and Its Political/Social Relevance for Western Europe', p. 134. Pentecostals interested in this subject should examine Luke Timothy Johnson's, *The Literary Function of Possessions in Luke–Acts* (SBLDS 39; Missoula: Scholars, 1977). While the title suggests primary focus on social justice, he spends considerable time linking the convergence of social concerns with the prophetic nature of the early community. Though not of Pentecostal persuasion, Johnson proves valuable to Pentecostal readers not only for his pioneering efforts in literary criticism, but also for his appreciation of the centrality of justice in the Spirit-led ministry of Jesus and the emerging apostolic community.

Pentecost beyond the many nations, cultures, ethnicities, and languages of the world. He coins the term 'pneumatological imagination' in order to offer theological rationale for enlarging the integrity of difference and otherness, specifically, to open space for those with physical and intellectual disabilities.[12] Yong interrogates the prevalent cultural emphasis on the veneration of 'normalness' as a contrast to the 'grotesque'. For Yong, a contemporary reading of Jesus' ministry and the ensuing Pentecost narrative must makes 'imaginative' room not only for the disabled, but also for a larger marginalized community that includes imperfect bodies unable to meet the cultural standards of slimness and eternal youth. In short, Yong places contemporary 'ableism' alongside the racial, ethnic, and sexist exclusion of the first century. In an earlier cited work, Yong wrestles with implications of contemporary inclusivity in relation to homosexuals. He suggests that current attempts to embody the breaking of barriers may require fresh examination of sexual barriers. Yong cites a controversial sermon entitled 'What Doth Hinder Me? The Conversion of a Black Homosexual as Recorded by St. Luke' delivered by African-American James Tinney.[13] Tinney claims that 'eunuchs in the Ancient Near Eastern world were at least disposed toward homosexuality, if not practicing homosexuals'. Though Yong notes the limited evidence for such a position, he asserts that the notion of Pentecost and inclusivity requires that Pentecostals think and dialogue further about Christian marginalization and exclusion of homosexuals and the homosexual community.[14]

---

[12] Amos Yong, *Theology and Down Syndrome: Reimagining Disability in Late Modernity* (Waco: Baylor University Press, 2007), pp. 10-11. For Pentecostal implications of Yong's work, see Jeff Hittenberger and Martin William Mittelstadt, 'Power and Powerlessness in Pentecostal Theology: (review of Amos Yong, *Theology and Down Syndrome: Reimagining Disability in Late Modernity*), *Pneuma* 30 (2008), pp. 137-45.

[13] Amos Yong (*The Spirit Poured Out on All Flesh: Pentecostalism and the Possibility of a Global Theology* [Grand Rapids: Baker, 2005]) cites a sermon delivered by James Tinney at the Metropolitan Church of Philadelphia, November 15, 1981 ('What Doth Hinder Me? The Conversion of a Black Homosexual as Recorded by St. Luke', [typescript available from the Associated Mennonite Biblical Seminary Library, Elkhart, IN]).

[14] I mark Tinney as controversial not primarily because of his homosexual predilection, but rather the reaction he receives from Pentecostal communities. Though Tinney maintains Pentecostal identity throughout his life, the conservative moral impulse of Pentecostals makes for a tumultuous relationship. See C.E. Jones, 'Tinney, James Steven', *NIDPCM*, p. 1143.

I conclude with important but less voluminous voices. John Christopher Thomas looks at the internal conflict surrounding table fellowship in Acts 6.1-7 and implores Pentecostals not only consider questions of unity and diversity, inclusion and exclusion, but also ministry potential. According to Thomas, Luke utilizes this scene not only to emphasize the need for a unified community, but as an opportunity for the formative community to diversify its organization through inclusion of a Gentile ministry team.[15] James Hernando finds in the story of Zacchaeus not only the conversion of an 'arch villain in Jewish society', but also a surprisingly paradigmatic agent of justice on account of his encounter with Jesus.[16] In a later article, Hernando addresses the beloved parable of the good Samaritan. In summarizing its social import, he captures Jesus' ability to invert the question 'Who is the neighbor I ought to love?' with 'Who showed the love of God and demonstrated he was a neighbor?'[17] On a more popular level, Ron Kydd celebrates Pentecostal longing to imitate the life of Jesus under the anointing and power of the Spirit. But Kydd also laments that imitation of Jesus often remains reduced to mere proclamation. Kydd remarks on the Canadian scene: 'When Pentecostalism was young we did not have an outreach to the poor, we were the poor! We just reached out to ourselves and we were reaching the poor!'[18] However, as Canadian numbers increase and the Canadian economy improves after World War II, Pentecostals experience significant upward mobility. Unfortunately, Kydd's rejoinder echoes Dempster's plea and offers little consolation: 'Since then we have become the rich and we still do not have any approach to the poor'.[19] Commenting on Jesus' ministry, Kydd implores Pentecostals to enlarge kingdom ministry of the Lukan Jesus:

---

[15] John Christopher Thomas, 'Unity and Diversity: Obstacle or Opportunity' in *Ministry and Theology: Studies for the Church and Its Leaders* (Cleveland, TN: Pathway Press, 1996), pp. 71-84.

[16] James D. Hernando, 'The Church as a Transformational Agent in Society: The Story of Zacchaeus, Luke 19:1-10. Part 1' *Encounter* 1:1 (Summer 2004): n.p. Online: http://www.agts.edu/encounter/articles/2004_summer/zaccheus.pdf.

[17] Hernando, 'The Church as a Transformational Agent in Society: The Parable of the Good Samaritan, Luke 10:25-27' *Encounter* 1:2 (Fall 2004): n.p. Online: http://www.agts.edu/encounter/articles/2004_fall/hernando.htm.

[18] Ron Kydd, 'To See is to be Called', *Pentecostal Testimony* 77:1 (January 1996), p. 11.

[19] Kydd, 'To See is to be Called', p. 11.

In Luke 4 Jesus proclaimed that He would take the gospel to the streets. He went to the big and the small, the rich and the poor, he went to the broken. You and I are called to these people. If we are filled with the Holy Spirit He will show us those people and he will help us to understand what needs to be done. I believe that he will give us the courage, perseverance, the love to hang in with those people until the grace of God becomes a reality of their lives.[20]

Though Kydd does not use technical language, he clearly views Luke 4 as programmatic prophecy to be fulfilled not only through the life of Jesus and the apostolic community, but a present 'today' reality (Lk. 4.21; 19.9).

In sum, these scholars recognize that sustainability of a prophetic voice for the Pentecostal community must be intricately linked to social healing and justice. They capture Luke's hope for a greater connection between Spirit, justice and community. Miroslav Volf says it well: if Pentecostals affirm a life of active eschatological expectation, continuity between God's present reign and the reign to come will 'guarantee that noble human efforts will not be wasted'.[21] Pentecostal scholars will surely continue exploration of justice themes in Luke–Acts in order to facilitate contemporary response to the link between Spirit-enablement and Spirit-living.

---

[20] Kydd, 'To See is to be Called', p. 12. I would argue that in personal practice many Pentecostals are generous and inclined to justice, however, few are afforded proper theological instruction and reflection on the subject often due to fear that such an emphasis may threaten missions as proclamation. For data, see Agnieszka Tennant, 'Tallying Compassion', *Christianity Today* (February, 2003), p. 56. She interviews Ram A. Cnaan (*The Invisible Caring Hand: American Congregations and Provision of Welfare* [New York: New York University Press, 2002]) who dispels the myth that mainline churches are more involved with social services than evangelical churches. His research indicates that both groups spend an equal amount of resources in the social arena (pp. 56-59).

[21] Miroslav Volf, 'On Loving With Hope: Eschatology and Social Responsibility', *Transformation* 7 (July/Sept 1990), p. 29. I would also recommend Volf's *Work in the Spirit: Toward a Theology of Work* (Eugene: Wipf & Stock, 2001). While this work is primarily theological, students and scholars of Luke–Acts should be inspired to draw upon Volf's holistic approach to vocation. See final section.

4.2 THE GOOD NEWS OF PEACE

Lukan emphasis upon 'Peace on earth, good will toward men' (Lk. 2.14) and Jesus as 'Prince of Peace', compels many early North American Pentecostal bodies to adopt a pacifist stance.[22] So also British Assemblies of God scholar Donald Gee states: 'the only answer for the Christian is contained in the immortal words of Peter, 'We ought to obey God rather than men' (Acts 5.29). For many, Conscientious Objection becomes the only possible course, however serious the consequences'.[23] Though pacifism continues to wane within Pentecostal circles, numerous scholars emphasize Luke's interest in the peace motif. Robert Reid provides an important point of departure. He follows a growing list of scholars who locate Luke's notion of the kingdom of Jesus as an alternative to the rule of Caesar, the supposed Savior and Lord of humanity.[24] Luke forces Christians to wrestle with the propaganda offered by the empire under the banner of *Pax Romana* or the new message based upon the good news of Jesus, *Pax Christi*.

Charismatic Catholic scholar J. Massyngbaerde Ford situates peacemaking within the context of Lukan hospitality. In *My Enemy is My Guest*, she begins with Luke's frequent references to Jesus' table fellowship alongside outcasts and enemies (Lk. 5.29; 15.1-2; 19.1-10). According to Ford, Luke promotes the victory of God through peace, forgiveness, and acceptance of enemies rather than through military struggle and violence. Hence, the Lukan Jesus show clemency to Samaritans (9.51-56), refuses retaliation (13.1-9), demonstrates restraint at the Temple cleansing (Lk. 19.45-46; compare Mk 11.15-19; Mt. 21.12-13), prays for his executioners (23.34), and suffers as a paradigmatic martyr in keeping with his words of

---

[22] See Jay Beaman, *Pentecostal Pacifism: The Origin, Development, and Rejection of Pacific Beliefs among the Pentecostals* (Hillsboro, KS: Center for Mennonite Brethren Studies, 1989), p. 24. Beaman cites some thirty Pentecostal bodies with a history of pacifism including the Assemblies of God, Pentecostal Assemblies of Canada, Church of God (Cleveland, TN), Pentecostal Holiness Church, and United Pentecostal Church International.

[23] Beaman, *Pentecostal Pacifism*, p. 65.

[24] Robert G. Reid, "Savior' and 'Lord' in the Lukan Birth Narrative: A Challenge to Caesar?' (paper presented at the annual meeting of the Society for Pentecostal Studies, Cleveland, TN, March 2007).

non-retaliation in self-defense (6.27-36).[25] At the grassroots level, the Lukan view of God's hospitality makes room for everyone; Luke implores believers to place no limitations on the invitation to 'dinner' including intentional fellowship with strangers and enemies.

Joel Shuman suggests that increasing militarism among contemporary American Pentecostals marks their near loss of self-understanding as a community of radical disciples.[26] Shuman reflects upon the Gospels and laments the rejection of the cross and the life of Jesus as the way of dealing with conflict. In turning to Acts, Shuman proposes that Pentecost signifies a new eschatological event whereby the divisions of Babel are reversed. Glossolalia symbolizes new possibilities for social and political relationships in stark contrast to Babel-like violence. According to Shuman, the import of glossolalia must not be restricted to utterance; 'it is instead a community whose memory of its Savior creates the miracle of being a people whose very differences contribute to their unity'.[27] He links this event to Peter's employment of Joel's prophecy so that the glossolalia of Pentecost anticipates the grand gathering of a great multitude beyond numerical comprehension from every nation, tribe, and language (Rev. 7.9). As such, Pentecost initiates the present reality of an alternative community, a people 'filled with the Spirit' to bring a peaceable vision of God's kingdom not bound by national allegiance.[28]

In a recent essay, I address the convergence of 'Spirit and Peace in Luke–Acts' and argue that Spirit-inspired witnesses solicit intentional embrace of the counter-cultural gospel of peace. Luke not only follows enthusiastic anticipation with fulfilled peace through the formation of an alternative community, but also does not avoid the implications of the rejection of peace as paramount to rejection of the gospel. An underlying political context marked by Roman

---

[25] J. Massyngbaerde Ford, *My Enemy is My Guest: Jesus and Violence in Luke* (Maryknoll, NY: Orbis, 1984).

[26] Joel Shuman, 'Pentecost and the End of Patriotism: A Call for the Restoration of Pacifism among Pentecostal Christians', *JPT* 9 (1996), pp. 71-72.

[27] Shuman, 'Pentecost and the End of Patriotism', pp. 95-96.

[28] Shuman cites Stanley Hauerwas ('The Church as God's New Language', in *Christian Existence Today* [Durham, NC: Labyrinth, 1988]). The church provides an 'alternative to Babel, to fear one another, and finally then to war … We do not just have an alternative, we are the alternative. We do not just have a story to tell but in the telling, we *are* the story being told' (p. 48, emphasis original).

occupation, war, brutality, and persecution stands as a critical back-drop for Luke's integration of gospel and peace. Luke uses the word 'peace' fourteen times in the Third Gospel and seven times in Acts, compared to minimal usage in Matthew (four), Mark (one), and John (six).[29] In short, whereas a broken world remains inclined toward power, self-interest and conflict, Luke presents the alterna-tive way of peace, a message of radical love based on God's desire for communities built upon human inclusivity. Spirit-led characters announce the coming of Jesus who incarnates the gospel of peace. As Jesus models this gospel of peace, his followers continue to em-body and proclaim his life and message. Finally, given the centrality of a Spirit-inspired gospel of peace, I suggest that the convergence of Spirit and peace in Luke–Acts provides possibilities for dialogue between Anabaptists and Pentecostals.[30]

Paul Alexander proves to be the most prolific scholar concerning Pentecostals and pacifism. Time and again, he implores Pentecostals to revisit their early heritage of nonviolence and peacemaking as continuous with Luke's story of Jesus and the church. He states: 'their theology, ethics, worldview, hermeneutic, ideology, or lifestyle, one thing is clear: Jesus was in the center of their thinking and do-ing, their words and deeds'.[31] Given Pentecostal emphasis on the paradigmatic nature of Jesus' life, Alexander interrogates Pentecos-tals for their marginalization of Jesus' stand on oppression, exploi-tation, greed, nationalism, and violence.[32] Alexander refers to the temptation scene in Lk. 4.1-13, where Jesus rejects the real options of safety, security, control, and coercion and instead redefines the

---

[29] Luke 1.79; 2.14; 2.29; 7.50; 8.48; 10.5; 10.6 (2); 11.21; 12.51; 14.32; 19.38; 19.42; 24.36. Acts 7.26; 9.31; 10.36; 12.20; 15.33; 16.36; 24.2. Luke's use of peace produces only one parallel use in Mark (5.34 par. Lk. 8.48) and another parallel use in Matthew (10.34 par. Lk. 12.51).

[30] While commentators provide specific exegesis on the ensuing texts, few at-tempt to make literary and theological connections. I find the following works most helpful in the exegesis below: Paul Borgman, *The Way According to Luke: Hearing the Whole Story of Luke–Acts* (Grand Rapids: Eerdmans, 2006); John Kil-gallen, ''Peace' in the Gospel of Luke and Acts of the Apostles', *Studia Missionalia* 38 (1989), pp. 55-79; and Willard Swartley, *Covenant of Peace: The Missing Peace in New Testament Theology and Ethics* (Grand Rapids: Eerdmans, 2006).

[31] Paul Alexander, *Peace to War: Shifting Allegiances in the Assemblies of God* (C. Henry Smith Series 9; Telford, PA: Cascadia, 2009).

[32] Paul Alexander, 'A Theology for Pentecostal Peace Making' (paper pre-sented at the annual meeting of the Society for Pentecostal Studies, Lakeland, FL, 14-16 March 2002), p. 455.

use of economic power, nationalism, and violence. In turning to Acts, Alexander states: 'Christology shows us how to live and die while making peace, pneumatology enables it'.[33] As the Lukan Jesus relies upon the Holy Spirit through his temptation, the early church is well positioned to testify to the power of the Spirit and enable followers to live peaceably as the new people of God. Through Pentecost, the early church (and Pentecostals) experiences God's victory over violence caused by the divisions of Babel; Pentecost reverses Babel and opens possibilities for harmonious human, social, and political relationships.[34]

In an earlier paper, Alexander calls upon Pentecostals to join him in forming a Pentecostal organization committed to peace and justice.[35] Since Pentecostals place large emphasis upon Jesus as one filled, led, empowered, and anointed by the Spirit (Lk. 4.1, 4, 14) and upon Jesus' encouragement of his followers to emulate his life in the Spirit (Lk. 24.46-49), Alexander reiterates his call for imitation of Jesus' rejection of violence and the sword. Jesus counters the life inclined toward safety, security, wealth, and power with the way of service, suffering, and death.[36] Given Jesus' teaching on money, provisions, sandals, and the sword, Alexander addresses specifically the arrest of Jesus in Luke 22, a scene often used as justification for the use of the sword. While Jesus calls for the disciples to buy a sword, Alexander argues that this request requires interpretation in light of temptation; 'two swords' are hardly 'enough' for defense, but demonstrative of their temptation. Peter follows his misunderstanding of the impending suffering, death, and resurrection of Jesus with a vicious attack by the sword to which Jesus responds with rebuke and tender mercy to the victim.[37] In speaking of Peter, Alexander then asserts: 'it is not by accident that this incident occurs before the day of Pentecost … He was quite different

---

[33] Alexander, 'A Theology for Pentecostal Peace Making', p. 467.

[34] Alexander, 'A Theology for Pentecostal Peace Making', pp. 469-70.

[35] Now called 'Pentecostals and Charismatics for Peace and Justice' (www.pcpj.org).

[36] Paul Alexander, 'Spirit-Empowered Peacemaking: Toward a Pentecostal Peace Fellowship', *JEPTA* 22 (2002), pp. 99-100. See also 'Spirit-Empowered Peacemaking as Opportunity: Toward a Pentecostal Charismatic Peace Fellowship' (paper presented at the annual meeting of the Society for Pentecostal Studies, Lakeland, FL, 14-16 March 2002).

[37] Luke does not associate this act of violence with Peter (but see Jn 18.1-11).

afterwards'.[38] The arrival of the Spirit creates the possibility for individuals and communities to lead lives according to Jesus and the manner of grace received.[39]

In sum, the words of Jürgen Moltmann strike a chord by way of a telling cross-examination: 'where are the "charismata of the 'charismatics'" in the everyday world, in the peace movement, in the movements of liberation'.[40] Like Moltmann, Alexander laments the stark contrast between first generation Christians and contemporary Pentecostals, who have 'outgrown the narratives of Jesus and Acts and have adopted what they consider to be a more responsible managing of the affairs of the world. They now live in a different story'.[41] Though Pentecostals typically utilize narrative as the primary means for protection of tongues as the one and only initial physical evidence for Spirit baptism, they have stopped using the narrative of Jesus' life and the early church for their ethics of war and peacemaking. Alexander decries a contemporary understanding of Pentecost, formerly understood as empowerment to live and die like Jesus evidenced by a border-crossing, self-giving, reconciling, and cross-bearing witness, now focused primarily upon entry into ecstatic experience.[42]

4.3 SUFFERING AND PERSECUTION

As people of the Spirit, Pentecostals are at times rightly accused of triumphalism. Pentecostals with their emphasis upon reception of the Spirit easily become susceptible to an uncritical sense of invincibility. But numerous scholars return to the Lukan story only to discover a more balanced approach. In a review of essays by Stron-

---

[38] Alexander, 'Spirit-Empowered Peacemaking', p. 99. Alexander also points to Peter's later teaching 'Let him turn aside from evil, and let him do good. Let him seek peace and pursue it … if you suffer for good, good for you! For you don't fear what they fear [death]' (1 Pet. 3.14).

[39] Alexander cites Frank Macchia's summary of a Pentecost experience: 'an experience with God that continually urges the people of God to move beyond the confines of private piety or even church fellowship to the global issues of justice, peace, and the redemption of the world' (Macchia, 'The Struggle for Global Witness', p. 18.)

[40] Jürgen Moltmann, *The Spirit of Life: A Universal Affirmation* (Minneapolis: Fortress, 2001), p. 186.

[41] Alexander, *Peace to War*, p. 335.

[42] Alexander, *Peace to War*, pp. 330, 338.

stad, Paul Elbert calls for further attention to the persecution motif: 'the category of suffering … has something significant to offer to our understanding of this aspect of Christian life. Would not this perspective also help in understanding the charismatic experience of the Lukan Paul, a main player in Stronstad's hermeneutical search?'[43] Given increasing attention to the persecution of global Christians, it comes as no surprise that Pentecostal scholars begin to address Elbert's concern. I consider first a number of essays focusing on single Lukan episodes.

Randall Holm examines the Stephen narrative (Acts 7) in an attempt to import the significance of Stephen's polemical words into the contemporary church. In the hands of Luke, Stephen's martyrdom functions as an ironic geographic segue to church expansion beyond Jerusalem and into the Gentile community. At the level of the story, witnesses must either resist the Holy Spirit and be complicit in Stephen's death or cast their own lot with the 'Son of Man standing at the right hand of God' (Acts 7.56). Holm raises important issues concerning Pentecostal reflection upon history, specifically a call to move beyond nostalgic desire for the 'old and venerable' to a rigorous spiritual formation and discipline aligned with God's purposes/destiny that may include opposition.[44]

In the first of two moving essays, Robert Gallagher offers pastoral autobiography in conjunction with the 'little Pentecost' (Acts 4.23-31). He laments how his ideas of ministry success generally parallel the contemporary values of western society without critical evaluation. By way of a fresh reading of Acts 4, Gallagher recognizes Luke's emphasis on the early church pattern of prayer, Spirit and mission and calls for contemporary readers to view mission flowing out of 'beingness' rather than 'doingness'.[45] By focusing on being, the gospel enables followers of Jesus, early and contemporary, to endure opposition. In the second paper Gallagher paradigmatically parallels the journey of his wife Dolores as she struggles

---

[43] Paul Elbert, 'Spirit, Scripture and Theology Through a Lukan Lens: A Review Article', *JPT* 13 (1998), pp. 59-60.

[44] Randall Holm, 'Acts 7 and the Destiny of the Holy Spirit' (paper presented at the annual meeting of the Society for Pentecostal Studies, Wilmore, KY, March 2003), p. 15.

[45] Robert Gallagher, 'From Doingness to Beingness: A Missiological Interpretation of Acts 4:23-31' (paper presented at the annual meeting of the Society for Pentecostal Studies, Tulsa, OK, March 2001).

and eventually dies of colon cancer to the respective tragedies and triumphs of James and Peter as recorded in Acts 12. Gallagher locates his family story alongside the persecution of the church in Jerusalem (Acts 12.1-5) and Peter's miraculous escape from prison (Acts 12.6-11).[46]

Finally, Peter Wallace Dunn highlights a specific scene in the apocryphal *Acts of Paul*, where Paul converts and baptizes a lion. In a twist of fate, when Paul eventually encounters this same lion in the arena at Ephesus, the lion refuses to devour the defenseless apostle. Dunn locates this second century story alongside numerous Lukan texts. The apocryphal Paul stands in the same tradition as first century Christians who hear Jesus' predictions concerning persecution (Lk. 12 and 21) and their fulfillment (cf. Acts 4.8).[47]

In a full length monograph entitled *Spirit and Suffering in Luke– Acts*, I contend that Pentecostals in their zeal to defend basic Pentecostal themes such as Spirit baptism have not adequately explored the biblical context of suffering and persecution in the life of Jesus, the disciples and the early church. I conclude that Luke's ability to sustain elements of triumph and tragedy, acceptance and rejection of the gospel provides a model for pneumatic discipleship. I examine the following six passages, three in the Third Gospel and three in Acts: (Lk. 2.25-35; 4.16-20; 12.1-12; Acts 3-5; 7; 20.18-35).

1) The somber words of Simeon near the climax of the Lukan birth narrative launch the intersection of Spirit and suffering (Lk. 2.25-35). Simeon's inspired words serve as a Lukan literary prophecy; God's work in Jesus brings all people to a point of decision and place rejection and opposition to Jesus in the plan of God.

2) The Spirit-led Jesus meets rejection and persecution in his inaugural mission (Lk. 4.16-30). While worshiping in the syna-

---

[46] Robert Gallagher, 'Hope in the Midst of Trial: A Missiological Interpretation of Acts 12:1-11' (paper presented at the annual meeting of the Society for Pentecostal Studies, Milwaukee, WI, March 2004). Both of Gallagher's essays are published in *Mission in Acts: Ancient Narratives in Contemporary Context* (ed. Gallagher and Paul Hertig; American Society of Missiology 34; Maryknoll: Orbis Books, 2004), pp. 45-58 and 157-166.

[47] Peter Wallace Dunn, 'The Charismatic Gifts in the *Acts of Paul*: Second Century Trends' (paper presented at the annual meeting of the Society for Pentecostal Studies, Kirkland, WA, March 2000), pp. G1-11.

gogue at his hometown of Nazareth, the Lukan Jesus, also under the direction of the Holy Spirit (3.15-16, 22; 4.1, 14), experiences rejection, thereby serving as Luke's first explicit example of Simeon's forecast of acceptance and rejection. These words also serve a paradigmatic purpose for Luke's readers: future witnesses of Jesus will not only proclaim the message of Jesus, but may also experience a similar fate, namely, acceptance and rejection.

3) In Lk. 12.1-12 by way of another literary prophecy, the Lukan Jesus assures his disciples that the same Spirit will produce bold witness in the midst of opposition. Luke places the disciples in continuity with their master; pneumatic discipleship will also receive a divided response.

4) In Acts 3-5, Luke advances the first fulfillment of Jesus' words in Lk. 12.1-12; Peter, John and the other apostles experience the triumph and tragedy of the new mission; when confronted with the decisive choice between confession and denial, the Holy Spirit inspires bold witness (Acts 4.8, 31).

5) Stephen becomes the first Christian martyr and mirrors the death of Jesus in Acts 7. For Luke, Stephen's story not only cultivates bold commitment in the face of opposition, but also locates such witness in continuity with Old Testament agents like Joseph, Moses, and the prophets.

6) Finally, Paul experiences not only remarkable missionary success, but rejection, abuse, and imprisonment. Ironically, Luke roots this persecution in divine providence; Paul's journey to Rome places him in continuity with Jesus. As the journey of Jesus in the Third Gospel serves as a voyage of his ordained suffering, so also the Lukan Paul goes to Rome, not as a free man but as a prisoner in chains and ultimately 'bound by the Spirit' (Acts 20.22). Paul also offers a fitting 'farewell discourse' to the Ephesian elders and by inference, future witnesses of Jesus (Acts 20.18-35). By implication, Paul's life, directed by the Spirit, serves as an example to the Ephesian community. When under duress, they (and Luke's readers) need not lose heart, for present and/or potential future persecution places them in continuity not only with the prophets, Jesus, the Apostles and Stephen, but also their own pastor, Paul.

In sum, Pentecostals must see in Luke–Acts, believers caught in the midst of opposition not only survive, but also thrive on account of Spirit enablement.[48]

Two further scholars echo these conclusions and view Christian history as a continuation of the Acts story. James Bradley notes the pattern of miracle and martyrdom in the post-apostolic church and cites how numerous church fathers place themselves in direct continuity with the primitive church in Acts.[49] Luke Wesley jumps into the 21st century and provides an insider portrait of the Church in China as a paradoxical combination of 'Pentecostal, Powerful, and Persecuted'.[50] Wesley substantiates firsthand the convergence of Spirit and suffering. On the one hand, he considers first the lives of Chinese Christians connected with the state church and concludes that their minimal threat of persecution makes texts which promise power for bold witness in the face of opposition (e.g., Lk. 12.11-12; Acts 1.8; 7.55) less important. On the other hand, house church believers, the majority Pentecostal, must make a different choice. Their context shapes how they read and appropriate Scripture. For these Chinese Christians, 'the stories in the book of Acts take on new meaning. The experiences of Peter, Stephen, and Paul often parallel their own. House church believers identify with early church vulnerability, weakness, and the need for divine strength'.[51] When these believers face persecution or its ever-present threat, texts which promise God's power for bold witness in the face of opposition take on tremendous significance.[52] At the other end of the spectrum, Wesley challenges Western readers to reflect afresh on the book of Acts. The experiences of countless Christians in China (and elsewhere) not only call for a new recognition that persecution

---

[48] Martin William Mittelstadt, *The Spirit and Suffering in Luke–Acts: Implications for a Pentecostal Pneumatology* (JPTSup 26; London: T & T Clark, 2004). See my brief synopsis, 'Life in the Spirit and the Way of the Cross', *Enrich: A Journal for Pentecostal Ministry* 4.2 (Fall 2005), pp. 26-30 and a more recent analysis of further work on suffering in Luke–Acts entitled: 'Spirit and Suffering in Contemporary Pentecostalism: The Lukan Epic Continues' in *Defining Issues in Pentecostalism: Classical and Emergent* (Eugene, OR: Pickwick Publications, 2007), pp. 144-74.

[49] James E. Bradley, 'Miracles and Martyrdom in the Early Church: Some Theological and Ethical Implications', *Pneuma* 13 (Spring 1991), p. 65.

[50] Luke Wesley, *The Church in China: Persecuted, Pentecostal, and Powerful* (AJPSS 2; Baguio: AJPS Books, 2004).

[51] Wesley, *The Church in China*, p. 96.

[52] Wesley, *The Church in China*, pp. 100-101.

and Pentecostal power go hand in hand, but also a new global part-nership.[53]

Finally, note the collection of essays on suffering and martyrdom through Pentecostal/Charismatic lenses, the first of its kind. Two essays by Keith Warrington and Jon Newton offer brief remarks on suffering and martyrdom in Luke–Acts with contemporary implications.[54] Warrington examines the current climate of persecution in Africa, the Middle East, Central and Eastern Europe, as well as Asia and calls for ongoing development of a biblical theology of suffering. As many disestablished and disenfranchised Pentecostals move about in a global and post-Christendom world, the Lukan narratives filled with the stories of apostles on trial, and preachers 'run out of town' should prove more and more relevant.

4.4 ECUMENISM AND INTERRELIGIOUS DIALOGUE

The numerical emergence of Pentecostalism thrusts Pentecostal scholars into exciting ecumenical dialogue. According to Allan Anderson, Pentecostalism constitutes various 'movements with an em-

---

[53] Wesley, *The Church in China*, p. 103. See poignant Acts-like examples in Luke Wesley's *Stories from China: Fried Rice for the Soul* (Waynesboro, GA: Authentic Media, 2005). Note the following example of Sister Li, an imprisoned young Chinese evangelist.

> The old routines in the prison changed … they would sing songs and study the Bible. This went on for several days. The guards could hear the singing and the preaching, so one day the chief officer called Sister Li into his office and said to her, 'Your songs are very nice, but you cannot preach. This is not a church, it's a prison.' Sister Li answered, 'We cannot sing, if we cannot preach.' He told her not to preach or sing anymore. But she and the others continued to do so.

Upon Sister Li's release after twenty days, Wesley continues:

> As the police officer escorted her to the local bus station, he shared with her that his mother was a Christian. He indicated that Sister Li and her songs had made a big impact on his life (p. 45).

This story and many others are reminiscent of episodes in Acts: 4.23-31; 5.29; 16.16-34.

[54] Keith Warrington, 'A Spirit Theology of Suffering', *The Suffering Body: Responding to the Persecution of Christians* (ed. Cecil M. Robeck and Harold Hunter; Peabody: Paternoster Press, 2006), pp. 24-36; Jon Newton, 'Toward a Pentecostal Martyrology', *Australasian Pentecostal Studies* (2008): n.p. Online: http://pcbc.web journals.org/Issues.asp?index=358&id={9960F980-CE81-42AA-8AAD-5F4CD4F27103}

phasis on the experience of the power of the Holy Spirit with accompanying manifestation of the imminent presence of God'.[55] For Anderson, such a broad definition offers enormous unifying potential for genuine ecumenical encounters. With this in mind, I begin with Frank Macchia, a Pentecostal representative of the Pentecostal/Roman Catholic Dialogue. He insists that any attempt at inward domestication of the Acts 2 narrative by any one movement or ecclesial community runs contrary to Pentecost.[56] Pentecost functions by nature as an ecumenical event. Macchia recognizes the historic tension of Pentecostals toward ecumenism, not the least due to their designation as a 'sectarian' movement. But with no primary points of departure from the orthodox affirmations of Christian faith, Macchia argues against such a label. He implores not only Pentecostals but also the Church universal to consider true Pentecost as a means of breaking sectarian scandal and promotion of cultural and ecclesiastical divisions. Moreover, Macchia suggests that the very existence of Pentecostalism as a marginalized movement may provide prophetic insight and criticism valuable for the whole people of God. He finds in Acts a firm foundation, a story that incorporates both male and female prophets, rich and poor, and young and old (2.17-18). The unifying work of the Spirit sweeps up diversity via the formation of a harmonious Jewish and Gentile community. Luke does not speak of the unity of the 'people of God' in some abstract sense, but, true to Joel 2, the events of Acts 2 break down seemingly insurmountable social, cultural, and religious boundaries. According to Macchia, Luke views visible disunity of diverse groups scandalous whereas authentic Spirit-encounter fosters unity.[57] Macchia envisions the ever-contemporary Lukan story symbolically eliciting future realizations of unity yet unforeseen; Luke continues to speak by accenting ongoing efforts of the people of God to redefine their identity in light of an ever-expanding catholicity.

---

[55] Allan Anderson, 'Diversity in the Definition of 'Pentecostal/Charismatic' and Its Ecumenical Implications' (paper presented at the annual meeting of the Society for Pentecostal Studies, Lakeland, FL, March 2002), p. 744.

[56] Frank Macchia, 'The Tongues of Pentecost: A Pentecostal Perspective on the Promise and Challenge of Pentecostal/Roman Catholic Dialogue', *Journal of Ecumenical Studies* 35 (1998), pp. 1-18.

[57] Macchia, 'The Tongues of Pentecost', p. 2.

Charismatic Catholic scholar Ralph Del Colle offers an important invitation for Pentecostal/Catholic dialogue based upon Luke's portrayal of Mary.[58] Though the Catholic/Pentecostal dialogue ventures forward, Del Colle notes the limited attention given by Pentecostals to Catholic piety and devotion relating to veneration of Mary.[59] Ironically, Del Colle turns to the prominent role of Mary in the Lukan narrative. According to Del Colle, 'the Church exists in the outpouring of the Spirit, similar to Mary conceiving Christ by the Spirit coming to her'. Given the pattern of prayerful yielding of the Lord by those in Topeka and Azusa, Del Colle continues: 'at this point I simply note that the Marian posture before God and the Spirit is not at all strange to the Pentecostal imagination ... An integral dialogue on Mariology begins with the Christian assembly awaiting the promise of Pentecost'.[60] Similarly, the prolific yet seldom cited Raniero Cantalamessa, longtime Charismatic preacher to the papal household, speaks of Mary as 'the most sublime example of a Spirit-filled person'.[61] His lament is poignant: 'It is painful to think that among the Christian denominations most hostile to Mary are certain Pentecostal groups'.[62] In sum, Del Colle and Cantalamessa recommend that Luke's investment in such pneumatological activity may provide a bridge for further discussion on the controversial Mary.

Similarly, a recent conversation between Robert Menzies and Cornelius van der Kooi produces possibilities for dialogue between Pentecostal and Reformation approaches to Acts. In response to a paper by Robert Menzies, Cornelius van der Kooi assesses Menzies' argument for Pentecostal emphasis upon the distinction between the soteriological and charismatic work of the Spirit and the claim

---

[58] Ralph Del Colle, 'Mary, The Unwelcome (?) Guest in Catholic/Pentecostal Dialogue' (paper presented at the annual meeting of the Society for Pentecostal Studies, Milwaukee, WI, March 2004).

[59] See the 'Perspectives on Mary', in the 'Final Report of the Dialogue between the Secretariat for Promoting Christian Unity of the Roman Catholic Church and some classical Pentecostals, 1977-1982', *Pneuma* 12.2 (Fall 1990), pp. 107-111.

[60] Del Colle, *Mary*, pp. 11-12.

[61] Raniero Cantalamessa, *Mary: Mirror of the Church* (trans. Frances Lonergan Villa; Collegeville, MN: Liturgical Press), p. 177.

[62] Cantalamessa, *Mary: Mirror of the Church*, p. 177.

for the universal potential for prophetic gifts.[63] While Van der Kooi affirms Menzies' basic thesis, he remains cautious concerning universality in order not to diminish the sovereignty of God.[64] Given the common Orthodox claims of both traditions, further dialogue not only seems inevitable but necessary.

The ground-breaking work of scholar Amos Yong exhibits similar ecumenical zeal but does not limit his comments to a specific tradition. He proposes a Spirit-Christology based upon Luke–Acts as the impetus for ecumenical missiology.[65] Under the guidance of the Spirit, Jesus heralds and ushers in the kingdom of God (Lk. 4.18-19). His life embodies the work of the Spirit from conception (Lk. 1.35) and dedication (Lk. 2.23-32), through growth and maturation (Lk. 1.80, 2.52), baptism (Lk. 3.21-22) and temptation (Lk. 4.1, 14), inauguration and ministry (Lk. 4.18-19), and death (Lk. 23.46).[66] In Acts, the gift of the Spirit continues the work of Jesus. Yong cites seven dimensions of this activity including: 1) personal (Acts 2.38; 9.17-18; 22.16); 2) family (Acts 2.39; 11.14; 16.14-15; 16.31-33; 18.8a); 3) ecclesial (the creation of a new people of God); 4) material (Lk. 1.52-53; 6.20-21, 24-25; Acts 6.16); 5) social (breaking down racial, class and gender barriers); 6) cosmic (Acts 2.19-21); and 7) eschatological (Acts 3.19-21).[67] These dimensions of Spirit-Christology and Spirit-Soteriology lead naturally toward the development of a pneumatic based ecclesiology and ecumenism. Concerning the church, Yong concludes: 'Jesus the Savior; healer; sanctifier; baptizer and coming King becomes the body of Christ as the saving, healing, sanctifying, baptizing and … eschatologicalizing … presence and activity of God by the Spirit'.[68] In a response to Yong, Anabaptist scholar Thomas Finger offers a fitting rejoinder. Finger suggests Mennonites and Pentecostals might find common ground via Lukan soteriology. While many scholars claim Luke offers a minimalist view of atonement, Finger suggests Mennonites and

---

[63] Robert Menzies, 'Luke's Understanding of Baptism in the Holy Spirit: A Pentecostal Perspective', *PentecoStudies* 6 (2007), pp. 108-126; Cornelius van der Kooi, 'The Wonders of God: A Reformed Perspective on Luke's Baptism in the Holy Spirit', *PentecoStudies* 7 (2008), pp. 34-45.

[64] Van der Kooi, 'The Wonders of God', pp. 44-45.

[65] Amos Yong, *The Spirit Poured Out*.

[66] Yong, *The Spirit Poured Out*, pp. 86-90.

[67] Yong, *The Spirit Poured Out*, pp. 91-96.

[68] Yong, *The Spirit Poured Out*, p. 166.

Pentecostals might find common ground in the *Christus Victor* motif.[69] By placing the work of the Spirit under broader ecclesial parameters, the Spirit poured out on all flesh only increases ecumenical possibilities.[70]

In a more recent work entitled *Hospitality & the Other*, Yong offers the most innovative attempt to date at connecting Lukan theology to interreligious dialogue.[71] He constructs a platform for the Christian doctrine of hospitality by recommending that followers of Jesus counter interreligious violence, war, and terrorism with the Spirit of Pentecost. Yong envisions a new kind of interreligious encounter where the diverse tongues of Pentecost open up a way to imaginative Christian practices in a pluralistic world. With Pentecost as the foundation for God's hospitable embrace, Yong returns to the Third Gospel and the Lukan Jesus as the embodiment of God's hospitality. First, Jesus serves as an exemplary recipient of hospitality. His lowly birth in a manger and final burial in the private tomb of Joseph of Arimathea bracket a life that relies on the goodwill of many. Jesus lives his life as the consummate guest in numerous homes. Furthermore, in ironic fashion, Jesus the 'homeless' guest becomes Jesus the host, the agent of God's redemptive hospitality. Jesus often breaks with convention by entering into suspect homes, failing to wash, and rebuking hosts in order to embrace outsiders, the oppressed and marginalized of the ancient world. In another twist, accusers generally fail to understand and/or receive Jesus' acts of hospitality and in so doing reject the hospitality of God. Finally, Yong finds in Jesus' parable of the Good Samaritan a principal lesson for interreligious hospitality. Yong establishes Jesus' teaching

---

[69] Thomas Finger, 'The Possibilities of a Lucan Hermeneutic: Some Mennonite Reflections on Amos Yong's Theology' (paper presented at the annual meeting of the Society for Pentecostal Studies, Durham, NC, 13-15 March 2008), pp. 1-14.

[70]Note also Yong's later essay 'Poured out on All Flesh: The Spirit, World Pentecostalism, and the Renewal of Theology and Praxis in the 21st Century', *PentecoStudies* 6.1 (2007), pp. 16-46. See also Shane Clifton, review of Amos Yong, *The Spirit Poured Out on All Flesh: Pentecostalism and the Possibility of Global Theology*, *Australasian Pentecostal Studies* 9 (2006): n.p. Online: http://aps.webjournals.org/articles/1/03/2006/6669.htm?id={ED4C92D8-DC69-4076-AE074F678C173F C0}.

Pentecostals interested in Spirit and ecumenism should consult the early but invaluable work of the long time dialogue partner, Jürgen Moltmann, *The Church in the Power of the Spirit* (San Francisco: Harper and Row, 1975).

[71] Yong, *Hospitality and the Other* (introduced in section 1.3)

relating to Jewish and Samaritan tension as an illustration of mutual encounter of the 'other' first century religion. Yong turns to Acts and notes Luke's extension of the life and teaching of the Lukan Jesus via the emerging Christian community. In continuity with the Israelite story, Christians must also depend upon diasporic hospitality (Acts 8.1-4; 11.9-20; Jas 1.1; 1 Pet. 1.1); while aliens and strangers in this world, early Christians, as perpetual guests of God and others, imitate the Israelite posture when serving as hosts.[72] Yong then links exegesis of Luke–Acts (and the larger biblical story) to contemporary Christianity. Like Jesus, early Christians are recipients and conduits of God's hospitality (Acts 1.1). Whether through household relationships and table fellowship or journeying and itinerancy, followers of the Way model reception and extension of the redemptive and pneumatological hospitality of God envisioned on the Day of Pentecost. As early Christians improvised the reception and extension of Jesus' hospitality, so also contemporary Christians must continue improvisation and extension of early Christian hospitality. If Pentecost symbolizes the ever-available extent of God's abundant hospitality 'for all who are far off' (Acts 2.39) and if gifts of the Spirit provide innovative power for God's people as guests and hosts, sometimes simultaneously, then *missio dei* must center not only on mere enlargement of the church, but authentic expression of the kingdom of God.[73] Christians must discern the Spirit's presence and 'perform' appropriate practices in concert with the hospitable God. They must embody Christ's incarnational vulnerability and open up theological and relational 'free space' not only to serve as hosts for the gospel but also risk being guests of others.[74] While Yong offers few specifics, he calls for an artistic ecclesiology marked by congregational hospitality. He implores individual Christians and institutional Christianity to begin with orthopraxis, that is, basic accommodations, a welcoming public face, a dialogical posture, and a commitment to public service. Pentecostals ever interested in the life of the Spirit should welcome Yong's theological and practical extension of Pentecost and the narrative of Luke–Acts. Twenty-first century Christians must imagine fresh possibili-

---

[72] Yong, *Hospitality and the Other*, p. 124.
[73] Yong, *Hospitality and the Other*, pp. 126-27.
[74] Yong, *Hospitality and the Other*, p. 132.

ties for performative encounters with those of current world religions.

In *Beyond the Impasse*, Yong produces a bold and pioneering analysis of Pentecost as a starting point for interreligious dialogue. He affirms the ecclesiological wooing of the Spirit that draws Parthians, Medes, Elamites and the like into the body of Christ. In contemporary light, Yong seeks to broaden the activity of the Spirit across similar dimensions. The Spirit 'in the last days' extends universally beyond the time and space of the Pentecost event by transcending the institutional boundaries of the church.[75] According to Yong, the same Spirit of Pentecost at work retroactively in Melchizedek, Abimelech, Jethro, Rahab, Ruth, Naaman, the Queen of Sheba, and Magi from the East works in Cornelius and others who enjoy a right relationship with God under the terms of a wider covenant.[76] Yong's provisional conclusions continue to challenge traditional christological boundaries. As a Malaysian-American Pentecostal, Yong believes contemporary witness must utilize Berean discernment in order to discover the Spirit already at work within religious symbols of non-Christian faiths.[77] In a later and related essay, Yong addresses similar concerns. Though countless Pentecostals maintain an exclusivist stance with regard to other religions, he suggests an interreligious posture based upon 'the inviting Spirit'. The same Spirit who implied his universal hospitality through announcing Pentecostal transformation through the many disparate cultures also expects the contemporary church to adopt a variety of practices in the body and in the world.[78] Passion built upon a creative pneumatological approach to a theology of religions should prove to be fertile ground for a post-9/11 world in desperate need of the unifying power of Pentecost. It remains to be seen if the stimulating work of Yong and other Pentecostal scholars will provide sustainable ecumenical and interreligious results.

---

[75] Amos Yong, *Beyond the Impasse: Toward a Pneumatological Theology of Religions* (Grand Rapids: Baker Academic, 2004), p. 40.

[76] Yong, *Beyond the Impasse*, p. 140.

[77] Yong, *Beyond the Impasse*, pp. 142, 191.

[78] Yong, 'The Inviting Spirit: Pentecostal Beliefs and Practices Regarding the Religions Today', in Studebaker (ed.), *Defining Issues in Pentecostalism*, pp. 29-45.

4.5 GLOBAL READINGS—'TO THE ENDS OF THE EARTH'

Anyone with even minimal experience in Pentecostal circles would attest to the pivotal role of Acts 1.8 in Pentecostal lore. The global missiological emphases of Acts 1.8 have long been rehearsed. In fact, according to global theologians such as Philip Jenkins, Allan Anderson, and Amos Yong, the face of contemporary Christianity no longer centers in Rome or Canterbury, but perhaps in Seoul, Beijing, Singapore, Bombay, Lagos, Sao Paulo, and Mexico City.[79] In light of the global success of Christianity in general and Pentecostal/Charismatic Christianity in particular, is it not time to enlarge 'academic' proclamation of the gospel to the 'ends of the earth' via development of Lukan scholarship from indigenous Pentecostals around the world?

Swiss Theologian Walter Hollenweger presses for such openness. He laments any colonial evangelistic efforts of the West that consistently offer a mono-cultural interpretation of the gospel to the nations. He entreats Pentecostals to revisit the conversion of Cornelius in Acts 10 with an eye to the conversion of Peter. It is in fact Peter's conversion that propels the gospel beyond Jewish confinement to inclusion of the Gentiles. Peter comes to understand that 'God treats all men alike', 'He has no favorites', and 'God is no

---

[79] See Yong, *The Spirit Poured Out*, p. 20; Allan Anderson, *An Introduction to Global Pentecostalism* (Cambridge: Cambridge University Press, 2004); and Philip Jenkins, *The Next Christendom: The Coming of Global Christianity* (New York: Oxford University Press, 2002). Jenkins observes: 'For the foreseeable future, the characteristic religious forms of Southern Christianity—enthusiastic and spontaneous, fundamentalist and supernatural oriented—look massively different from those of the older centers in Europe and North America' (p. 92). He continues: 'Southern churches should continue to offer a powerful and attractive package for potential converts, both North and South. They can plausibly present themselves as modern-day bearers of an apostolic message that is not limited by geography, race, or culture, and claims of signs and wonders will serve as their credentials' (p. 160). Note also the following works. While the authors do not focus specifically on Luke–Acts, the works remain important for their global perspective. Allan Anderson, 'The Pentecostal Gospel and Third World Cultures' (paper presented at the annual meeting of the Society for Pentecostal Studies, Springfield, MO, March 1999). See also the essays by Ivan Satyavrata, 'Contextual Perspectives on Pentecostalism as a Global Culture: A South Asian View', and Vinay Samuel, 'Pentecostalism as a Global Culture: A Response', in *The Globalization of Pentecostalism: A Religion Made to Travel* (ed. Murray Dempster, Byron Klaus, and Douglas Petersen. Irvine, CA: Regnum Press, 1999), pp. 253-58.

respecter of persons' (Acts 10.34). Peter then wins over the apostles by citing that genuine evangelism must allow listeners to be part of the communication—in other words, the evangelist must respect-fully hear the voices of the evangelized.[80] If the New Testament contains numerous christologies, liturgies, theologies, and ethics, how much more must contemporary Pentecostals with roots in so many diverse cultures say farewell to a streamlined and universal theology?[81] He observes that Western churches probably owe more to their Celtic and Germanic ancestors and to Greek and Roman culture than to biblical predecessors (e.g., burial rites, buildings, lit-urgies, liturgical vestments, and church music). He continues: 'if we educate African theologians according to our literary understanding of theology and we are successful in this, we do not only make them useless to their African context but we also lose the possibility for true dialogue, since then they only mirror our thinking'.[82] He implores contemporary Pentecostals to view Luke–Acts as a win-dow to open new possibilities for global pneumatologies: 'The Holy Spirit cannot be monopolized, restricted or confined—no group can claim authority over it'.[83] Hollenweger challenges Pentecostals to practice what they preach: the Spirit poured out on all flesh (Acts 2.17). In this vein, Hollenweger would approve the sentiments of African scholar Gbolohan Olukayode Akinsanya, who laments Western misunderstanding of the African concept of the Supreme Being or the Most High God. Akinsanya turns to the words of Paul at Lystra (Acts 14.15b-17) and affirms the self-revelation of God in all cultures, particularly African.[84]

Murray Dempster echoes Hollenweger's desire for a global theo-logical worldview. Dempster notes that beyond historical criticism rightfully emphasized and conditioned by time and social location,

---

[80] Hollenweger, 'Evangelism: A Non-Colonial Model', *JPT* 7 (1995), p. 122. In addition to Hollenweger's argument, note Peter's words in Acts 2.39. Peter does not yet understand the meaning of the gospel message 'for all who are far off.'

[81] Lynne Price, *Theology Out of Place: A Theological Biography of Walter J. Hollenweger* (JPTSup 23; Sheffield: Sheffield University Press, 2003), p. 46.

[82] Price, *Theology Out of Place*, p. 72.

[83] Price, *Theology Out of Place*, p. 147.

[84] Gbolohan Olukayode Akinsanya, *'You Shall Receive Power': The Establishment of the Pentecostal Movement in the Nigerian Context* (PhD diss., Drew University, 2000), p. 22. Akinsanya also notes continuity between Luke's understanding of Pauline theology with Paul's statements in Rom. 1.19-20.

the more telling factor in hermeneutical theory is the function of history and culture alive in the interpreter.[85] In the same manner a feminist or liberationist interpreter locates a specific socio-cultural period, so also contemporary global locations must be considered when analyzing multifaceted Pentecostal contexts. The global growth of Pentecostalism lays in its adaptability for diverse language, music, and cultural relevance in the religious terrain in which it lives.[86] Harold Hunter cites his own travels in an attempt to call for global readings. Hunter believes that as the world 'decreases in size', there follows a similar demand that all traditions devote attention to living out their shared identity in Christ. As a Pentecostal, Hunter challenges western Pentecostals to move beyond introspection. In order to remain globally relevant Pentecostals must engage responsibly other Christians, other religions, and the whole of creation.[87] Both Dempster and Hunter believe that Luke–Acts scholarship in the next generation must flesh out a global worldview comparable to the Pentecost event.

Hispanic scholar Samuel Solivan notes the cultural significance of Acts 2; the words 'tongues' or 'language' (γλῶσσαι), 'dialects' (διάλεκτοι), and 'ethnos' (ἔθνος) play an important role concerning pluralism, racism, and globalization. According to Solivan, Acts 2 resists the use of any particular language and culture (English and White European) as the primary matrix for civility, intelligence, and self-worth. He writes: 'to the colonized and oppressed of Acts 2, the Holy Spirit rekindled the respect for and importance of language and culture as God's intent for the liberation of all people'.[88] Solivan calls for attentiveness to cultural particularities as a means of breaking down global prejudice and ethnocentrism. Elsewhere, Solivan embraces classic Pentecostal emphasis upon power for service, mission and evangelism as indicated through Acts 2 but alongside an ethnic reading of Pentecost. Solivan suggests readers take a

---

[85] Murray Dempster, 'Paradigm Shifts and Hermeneutics: Confronting Issues Old and New', *Pneuma* 15 (1993), p. 132.

[86] Dempster, 'Paradigm Shifts and Hermeneutics', p. 135.

[87] Harold D. Hunter, 'Two Movements of the Holy Spirit in the 20th Century? A Closer Look at Global Pentecostalism and Ecumenism' (paper presented at the annual meeting of the Society for Pentecostal Studies, Lakeland, FL, March 2002), p. 72.

[88] Samuel Solivan, *The Spirit, Pathos and Liberation: Toward an Hispanic Pentecostal Theology* (JPTSup 14; Sheffield: Sheffield Academic Press, 1998), p. 116.

scriptural 'underview' and thereby discover fresh insights to the question 'what meaneth this?' (Acts 2.12). Solivan views the Feast of Pentecost as a symbolic in-gathering of the wheat harvest, a metaphor for God's great harvest. Pentecost functions as a Jewish picture of a global phenomenon. The feast captures God's desire to gather peoples, tribes, and nations of the world—that they might be one.[89] The outpouring of the Spirit introduces the Roman world to a spiritual revolution that replaces *Pax Romana* with *Pax Christi*. In turn, the gospel breaks cultural boundaries by overturning centuries of oppressive social structures and relationships.[90] For both Jewish and Gentile Christians, the Pentecost event provides a new set of possibilities and expectations for the formation of a community that ought to reflect the global gathering (built upon reconciliation) between peoples separated since the Fall in Genesis 2 and Babel in Genesis 11.[91]

Frank Macchia explores the cultural relationship between Babel and Pentecost. While Macchia agrees with a common view of Pentecost as the reversal of Babel, he chooses to highlight cultural fulfillment.[92] At the tower of Babel, humanity fails in the quest for homogenous and centralized security; in fact, the confusion of tongues and the scattering of the peoples may indeed signify the grace of God. In Acts, Luke focuses upon the scattering of the peoples through the world as a reversed-providential fulfillment; followers of Christ scatter across the face of the earth with the hope that humans find and encounter God (Acts 17.26-27).[93] Macchia concludes:

> God destroyed the oppressive, monolithic unity by dispersing the tongues and peoples of the world so that they would give up

---

[89] Samuel Solivan, 'Cultural Glossolalia in Acts 2: A Theological Reassessment of the Importance of Culture and Language' (paper presented at the annual meeting of the Society for Pentecostal Studies, Wheaton, IL, November 1994), p. 14.

[90] Solivan, 'Cultural Glossolalia in Acts 2', p. 25.

[91] Solivan, 'Cultural Glossolalia in Acts 2', p. 3.

[92] Frank Macchia, 'Babel and the Tongues of Pentecost: Reversal or Fulfillment?—A Theological Perspective', in Mark J. Cartledge (ed.), *Speaking in Tongues: Multi-Disciplinary Approaches* (Studies in Pentecostal and Charismatic Issues; Waynesboro: Paternoster Press, 2006), pp. 34-51.

[93] Macchia, 'Babel and the Tongues of Pentecost', p. 43.

any idolatrous illusions and find and glorify God … in the midst of a higher and more differentiated unity in diversity.[94]

According to Macchia, the event of Pentecost functions as protest against domestication of the gospel to a single idiom or culture. In her essay 'Missionary Tongues', Jenny Everts argues that those (including Pentecostals) who equate tongues merely with 'foreign' language have been slow to realize potential cultural and ethical implications. When tongues are understood as the new spiritual language of the new community created by the Spirit, long existing social, cultural, national and linguistic barriers are removed. Everts cites the resolution of seemingly insurmountable religio-cultural barriers that divide Jews in Acts 10 and the religious integration of the followers of John the Baptist into the Christian community in Acts 19.[95]

Early fulfillment of the pleas above may be found in the work of three Pentecostal scholars intent on reading Luke–Acts through a non-Western lens. Peter Gräbe looks at specific Pentecostal settings in Africa and concurs with the symphonic call of Hollenweger. Gräbe believes an African Pentecostal worldview remains significantly more open to experiencing God's power in very concrete and tangible ways than Western counterparts. Gräbe investigates the biblical basis for this Pentecostal focus on the power of God in both the miraculous dimension as well as the perspective of power in the midst of weakness and concludes that African behavior centers more on the purpose of acquiring life, strength, and vital force. As a continent so often overwhelmed with sickness, death, poverty, misfortune, sorcery, oppression, injustice, witchcraft, evil spirits, famine, floods, and so on, there is a longing for a source of power outside oneself that will enable one to cope.[96] The Lukan message of God's life-giving power, which delivers from evil and allows one to feel safe in a hostile world, is particularly and uniquely relevant to

---

[94] Macchia, 'Babel and the Tongues of Pentecost', p. 45.

[95] Jenny Everts, 'Missionary Tongues?' (paper presented at the annual meeting of the Society for Pentecostal Studies, Guadalajara, Mexico, November 1993), p. 9.

[96] Peter Gräbe, 'The Pentecostal Discovery of the New Testament Theme of God's Power and Its Relevance to the African Context', *Pneuma* 24 (2002), p. 240.

the existential world of Africa.[97] Writing on the rapid growth of Pentecostalism in Latin America, Douglas Petersen points to the role of assertive personalities, 'people with personal reasons to reject the *status quo* and who are in search of change'.[98] He notes the perspective of José Comblin, Catholic liberation theologian. Comblin describes Pentecostals not as alienated and withdrawn from the world, but tenacious, persistent, and determined while ostracized and abused. Petersen suggests Luke's use of the term 'boldness' for the success of Latino Pentecostals.[99]

Though the geographic direction of the Acts narrative moves West, Luke teases his readers with global implications for the gospel by way of a short scene of the encounter between Philip and an Ethiopian Eunuch (Acts 8). Today, just as the early church expanded to the east and to the south, contemporary Christianity moves in a similar direction. Given unparalleled growth in Africa, Asia, Latin and South America, western Pentecostals must create space for indigenous contributions to Luke–Acts research. Undoubtedly, non-Western scholars will create possibilities for dialogue based upon the unique questions and concerns of their own contexts, thereby promoting a Pentecostal complexity.

4.6 LUKE–ACTS IN A POSTMODERN AGE

Veli-Matti Kärkkäinen suggests that the advent of post-modernity offers significant possibilities for exploration between the lives of the earliest Pentecostals and contemporary Pentecostals. In the same way early Pentecostals react to cultural dynamics, so also contemporary Pentecostals in a postmodern world are afforded similar possibilities. Like their early twentieth predecessors, current twenty-first century Pentecostals strive to fill the void of an 'affectionless' and primarily 'cerebral' pursuit of God. Pentecostals never rest

---

[97] Gräbe, 'The Pentecostal Discovery of the New Testament Theme of God's Power and Its Relevance to the African Context', p. 241. Writing in Amharic, Melisachew Mesfin of the Full Gospel Believers Church in Mulu Wengel provides an expository analysis through Ethiopian lenses: *'To the Ends of the earth': Exposition of the Book of Acts (Amharic)* (Addis Abada, Ethiopia: Melisachew Mesfin, 2006).

[98] Douglas Petersen, *Not By Might Nor By Power: A Pentecostal Theology of Social Concern in Latin America* (Irvine, CA: Regnum Books, 1996), p. 87.

[99] Petersen, *Not By Might Nor By Power*, p. 88. See further section 4.3.

comfortably in mere mechanical rationalistic pursuit of God, but view knowing God in the context of active relationship(s).[100] Like Kärkkäinen, Scott Ellington implores Pentecostals not to yield primarily to rationalist approaches to Scripture. Pentecostals ought to utilize doctrine to describe and verbalize lived experience. Since Luke reveals a world at least in part unknown by the reader, Ellington invites readers to search for ways to merge their world unashamedly with the rationality and affections demonstrated within the Lukan story.[101]

A number of scholars look at the Lukan narratives as a means of prophetic posturing toward a world consumed with postmodern ideals. Harvey Cox, a regular observer of Pentecostal theology and practice, looks specifically at the Ephesian Christians in Acts 19. He compares the religion-based consumer conflict created between the prophetic voice of Paul (and the new Christian community) to proponents of the goddess Diana. Cox calls upon Pentecostals to echo Paul's exposure of the Ephesian market god as 'gods that are no gods'. Instead, through insightful prophetic critique, Pentecostals, like Paul, must challenge the insatiable Western appetite for consumerism and acquisition.[102] In another context, Cox offers similar commentary:

> Behind descriptions of market reforms, monetary policy, and the convolutions of the Dow, I gradually made out the pieces of a grand narrative about the inner meaning of human history, why things had gone wrong, and how to put them right. Theologians call these myths of origin, legends of the fall, and doctrines of sin and redemption. But here they were again, and in only thin disguise: chronicles about the creation of wealth, the seductive

---

[100] Veli-Matti Kärkkäinen, 'Pentecostal Hermeneutics in the Making: On the Way from Fundamentalism to Postmodernism', *JEPTA* 18 (1998), pp. 94-95. See further debate via Paul W. Lewis, 'Postmodernity and Pentecostalism: A Survey and Assessment', *AJPS* 1 (2002), pp. 34-66 and Mathew S. Clark, 'Pentecostal Hermeneutics: The Challenge of Relating To (Post)-Modern Literary Theory', *AJPS* 1 (2002), pp. 67-92.

[101] Scott Ellington, 'Pentecostals and the Authority of Scripture', *JPT* 9 (1997), pp. 16-38.

[102] Harvey Cox, "Pentecostalism and the Global Market Culture': A Response to Issues Facing Pentecostalism in a Postmodern World' in *The Globalization of Pentecostalism: A Religion Made to Travel* (ed. Murray Dempster, Bryon Klaus, and Douglas Peterson. Irvine, CA: Regnum Press, 1999), pp. 386-95.

temptations of statism, captivity to faceless economic cycles, and, ultimately, salvation through the advent of free markets, with a small dose of ascetic belt tightening along the way, especially for the East Asian economies.[103]

In continuity with this statement, he makes the connection to the Lukan story:

What does Athens have to do with Jerusalem? What does secularization have to do with religious proliferation and pluralism? The answer to both questions is the same. Athens and Jerusalem have created a whole history through their interaction with each other, and so have religion and secularization. In both cases, as soon as one achieves a kind of dominance, the other swoops back from exile to challenge it. When reason and intellect begin to ride high, they invariably make unrealistic claims. And faith and intuition awaken to question their hegemony. Then, just as the sacral begins to feel its oats and reach out for civilizational supremacy, reason and cognition question its pretentiousness. In past eras, this seesaw battle often took centuries. Today, events move more swiftly.[104]

While Cox does not offer consistent reference to Luke–Acts, he calls upon Pentecostal scholars to read Luke's grand narrative in light of the global market crisis.

Marc Turnage examines Paul in Athens where Luke gives a rare glimpse of Paul's interaction with Greek philosophers. As Paul must adapt to the philosophical and cultural crossroads of Athens, so also Pentecostalism must adapt beyond modernity. While many Western Christians, particularly those closely associated with the Evangelical and Fundamentalist movements, demand that the world maintain the assumptions of modernism simply because they have canonized them, Pentecostalism, also part of the cultural shifts occurring through the world, stands at an axis of prime opportunity. Theological and ideological paradigms in place for centuries need to be rethought, removed, or recreated not in an effort towards

---

[103] Harvey Cox, 'The Market as God', in *The Atlantic* 283.3 (March 1999): n.p. Reprinted online: http://speakingoffaith.publicradio.org/programs/atheism-religion/cox_marketasgod.shtml.

[104] Harvey Cox, *Religion in the Secular City: Essays in Honor of Harvey Cox* (ed. Arvind Sharma; Harrisburg, PA: Trinity Press International, 2001), p. xix.

trendiness, but contextually to an ever-evolving, pluralistic world. Turnage looks to Paul as a model of liberal education: Paul proclaims the gospel effectively because of his ability to converse with pagan ideologies and philosophies. According to Turnage, students of Pentecostal-Charismatic Christianity need similar training in order to engage current cultural contexts?[105]

Adam Ayers proposes critical engagement of the entertainment industry in hopes of securing the postmodern audience. He encourages Pentecostals to interact with Hollywood (a scandalous thought only a generation ago) via tongues. Ecstatic speech functions as a behavioral means of creating integration, subjective identification, and overt affiliation within the community of the disciples begun at Pentecost. Concerning the tongues at Pentecost, Caesarea, and Ephesus (and the implicit tongues in Samaria), he concludes 'their apparent meaninglessness is precisely their meaning'.[106] He compares the rousing gibberish of Cinderella's fairy godmother ('Salaga-doola, mechicka moo-la, Bibbidi-Bobbidi-Boo!') to the magic of tongues. It is doubtful that this children's chorus, intended to express mystery, magic, and childish wonder, would be able to convey similar existential, human intention and meaning by using a song with the chorus, 'This is mysterious and magical!' In other words, 'Bibbidi-Bobbidi-Boo' become the best words for the job, both as an expression and as a song, by virtue of not being words at all.[107] For Ayers, Luke–Acts employs a similar mystery via the manifestations of tongues: tongues leave participants and onlookers wonderstruck. Supernaturally and paradoxically, 'gibberish must function *as* gibberish in order to fulfill meaning where ordinary words would be gibberish'.[108] Ayers argues that supernatural utterance functions as artistic expression and need not be analyzed by a narrow set of linguistic criteria. He suggests such an approach to the Lukan narratives would prove highly relevant to Postmoderns

---

[105] Marc Turnage, 'The Early Church and the Axis of History and Pentecostalism Facing the 21st Century: Some Reflections', *JEPTA* 23 (2003), pp. 4-29.

[106] Adam Ayers, 'Can the Behavior of Tongues Utterance Still Function as Ecclesial Boundary? The Significance of Art and Sacrament', *Pneuma* 22 (2000), p. 288.

[107] Ayers, 'Can the Behavior of Tongues Utterance Still Function as Ecclesial Boundary?', p. 287.

[108] Ayers, 'Can the Behavior of Tongues Utterance Still Function as Ecclesial Boundary?', p. 288.

drawn to a world of meaning found through magic and imagination.

Blaine Charette also calls for potential engagement of Pentecostal core beliefs and values in the arena of film. Maybe in the not too distant future, a Pentecostal gospel scholar will contribute to a production of 'Jesus on the silver screen' and bring to bear through the visual arts some of Charette's concerns, such as proper emphasis upon Jesus' messianic anointing and Spirit Baptism through Pentecostal lenses.[109]

Artistic exegesis now includes dramas, short stories, and poetry. First, Walter Hollenweger (noted above) occasionally couples his academic pursuits with short plays; he dramatizes biblical stories so that local communities might engage the content and history of the biblical text in a lively interactive manner. A drama entitled: *'Besuch bei Lukas'* contains artistic exegesis on Exodus 14; 2 Cor. 6.4-11; Lk. 2.1-14 and 19.1-10. Hollenweger brings ancient characters to life with dramatic flair. He portrays Zacchaeus as a 'stinking rich financier' criticized by a cold bishop for colonialism and capitalist abuse. The narrative concludes with commentary and a bibliography suggesting further study resources.[110] In successive acts of another drama, *Das Wagnis des Glaubens* (translated *The Adventure of Faith*), Hollenweger simulates Philip's baptism of the Ethiopian Eunuch, Peter's fraternizing with Cornelius, and Ananias' dealings with Saul/Paul. All three acts portray the events through the lens of an early church meeting and force critical reflection. The play encourages viewers to consider contemporary events in need of an encounter with Jesus in order to revisit the inclusivity of Christian tradition.[111]

Jerry Camery-Hoggatt composes a witty collection of short stories and personal illustrations that cut to the core of Christian conversation. In 'Moral Terror of the Inner Life', he tackles the 'four horsemen of the inner apocalypse' and suggests that a serious reading of Jesus' words in Lk. 12.1-3 should solicit a verbal pause. He

---

[109] Blaine Charette, 'Messiah Without Anointing: A Missing Element in Cinematic Portrayals of Jesus' (paper presented at the annual meeting of the Society for Pentecostal Studies, Wilmore, KY, March 2003).

[110] Walter Hollenweger, *Besuch bei Lukas* (Munich: Chr. Kaiser Verlag, 1986).

[111] Hollenweger, *Das Wagnis des Glaubens: Ein Spiel über die Mission für Sprecher, Instrumentalisten, Bewegungstheater und Gemeinde* (Munich: Chr. Kaiser Verlag, 1986).

laments the use of spiritual language and Scripture to validate our rage, buttress our power, affirm our perfection, or justify our withdrawal. Through a clever story, Camery-Hoggatt brings Jesus' words to life and demonstrates that people often focus upon and reveal the faults of others as a means of self-protection.[112]

Like Camery-Hoggatt, Kilian McDonnell's recent venture into poetry builds upon his life work as a contemplative theologian. A Benedictine monk, McDonnell's poetry reflects lifelong immersion in strict scriptural reading and liturgical prayer and appears as a personal and poetic *lectio divina*.[113] He writes 'out of the experience of stumbling toward God', not afraid of human frailty and earthy detail, with a combination of serious and comic elements.[114] As classical Pentecostals value testimony, charismatic scholar McDonnell writes for everyone, 'including non-monastics, who take the quest for God seriously and make prayer part of the rhythm of the day'.[115] The following table includes poems derived from the Lukan story.

Name	Reference	Collection	Theme
The Ox's Broad Behind	Lk. 15.12	YS, 36	Parable
Hogs and Salvation	Lk. 15.15	YS 38	Parable
The Younger Son	Lk. 15.18	SL, 38	Parable
Rolling the Stone from the Grave	Lk. 15.20	YS, 40	Parable
The Father of the Younger Son	Lk. 15.20	SL, 40	Parable
I Have Two Sons	Lk. 15.28	YS, 44	Parable
The Elder Son	Lk. 15.29	SL, 42	Parable
No One Loves Me	Lk. 15.30	YS, 42	Parable
The Father of the Elder Son	Lk. 15.32	SL, 44	Parable
God Drops and Loses Things	Lk. 15.8	GD, 28	Parable
Bottom Feeders	Lk. 5.29	GD, 24	Hospitality
Guess Who's Coming to Din-	Lk. 7.45	SL, 56	Hospitality

[112] Jerry Camery-Hoggatt, 'Moral Terror of the Inner Life: The Four Horsemen of the Inner Apocalypse', *Grapevine: The Spirituality of Gossip* (Scottsdale: Herald Press, 2002), pp. 148-61.

[113] In order of appearance, Killian McDonnell, O.S.B., *Swift, Lord, You Are Not* (Collegeville, MN: St. John's University Press, 2003); *Yahweh's Other Shoe* (Collegeville, MN: St. John's University Press, 2006); and *God Drops and Loses Things* (Collegeville, MN: St. John's University Press, 2009). Note the respective abbreviations: SL, YS, and GD.

[114] McDonnell, *Swift, Lord*, pp. 108-109.

[115] McDonnell, *Yahweh's Other Shoe*, p. 115.

ner

The Kitchen	Lk. 1.26	SL, 46	Hospitality/ Birth Narrative
The Robber Angel Comes	Lk. 1.26	GD, 20	Birth Narrative
This Night a Child is Born	2 Sam. 7.16 (Lk. 1.31-33)	SL, 50	Birth Narrative
The Visitation	Lk. 1.44	SL, 52	Birth Narrative
Something for the Census	Lk. 2.1	YS, 20-21	Birth Narrative
Mary Magdalene	Lk. 8.1-2	GD, 26	Women
The Prayer of the Impertinent	Lk. 11.8	GD, 31	Prayer
The One Called Judas	Lk. 22.47	YS, 32-33	Hope and Betrayal
The Palimpsest on Calvary	Mk 15. 40; Mt. 26.56; Lk. 23.49	GD, 41	Synoptic Analysis
After All the Words	(Acts 2)	SL, 105	Tongues/ Pentecost

McDonnell commits ten poems to the parable of the Prodigal Son (Luke 15). Included across the three volumes, he demonstrates an uncanny ability to communicate the unreasonable hope and the utter despair of the younger son, the undying passion of a father, and the confusion and pride of the older son. Also noteworthy, McDonnell offers a beautiful and yet sobering portrayal of 'The One Called Judas'. McDonnell finds in Judas not a money-mongering betrayer, but one on a quest for messianic hope yet unable to reconcile hope and confusion.

As pragmatic Pentecostals continue to engage Luke–Acts in a postmodern world, pioneers in film and literature should provide an excellent environment for further exploration.

THE CURRENT STATUS OF LUKE–ACTS
RESEARCH: OBSERVATIONS AND POSSIBILITIES

Pentecostal scholarship has come a long way.
But we are still in the very beginning stages of interpreting our own
tongues into the languages of others,
of interpreting the languages of others into tongues we can understand,
and of interpreting different languages to different groups from
our position betwixt and between.
Is this not itself part of the continuing miracle of the Day of Pentecost?
(Amos Yong)[1]

Even a cursory overview of pre-1970 Lukan scholarship shows little Pentecostal dialogue or maybe better stated little Pentecostal awareness/interest with major twentieth century Lukan scholars.[2] Early Pentecostals generally steer clear of synoptic debates and the dominant questions concerning the historical reliability of the Gospels and Acts. As the first Pentecostal scholars emerge in the post-1970 era, attention remains squarely focused on specific Pentecostal concerns, typically pneumatology and hermeneutics. However, in chapters three and four I summarize the recent surge of publications on a wide range of Lukan themes, many of which are beginning to impact both Pentecostals and non-Pentecostals alike. As Pentecostal scholars find newfound freedom beyond a defensive

---

[1] Amos Yong, 'Pentecostalism and the Theological Academy', *Theology Today* 64 (2007), p. 250.

[2] I have in mind the following scholars cited in section 1.1: F.J. Foakes Jackson and Kirsopp Lake, *The Beginnings of Christianity*; Henry Cadbury, *The Making of Luke–Acts*; and Martin Dibelius, *From Tradition to Gospel*. Minimal dialogue also occurs with the emergence of the influential volumes by Hans Conzelmann (*Acts of the Apostles* [ed. Helmut Koester; trans. James Limburg *et al.*; Hermenia; Philadelphia: Fortress Press, 1987; German rev. edn 1972] originally published in 1961 or Ernst Haenchen (*The Acts of the Apostles: A Commentary* [ed. R. McL. Wilson; trans. Bernard Noble and Gerald Shinn; Philadelphia: Westminster, 1971). Though Haenchen casts significant doubt upon the historicity of Acts, he causes little stir among Pentecostals.

mode, there seems to be little reason not to anticipate ongoing Pentecostal engagement on a vast array of issues in Luke–Acts. I agree wholeheartedly with the above appeal by Amos Yong; in the Spirit of Pentecost, may fruitful interpretation continue. With this in mind, I humbly offer some final observations on the status of Pentecostal research and possibilities for further research.

AN OPEN DOOR

While scholars continue to probe for new areas of exploration, I would like to suggest that the work in the thematic categories throughout this volume remains incomplete and requires further attention. As Pentecostal scholars continue to investigate the vital role of Lukan pneumatology and missions alongside hermeneutics and healing/exorcism, this should no longer be at the expense of other Lukan emphases or without dialogue and insight from the larger academic community. These categories remain central to Pentecostal identity and warrant ongoing attention in Pentecostal constituencies. Of course, this works both ways; as the employment of Pentecostal scholarship among non-Pentecostal scholars continues to improve, the sphere of Pentecostal scholars should only increase. Ecumenical dialogue between various Pentecostal communities such as Trinitarian and Oneness Pentecostals as well as classical Pentecostal and Roman Catholics requires substantial concentration with particular attention to Lukan emphasis upon soteriology, baptism, Mary, and ecclesiology/community. Furthermore, the ongoing interest in inter-religious unity in a world bent on tolerance and relativism will remain crucial concerns in 21st century Pentecostalism. Given Pentecostal emphasis upon evangelism, this promises to be lively and controversial. Whether in tolerant communities or restricted access communities, Pentecostals must continue to mine the Lukan narratives for relevant and culturally authentic means of gospel witness. Mixed messages surrounding the role of women and unending egalitarian and justice issues require ongoing inspection. Lukan stories such as the Samaritan and Ethiopian expansion remain poised to speak not only concerning evangelistic strategy, but also to Pentecostals in a global community filled with ethnic and racial tension. As Pentecostals continue to encourage transference of the Spirit, scholarly investment in Luke's social concerns must remain a critical component to extension of the gospel message. Finally, all of these concerns must be brought under the microscope of Luke's holistic commitment to personal and social transformation. In other words, how does Pentecostal proclamation of Luke's enthusiastic life of the Spirit interconnect with the quest for personal and societal transformation? How does a tradition often fixated on the evidential tongues translate this experience into everyday living? And as people of the Spirit, how will Pentecostals continue to engage questions surrounding guidance and discernment? Perhaps an integrative approach might also include the psychological and emotional components of guidance through the eyes of Lukan characters.[3] I turn now to several categories mentioned above, but I believe in need of principal assessment.

PENTECOSTALS AND WORLD CHRISTIANITY

Even though the previous chapter includes categorical sections on globalization and postmodernism, I believe these matters must continue to provide the primary lens for Lukan scholarship in the current generation. Given the recent work of scholars like Philip Jenkins on shifting global paradigms, Lukan scholars must give greater attention to the global south. In *The New Face of Christianity*, Jenkins explores Bible reading in the global south and includes chapters on old/new, rich/poor, men/women, north/south, and good/evil with endless illustrations under Pentecostal/charismatic banners.[4] With this in mind it seems prudent for current scholars to consider what Luke might say concerning global cosmologies and socio-economic crises. First, whereas many North American Christians including significant numbers within Pentecostal constituencies increasingly view concepts of exorcism and deliverance as fanatical, such concepts remain vital to the larger cosmological worldviews of Christians in the global south. Jenkins recounts plenty of examples, none more telling than the conversion of a Korean woman named Bokhee Lim. Christians in Yoido Pentecostal Church in Seoul, Korea pray boldly for her salvation and witness a remarkable transforma-

---

[3] See Matthew Elliot's *Faithful Feelings: Rethinking Emotion in the New Testament* (Grand Rapids: Kregel Publications, 2006).

[4] Philip Jenkins, *The New Face of Christianity: Believing the Bible in the Global South* (Oxford: Oxford University Press, 2006).

tion; Lim gives up her life as a shaman to follow Jesus. Jenkins cites Lim's testimony: 'Because it was a confrontation between a demigod and the almighty God, the demigod could do nothing but to be defeated in a groggy state without even having a real fight'. Lim collects the symbolic clothes and equipment of her former practice, burns them and destroys her backyard temple dedicated to her former god. Jenkins concludes this illustration with a poignant remark by contrasting suspicion surrounding such stories within Euro-American contexts against an Asian worldview. Ironically, such a story echoes the classical biblical stories of confrontations with alien gods as in the book of Acts, namely stories of power encounters, magic and sorcery.[5]

In light of the Pentecostal flavor of global Christianity, Pentecostal scholars must also prepare to address contemporary socioeconomic issues that intersect with Luke–Acts. For example, how might Pentecostals investigate Luke–Acts in order to address ethnic integration and/or the limits of assimilation? In various national and global media venues, questions surrounding immigration serve as headline news. How might scholars investigate the savvy Lukan Paul, who certainly recognizes the critical importance of citizenship at an appropriate time? On a larger scale, how might Luke–Acts function as a migration, emigration, and/or immigration narrative? Given Luke's emphasis on Paul's urban ministry, what might scholars say concerning evangelism and church planting in complex communities? Though Lukan scholars have rehearsed well the constant movement of the people of God in Luke–Acts as part of a grand salvation meta-narrative, how might Pentecostal scholars engage further Luke's focus upon displacement and hospitality? Whether stories of Abraham the immigrant, Joseph the slave, Moses the advocate for emigration, the itinerant Jesus or apostles on the move, Luke's story is one of people on the go—troubled, persecuted, yet recipients of gracious hospitality. The mass movement of contemporary Christians not unlike the migrations of first century converts should incline Pentecostal scholars to read Luke–Acts from such angles.[6]

---

[5] Jenkins, *The New Face of Christianity*, pp. 105-106, 112.

[6] Amos Yong, *The Holy Spirit in Luke–Acts & the Public Square* (Brewster, MA: Paraclete Press, forthcoming).

Note finally the closely related motif of hospitality. A serious reading of Luke–Acts and any extended experience within the Pentecostal tradition demonstrate respective interest in food and meal fellowship. Similarly, note Luke's dominant emphasis upon the hospitality of God toward outcasts and outsiders; God intends for those rejected by the world to find a place at the divine banquet. Pentecostal emphasis upon the inclusivity of the Pentecost narrative should incline scholars to re-envision hospitality inspired by the Spirit. Global economic crises call for fresh analysis of the gospel implications upon the family table and ecclesial communities in complex societies. Given the global expansion of Pentecostalism, scholars must pay closer attention to Luke's theology of the table, both literal and figurative.[7]

THE POLITICS OF THE GOSPEL

Due to the explosive growth of Pentecostalism in politically sensitive areas, contemporary Pentecostals need to explore further the socio-political implications of Luke–Acts. Earlier categories such as peacemaking, suffering and persecution will remain acute in a culture of violence. Luke augments his story with language well connected to the dominant and at times oppressive rule under the Roman Empire: Jesus' birth occurs during a worldwide census by Augustus (Lk. 2.1); Jesus launches his ministry during the reign of Tiberius (Lk. 3.1); Agabus predicts a famine throughout the entire world during the reign of Claudius (Acts 11.27-8); Aquila and Priscilla leave Rome due to Claudius' expulsion of Jews in Rome (Acts 18.2); and Paul stands in the presence of numerous Roman governing officials. Luke develops his portrait of Jesus around accolades such as Savior (Lk. 2.11; Acts 5.31; 13.23) and 'Prince of Peace' (Lk. 1.79; 2.14; Acts 10.36). Furthermore, in light of the prominent emphasis upon implications surrounding the Pentecost event, Pentecostals would do well to investigate the political significance of the diverse crowd mapped out in Acts 2.5-11. According to Gary Gilbert, Luke's list of nations expresses not merely the universal appeal and availability of the gospel, but also an alternative to a

---

[7] David Martin, 'Undermining the Old Paradigms: Rescripting Pentecostal Accounts', *PentecoStudies* 5.1 (2006), pp. 18-36.

powerful Roman ideology. Gilbert argues that Luke uses the list of nations to advance the expansive nature of the gospel and thereby undermine Roman propaganda. In so doing, Luke not only places the expansive rule of Jesus, the legitimate Savior and Lord over and against Caesar, but gives center stage to Jesus' mandate to reach the ends of the earth (Acts 1.8).[8] It seems reasonable to argue that Luke intends for first-century Christians to view the message of Luke–Acts as an attempt to look beyond the dominion of Caesar and embrace a newfound *oikoumene*. In short, Pentecostal investment in Acts 1 and 2 (specifically 1.8 and 2.1-4) should call for a fresh analysis of the revolutionary nature of the gospel in complex political systems. As Pentecostal numbers increase, age-old questions on pneumatology and mission must be located in a complex global world, increasingly postmodern and politically volatile. Undoubtedly, Jürgen Moltman's desire that 'the church in the power of the Spirit' be reinvented remains critical for every generation of Christians living in a highly violent and politicized world with competing voices.[9]

THE GOSPEL AND VOCATION

According to Miroslav Volf, if indeed Jesus pours out the Spirit upon all flesh, *charisms* must not become the possession of an elite ministerial class, but the entire Christian community irrespective of positions or status.[10] Unfortunately, within certain pneumatological approaches including a classical Pentecostal pneumatology, a common tendency remains to equate 'charismatic' with extraordinary service often by extraordinary people. Volf implores Christians to view work as service to others as in Paul's exhortation to the Ephesian elders. In reflecting upon Jesus' words, Paul states: 'It is more blessed to give than to receive' and connects these words to daily toil in service to the needy (Acts 20.35). In other words, 'every Christian has an obligation to help the poor when she has the

---

[8] I highly recommend the work of Gary Gilbert, 'The List of Nations in Acts 2: Roman Propaganda and the Lukan Response', *JBL* 121.3 (2002), pp. 427-529.

[9] I take this title from Jürgen Moltmann, *The Church in the Power of the Spirit: A Contribution to Messianic Ecclesiology* (New York: Harper & Row, 1977).

[10] Miroslav Volf, *Work in the Spirit: Toward a Theology of Work* (Eugene: Wipf and Stock, 2001), p. 112.

means to do so. It charges her not only to help the poor, but explicitly to *labor strenuously (kopaio) in order to have the means to do so*.[11] For this reason, a holistic analysis of vocation in Luke–Acts must view *charisms* not simply as elitist, restrictive, and extraordinary, but also ordinary and mundane. God's agents express the love and power of God not only through extraordinary miracles and healings, but also through humble, ordinary, and mundane service. In Luke's thought, such service functions as part and parcel of the gospel—its message and appropriation.

Volf also offers a much-needed corrective to work as busyness. Pentecostals so often focused upon mission as employed by Luke must not miss the call to their ascetic vocation. Beyond a product/results-based empowerment, Pentecostals need to mine the Lukan story in search of leisurely and playful vocation, that is, satisfaction in God for his own sake, as in Mary who sits at the feet of Jesus and simply enjoys his presence. Is it not ironic that Pentecostals, champions of divine encounter, often fall prey to a task-oriented utilitarianism and thus overlook the intimacy with the God they proclaim?[12]

LUKE, ACTS, OR LUKE–ACTS

In turning to another category, I offer the following observations and suggestions surrounding narrative territory. What of Pentecostal preference for Acts over Luke? Or conversely, how do Pentecostals respond to ever-increasing debate concerning the emergence of canonical criticism? I begin with the prevailing Pentecostal preference for Acts over the Third Gospel. While the title of this work suggests analysis of Luke–Acts, the data demonstrates clearly that in the early years of the movement, Pentecostals focus primarily on Acts as their 'bread and butter' text. Acts provides the basis for experience and serves to solidify and retain doctrinal positions. I arrive at this conclusion via the following evidence. First, commentaries on the Third Gospel as well as essays only on the Third Gospel remain minimal at best. The overwhelming majority of Pentecostal

---

[11] Volf, *Work in the Spirit*, p. 188. Emphasis original.
[12] Volf, *Work in the Spirit*, p. 152.

efforts on Luke–Acts remain primarily focused on Luke's second volume (see the appendix and the subsequent list of commentaries).

Second, Pentecostal scholarship seems squarely focused on limited passages/scenes and in turn limited issues in Luke–Acts. I offer the following thematic structure of Luke–Acts offered by Roger Stronstad from his influential *Charismatic Theology of St. Luke*.[13]

	LUKE	*ACTS*
Beginning	Birth, anointing of Jesus	Baptism, filling of disciples
Inaugural Proclamation	Jesus' Nazareth Sermon	Peter's Pentecost Sermon
Confirmatory Miracles	Casting out demons and healing the sick in Capernaum	Healing lame man at Beautiful Gate
Success	Widespread popular acclaim	Widespread popular acclaim
Opposition	Pharisees, leaders of the Jews	Sanhedrin, Jews of the dispersion
Travel	Itinerant ministry in Galilee, Judea	Missionary journeys of Peter and Paul
Arrest and Trial	Threefold trial: before Sanhedrin, Pilate, and Herod	Threefold trial: before Felix, Festus, and Agrippa
Consummation	The Cross	Rome

The italicized sections centering primarily on Jesus' inauguration and miracles and then the early chapters of Acts generate the most interest from Pentecostal scholars. Ironically, numerous areas remain essentially untapped including Acts. Except for a few contributions, Pentecostals focus little on Jesus' journey and instruction on the way to Jerusalem, the Passion and Resurrection narrative, and the ministry of Paul (Acts 13 and beyond). A glance at the literature reveals Pentecostal proclivity to Acts 1–10 (especially Acts 2—Pentecost), Acts 2, 8, 9, 10, and 19 for their importance in the

---

[13] Stronstad, *Charismatic Theology*, p. 34. Similarly, Stronstad identifies five two-part narrative categories in the Third Gospel and Acts: 1) beginning narrative; 2) inauguration Narrative; 3) reports of ministry with confirmatory miracles; 4) travel narrative; 5) trials narrative ('Signs on the Earth Beneath' [paper presented at the annual meeting of the Society of Pentecostal Studies in Lakeland, FL, 1991], p. 110.

initial evidence debate, Acts 10—on inclusivity (also Acts 8–9), but very little on the second half of Acts. Paul, the missionary and prisoner receives little attention. I suppose the marked decline of Spirit language in the second half of Acts may serve as a contributing factor. However, several facts are noteworthy: 1) the decline of overt reference to the Spirit does not suggest that the Lukan Paul functions apart from the Spirit. To the contrary, just as the Lukan Jesus arrives on the scene with heavy emphasis upon the Spirit, a decline in references to the Spirit does not suggest less direction or guidance by the Spirit. Both Jesus and Paul function under the guidance and power of the Spirit throughout their respective ministries; 2) given the missiological passion of Pentecostals in general and scholars specifically, it seems surprising that the second half of Acts does not receive greater notice. Paul the missionary is a man of many methods; he exhibits an entrepreneurial spirit by taking the gospel to previously unchartered theological, geographical, and cultural territory; whether free or in chains, he proclaims the gospel with considerable success.

With this in mind, the appearance of literary and narrative methodologies should bring the necessary balance and embolden Pentecostal scholars to consider the unity of Luke–Acts and the values to emerge from a continuous reading. In spite of the current victory of literary and narrative approaches to Luke–Acts and the near consensus in scholarship on the unity of Luke–Acts, I am unsure as to how well this is being communicated at educational and congregational levels.[14] How long until our educational institutions begin to teach Luke–Acts instead of or alongside separate courses like the Synoptic Gospels and Acts? Should Pentecostal scholars do more to encourage homiletical and devotional integration of the Third Gospel and Acts? Perhaps further Pentecostal efforts to link the Third Gospel and Acts will lead the way.

At the same time, what about a canonical approach to Luke and Acts pulling in the opposite direction? In a twist against the rising literary/narrative methodologies, Anthony Robinson and Robert

---

[14] The most influential work to challenge the unity of Luke–Acts remains the co-authored volume by Mikeal C. Parsons and Richard I. Pervo entitled *Rethinking the Unity of Luke–Acts* (Minneapolis: Fortress, 1993).

Wall study Acts in its canonical *Sitz im Leben*.[15] They do not begin reading Acts at its point of origin in the ancient world or as the second volume of a Lukan project. Instead, Robinson and Wall emphasize that the canonical division supplies new and separate roles for each text to perform within the New Testament. Within its canonical setting, the Third Gospel finds its meaning within the fourfold Gospels collection, while the 'Acts of the Apostles' is so-titled and located within the Christian Bible to introduce its canonical audience to the apostolic letters that follow. According to Robinson and Wall, Jesus properly understood in Acts must reflect a fourfold thematic continuity and not simply the Lukan Jesus.[16] Wall continues to unfold a canonical hermeneutic for Acts that is 'text-centered' rather than 'author-centered' in order to find primary meaning and application in light of ecclesial intent. He suggests the final shape of the New Testament moves the reader deliberately from the fourfold Gospels to Acts and thus a transfer of the history of God's salvation from messianic to apostolic. While the Gospels focus on the facilitation of the Spirit of God by which all things happen during Jesus' earthly ministry, Acts focuses upon Jesus' apostolic successors who fulfill God's ordained plan (as in Acts 1.16, 22; 2.23; 3.21; 4.28; 10.42). The historic designation 'Acts of the Apostles' emphasizes that the ecclesial interests of apostolic authority are different than the authorial interests in the Spirit.[17] Certainly the hermeneutical ebb and flow between literary and ca-

---

[15] Anthony B. Robinson and Robert W. Wall, *Called To Be Church: The Book of Acts for a New Day* (Grand Rapids: Eerdmans: 2006). Wall, an occasional visitor to the Society for Pentecostal Studies, presented his canonical vision via an essay as 'Purity and Power According to the Acts of the Apostles' (paper presented at the annual meeting of the Society for Pentecostal Studies, Cleveland, TN, March 1998. See also Wall's earlier work 'The Acts of the Apostles in the Context of the New Testament Canon', *Biblical Theological Bulletin* 18 (1988), pp. 15-23, and David E. Smith, *The Canonical Function of Acts: A Comparative Analysis* (Collegeville: Liturgical Press, 2002).

[16] Robinson and Wall, *Called To Be Church*, p. 1. They surmise:

When the Bible is read sequentially, as it should be, the strategic role of Acts within the biblical canon becomes more apparent. Not only will its many references to Israel's Scripture supply interpretative guidelines for reading the Old Testament as Christian Scripture; its placement between the four Gospels and the following two collections of Epistles implies that it has a bridge-building role in relating the gospel story of Jesus with the biblical writings of his apostolic successors (pp. 25-26).

[17] Robinson and Wall, *Called To Be Church*, p. 3.

nonical methodology will warrant further consideration of Wall's conclusions. Pentecostal scholarship to date reveals only minimal focus upon on the ecclesial role of Acts. Pentecostal scholars write endlessly on the 'Acts of the Holy Spirit' but what of the significance of its ecclesial role, namely, the 'Acts of the Apostles'? What kind of ecclesial/canonical significance may be gleaned by the separation of Luke and Acts. For starters, Pentecostals would do well to build on Wall's efforts and explore the convergence of the Spirit with the ecclesiastical formation of the apostolic/institutional community as described in Acts. What remains consistent? What components seem culturally flexible, adaptable from one generation or region to another? Furthermore, given the scholarly dominance on questions surrounding the relationship between the likes of Lukan and Pauline hermeneutics and pneumatologies, whither the Fourth Gospel? How might scholars so focused on the relationship between Lukan and Pauline unity and diversity enlarge the conversation by bringing Johannine theology and practice into the mix?

UNTAPPED POSSIBILITIES

Finally, I would like to suggest a number of motifs, to my knowledge relatively untouched, by Pentecostal scholars. Since Pentecostals tend toward Lukan pneumatology, the major traditional theological categories often remain unexamined. Just as the ecclesial concerns noted above warrant attention, so also Lukan Christology needs fresh appraisal through the various Pentecostal lenses. In view of the fact that Pentecostals have never exemplified a mere forensic approach to Jesus' salvific work, scholars should be able to offer further contributions to a Lukan view of Christology. Moving from Jesus to Paul, Pentecostals should also be engaging the questions surrounding the *New Perspective on Paul* and its implications for various Pentecostal contexts.

Given Pentecostal emphasis on music, how about an integrated study on the impact of Lukan themes on Pentecostal hymnology and worship? Since Pentecostals utilize songs as a means of divine encounter as well as for doctrinal and instructional purposes, it should not be surprising to discover a rich history of music dependent on Luke–Acts.

Surely the story of Jesus and the church is as much an adventure of faith now as in the first century. The gospel moves into the world stage with countercultural and prophetic vigor. Twenty centuries later, contemporary Pentecostals look back at the Lukan narrative in order to continue Jesus' story into the current generation. If the work of the last forty years serves as any indication, the future of Pentecostal scholarship in Luke–Acts is indeed bright.

A NOT SO FINAL WORD

In my former book, Theophilus, I wrote about all that Jesus began to do and teach.

(Acts 1:1, NIV)

The Christian understanding of the world is not only a matter of
'dwelling in' a tradition of understanding;
it is a matter of dwelling in a story of God's activity, which is
still continuing.
The knowledge which Christian faith seeks is knowledge of God who
has acted and is acting.
(Leslie Newbigin) [1]

Only a little more than a decade ago Pentecostals begin to speak of the need for an enduring scholarly identity. Voices like Cheryl Bridges Johns set in motion a quest for the maturation of Pentecostal scholarship. She states:

> In order to grow up the Pentecostal movement must embrace the fire, for the fire is not just found in its infancy. It is at the heart of the Pentecostal identity. In this fire there should emerge a new form of Pentecostal scholarship. It would not be a scholarship based on shame, assuming that scholarly work has to fit into the categories of others.[2]

In light of such statements, is it not a shock to hear a reputable scholar like François Bovon suggest that in the area of Lukan stud-

---

[1] Leslie Newbigin, *The Gospel in a Pluralist Society* (Grand Rapids, MI: Eerdmans, 1989), p. 51.
[2] Cheryl Bridges Johns, 'The Adolescence of Pentecostalism: In Search of a Legitimate Sectarian Identity', *Pneuma* 17 (1995), p. 17.

ies Pentecostal scholars have indeed arrived?[3] As I worked my way through Pentecostal contributions to Lukan scholarship, even I was shocked at its sheer volume. This in turn begs further questions. Are the constituencies Pentecostal scholars serve aware of these efforts? Are Pentecostal students given the opportunity to engage the scholarship of their own tradition? How well does Pentecostal scholarship move from universities and seminaries into the local church? Do pastors know and utilize the work of their own scholars? And finally, are scholars working in conjunction with the local church to impact their movement? I am reminded of the words of my teacher Ron Kydd:

> Theologian and Church really are supposed to be performing a *pas de deux* … We are to be functioning members of Christian communities, drawing many benefits from them and, in turn, enriching them with our insights and activities … It is hazardous for us to attempt to be lone rangers. We need the nurture of the Church. It also needs the strengths we offer. We and the Church are caught up in this intriguing *pas de deux*. We stumble a bit and miss the occasional step, but we have to keep dancing.[4]

According to the nineteenth century Russian literary critic Mikhail Bakhtin, the reading and analyzing of any text provides neither a first nor a last word. Meanings born in dialogue should never be finalized, that is, ended once for all. Instead, conscientious readers of a text must always be renewed in the process of subsequent and future development of the dialogue. Along the way readers encounter not only previously unseen or unknown treasures, but also suspended masses of forgotten contextual meanings, which at certain moments of the dialogue's subsequent development are recalled

---

[3] See the Introduction.

[4] Ronald Kydd, 'A Prolegomenon to Pentecostal Theologizing', p. 131. In concert with Kydd, see D. Michael Postlethwait's clever attempt to link emotional and intellectual components of Pentecostal theology and praxis ('Drunk No More: The Biblical Case For Sobriety and Intellectual Awareness in Acts 2' (paper presented at the annual meeting of the Society for Pentecostal Studies, Eugene, OR, 2009).

and invigorated both in renewed forms and in new contexts.[5] If Bakhtin is correct, readers must engage the still unfolding insights of others to complement and enlarge their own. In true Bakhtinian fashion, I am confident that as the complementary dialogue between Pentecostals and non-Pentecostals, scholars and the church forges forward, the future of Luke–Acts research in the Pentecostal tradition will prove most rewarding. May our efforts strive for collaborative engagement with our respective academic and ecclesial communities! In true Lukan fashion, may Pentecostal scholars continue to write about 'all that Jesus began to do and teach'. In the spirit of an open-ended Acts, may we hear what the Spirit is saying to the academy and the church!

---

[5] Mikhail Bakhtin, *Speech Genres and Other Late Essays* (ed. Caryl Emerson and Michael Holquist; trans. Vern W. McGee; Austin: University of Texas Press, 1986), p. 170.

APPENDIX

COMMENTARIES / PASTORAL TOOLS

Due to the overwhelming amount of devotional material and wide range of commentaries, I offer only general observations:

1. The majority of commentaries cited in the bibliography function primarily as popular tools to serve in sermon preparation or personal study. For example, early Pentecostals (like Myer Pearlman and E.S. Williams) tend to zero in on distinctive texts in order to offer devotional and homiletical resources for Sunday school teachers and preachers.[1] Even later commentaries by Charles Conn (1965), Oral Roberts (Luke: 1984), Jimmy Swaggart (Luke: 1996; Acts: 1997) fit this category.[2] Many of these commentators demonstrate no hesitation in sharing personal experience as part of their presentation. In fact, Roberts and Swaggart emphasize their personal experiences in contradistinction to 'scholars who write only for other scholars'.[3] A couple of early pieces are noteworthy. A.S. Copley produces what may be the earliest devotional and verse-by-verse exposition of Acts.[4] In 95 pages, Copley highlights key early Pentecostal motifs such as the work of the Spirit, miracles, divine guidance and the mission

---

[1] See section 1.3.

[2] Charles Conn, *The Acts of the Apostles* (Cleveland, TN: Pathway Press, 1965); Oral Roberts, *Matthew, Mark, Luke, John* (The New Testament Comes Alive: A Personal New Testament Commentary 1; Tulsa: Oral Roberts, 1984); Jimmy Swaggart, *Luke* (Jimmy Swaggart Bible Commentary 9) and *Acts* (Jimmy Swaggart Bible Commentary 11; Baton Rouge, LA: World Evangelism Press, 1996, 1997).

[3] Jimmy Swaggart, *Luke*, p. vi.

[4] A.S. Copley, *The Church of Christ Founded: Spiritual Studies in The Acts* (Kansas City: Grace and Glory, n.d.). In this guide, Copley refers to an earlier pamphlet, 'This is That' (Republished by Grace and Glory Publications in Mountain Grove, MO, n.d.). Though questions remain concerning these dates, the anonymous author of an historical survey of the 'Grace and Glory' movement entitled *Indelible Grace. An Account of Grace Pentecostal Assemblies* (no publisher, no date), writes of Copley: 'By 1918, many of the Grace and Glory study books and booklets had been published. They would later be revised and enlarged, but all their essential teachings had, by this date, been published' (p. 14).

of the church. Similarly, Balthasar Theodor Bard, an early Assemblies of God missionary to China, produces an impressive unpublished verse-by-verse commentary with heavy emphasis upon Pentecostal theology and praxis.[5]

2. No Pentecostal produces a thoroughgoing verse-by-verse commentary until the post-Dunn era. Various commentators serve their respective Pentecostal communities as in Assemblies of God scholars Stanley Horton (1981) and Robert Tourville (1983) and Church of God (Cleveland, TN) scholars French Arrington (1988) and Trevor Grizzle (2000).[6] Horton teams up a few years later with numerous contributors to edit the Luke commentary for the Complete Biblical Library (1987). Though these commentators do not respond specifically to Dunn, the timing of their work stands in continuity with the pre- and post-critical period based on the release of Dunn's *Baptism in the Holy Spirit* in 1970.

3. The limited number of commentaries surely stems from consistent unwillingness by non-Pentecostal editors and publishers to utilize Pentecostal scholars as part of New Testament commentaries that serve the broader Christian community. In light of this, denominational publishing houses (such as Gospel Pub-

---

[5] Balthasar Theodor Bard, *The Acts of the Apostles* (Unpublished Teaching Notes, ca. 1935). The typed manuscript is 394 pages. Since Bard taught in a Bible school in China, the manuscript may have served as his teaching notes.

[6] See numerous commentaries by Stanley Horton including *The Book of Acts* (The Radiant Commentary of the New Testament. Springfield, MO: Gospel Publishing House, 1981). This commentary is also published in Russian as *The Book of Acts: The Wind of the Spirit* [Russian] (Republic of Belarus: Life Publishers International, 2002).

See further Horton, editor of *Luke* (The Complete Biblical Library 4. Springfield, MO: Gospel Publishing House, 1988) and *Acts* (The Complete Biblical Library 4. Springfield, MO: Gospel Publishing House, 1987) Horton revises and expands his commentary in 2001 as *Acts* (The Logion Press Commentary; Springfield: Logion Press, 2001). Robert E. Tourville, *The Acts of the Apostles: A Verse-By-Verse Commentary from the Classical Pentecostal Point of View* (New Wilmington, PA: House of Bonn Giovanni, 1983); French L. Arrington, *The Acts of the Apostles: Introduction, Translation and Commentary* (Peabody, MA: Hendrickson, 1988). Note also the review by Charles Holman, 'Review of French L. Arrington, *The Acts of the Apostles: An Introduction and Commentary*, in *Old and New Issues in Pentecostalism*' (paper presented at the annual meeting of the Society of Pentecostal Studies, Fresno, CA, 1989). Trevor Grizzle, *Church Aflame: An Exposition of Acts 1-12* (Cleveland, TN: Pathway Press, 2000).

lishing House and Pathway Press) produce the earliest commentaries. It seems only a matter of time until Pentecostal scholars produce not only much needed commentaries for their constituencies, but also larger academic and ecclesial communities. Increasing awareness of Pentecostal efforts as seen throughout this volume, whether by way of academic monographs and various journals, should give rise to never before seen possibilities for Pentecostals among the dominant publishing companies.

4. There remains a strong emphasis on Acts over the Third Gospel. To my knowledge, there exists no critical commentary on Luke's gospel by a Pentecostal to date.[7] The new Pentecostal Commentary Series (Deo Publishing) edited by John Christopher Thomas expects to fill this void in the next few years.[8]

5. Even with the emergence of literary/narrative criticism, subsequent emphasis upon Luke–Acts as a two-volume work, and the various monographs on Lukan motifs based upon the Third gospel and Acts (e.g. Stronstad, Menzies, Shelton, Penney, Wenk, and Mittelstadt), Pentecostals have not produced to date a commentary on Luke–Acts, appropriating the two-volume model.[9] Given the pervasive Pentecostal interest in the life of Jesus as paradigmatic for the contemporary Christian, it comes as a surprise that a comprehensive Luke–Acts commentary written

---

[7] Editor Stanley Horton employs the following contributors: Dawn Hartman (1.1-2.17); James Shelton (2.18-4.13); Thomas Gilman (7.19-8.40); Marjorie Williams (8.41-9.62); Gary York (10.1-11.29); A.D. Beacham, Jr. (11.30-12.53); Keith McCaslin (12.54-14.35); Mark Krause (15.1-17.9); Joseph Wilser (17.20-19.27); David Dippold (19.28-21.16); Streeter Stuart, Jr. (22.63-23.56). I assume the sections not listed are written by Horton (4.14-7.18; 24.1-53).

[8] According to John Christopher Thomas, James Shelton is under contract for the commentary on the Third Gospel. The author of the commentary on Acts is still in question.

[9] Monographs on Luke–Acts cited in earlier sections include Stronstad, *Charismatic Theology*; Menzies, *Empowered for Witness*; Shelton, *Mighty in Word and Deed*; Penney, *Missionary Emphasis*; Wenk, *Community and Power*; and Mittelstadt, *Spirit and Suffering*. Concerning commentaries, I am thinking along the lines of the two-volume work by Robert Tannehill, *The Narrative Unity of Luke–Acts: A Literary Interpretation* (2 vols.; Philadelphia: Fortress Press, 1986 &1990) or possibly the earlier combination by Charles H. Talbert, *Reading Luke: A Literary and Theological Commentary on the Third Gospel* and *Reading Acts: A Literary and Theological Commentary on the Acts of the Apostles* (Reading the New Testament Series. New York: Crossroad, 1982 &1997). Both sets include a number of intervening years between volumes but presume a continuous reading of Luke–Acts.

through Pentecostal lenses has not yet appeared. A little known exception may be the contribution by French Arrington to the one-volume *'Life in the Spirit' New Testament commentary*. In a bold move, the editors, Stronstad and Arrington, divert from the tradition canonical sequence and produce a commentary beginning with John, Matthew, Mark, Luke, Acts, and Romans.[10] In the preface they offer the following reasons: '(1) to link Luke and Acts together, so that they can be seen as a continuous unified account...; (2) to retain Acts adjacent to the Pauline letters; and (3) to keep the Synoptic Gospels together'.[11] In his introduction to continuous commentary on Luke and Acts, Arrington provides the following outline (with assistance from Stronstad):

Gospel of Luke	*The Acts of the Apostles*
The Acts of Jesus (Content)	The Acts of the Apostles (Content)
The Narratives of Jesus (Genre)	The Narratives of the Apostles (Genre)
1. Preface (1.1-4)	1. Preface (1.1-11)
2. The Origins of Spirit-Anointed Community (1.5-3.38)	2. The Origins of the Spirit-Baptized/Filled Community (1.12-2.41)
3. The Ministry of the Spirit-Anointed Prophet: Christ in Galilee (4.1-9.50)	3. The Acts of the Spirit-Baptized/Filled Community (2.42-6.7)
	4. The Acts of Six Spirit-Filled Leaders (6.8-12.24)
-------	
4. Travel Narrative: The Journey of Jesus to Jerusalem (9.51-19.44)	5. Travel Narrative: The Acts of Paul: An Itinerant, Spirit-Filled Prophet (12.25-22.21)
5. Jesus: Rejected Prophet-King (19.45-21.38)	-------
6. The Trial, Death and Resurrection of Jesus (22.1-24.53)	6. Paul's Arrest and Trials (22.22-26.32)
-------	7. Paul is sent to Rome (27.1-28.31)

Arrington also follows numerous structural parallels: (1) the prefaces with a dedication to Theophilus (Lk. 1.1-4; Acts 1.1-5); (2) comparable filling with the Spirit as ministry inauguration

---

[10] French Arrington, 'Luke', and 'Acts', in *Life in the Spirit New Testament Commentary* (ed. Arrington and Stronstad; Grand Rapids: Zondervan, 1999), pp. 375-534 and 535-693, respectively.

[11] Arrington, 'Luke', and 'Acts', in *Life in the Spirit New Testament Commentary*. The editors, in moving John to the front, offer the following comment: 'As we meet these objectives, John has been moved to stand first. This location is appropriate since its prologue opens with the preexistence of Christ' (p. vii).

(Lk. 3.21-22; Acts 2.1-4); (3) forty-day periods of preparation and ministry (Lk. 4.2; Acts 1.3); (4) inaugural homilies (Lk. 4.16-30; Acts 2.14-40); (5) various words and deeds provoking conflict, unbelief and rejection (Lk. 4.31-8.56; Acts 3.1-12.17); (6) evangelization of Gentiles (Lk. 10.1-12; Acts 13.1-19.20); (7) the extended journeys of Jesus and Paul (Lk. 9.51-22.53; Acts 19.21-21.26).[12] Arrington's entry should pave the way for future scholars and publishers to consider the need for thoroughgoing Luke–Acts commentaries.

6. Finally, there remains a gaping hole concerning culturally and ethnically sensitive commentaries. A quick glance at the commentary list reveals total domination by global north scholars. Given the global presence of Pentecostal impulses, this gap requires immediate attention. Such commentaries will undoubtedly draw upon not only the personal and ecclesial concerns of the region, but also specific socio-cultural, ethnic, and political dynamics thereby bringing Luke's story and theology from the ends of the earth into the larger conversation.[13] It is time for African, Asian, and South American Pentecostals to articulate the biblical story through their eyes so as to enlarge the understanding and vision of global north scholars. The embrace between scholars of the global north and global south should prove a fruitful endeavor.

---

[12] Arrington, 'Luke', and 'Acts', in *Life in the Spirit New Testament Commentary*, p. 385. Other early hints at interest in a Luke–Acts commentary come from J. Ramsey Michaels, 'Luke–Acts', in *Dictionary of Pentecostal and Charismatic Movements* (ed. Stanley Burgess, Gary McGee and Patrick Alexander; Grand Rapids: Zondervan, 1988), pp. 544-61. The decision of the editors to combine the Third Gospel and Acts marks the beginning of the triumph of the two-volume literary approach.

See also George Montague, *The Holy Spirit: Growth of a Biblical Tradition. A Commentary on the Principal Texts of the Old and New Testaments* (New York: Paulist Press, 1976). Montague provides a summary of Luke–Acts and emphasizes Luke's two-volume ecclesial concerns. The disciples endowed with Jesus' own charismatic power extend fulfillment of Jesus as the Spirit anointed servant of Isaiah 61 and continue their journey into a new community of the Spirit foretold by Joel. Under the guidance of the Spirit of Jesus, disciples continue the prophetic presence and direction of the Spirit in the life of the early church.

[13] For starters, see Tokunboh Adeyemo (ed.), *Africa Bible Commentary: A One Volume Commentary Written by 70 African Scholars* (Grand Rapids: Zondervan, 2006). I have in mind a one-volume biblical commentary of global Pentecostal voices.

BIBLIOGRAPHY

Bibliographical references correspond in number to the sections above.

Works cited in previous sections are not repeated when they occur in later sections.

*Works duly cited are either not produced by Pentecostal/Charismatic scholars or not specifically in conversation with Pentecostal/Charismatic concerns. I include these sources because of their importance and potential influential upon Pentecostal exegesis and theology.

PART I. Introduction

Getting Started

Burgess, Stanley and Eduard M. Van Der Maas (eds.), *New International Dictionary of Pentecostal and Charismatic Movement*. Revised and Expanded Edition. Grand Rapids: Zondervan, 2002.

Dayton, Donald W. *Theological Roots of Pentecostalism*. Peabody: Hendrickson, 1987.

Dunn, James. *Baptism in the Holy Spirit: A Re-examination of the New Testament Teaching on the Gift of the Spirit in Relation to Pentecostalism Today*. London: SCM Press, 1970.

Hollenweger, Walter J. *The Pentecostals*. Peabody: Hendrickson, 1972.

Mittelstadt, Martin William. 'Reading Luke–Acts in the Pentecostal Tradition: The History and Status of Luke–Acts Research'. Paper presented at annual meeting of the Society for Pentecostal Studies. Cleveland, TN, March 8-10, 2007.

_____. 'Scripture in the Pentecostal Tradition: A Contemporary Reading of Luke–Acts'. Paper presented at the annual meeting of the Society for Pentecostal Studies. Pasadena, CA, Mar 23-25, 2006. Repr. Pages 123-41 in *Canadian Pentecostalism: Transition and Transformation*. Edited by Michael Wilkinson. Montreal: McGill/ Queens University Press, 2008.

Luke–Acts Research in the Twentieth Century

*Barrett, C. K. 'The Third Gospel as a Preface to Acts? Some Reflections'. Pages 1451-1466 in *The Four Gospels*, 1992: Festschrift Frans Neirynck. Edited by F. Van Segbroeck, et al. Vol. 2 of Bibliotheca Ephemeridum Theologicarum Lovaniensium. Edited by F. Van Segbroeck, C.M. Tuckett, G. Van Belle, and J. Verheyden. Louvain: Leuven University Press, 1992.

*Bovon, François. *Luc le théologien: Vingt-cinq ans de recherches* (1950-1975). Paris: Delachaux et Niestle, 1978.

*_____. *Luke the Theologian: Thirty-Three Years of Research* (1950-1983). Translated by K. McKinney. Pittsburgh Theological Monograph Series 20. Allison Park: Pickwick Publications, 1987.

*_____. *Luke The Theologian: Fifty-five Years of Research* (1950-2005). 3rd Rev. Ed. Waco: Baylor University Press, 2006.

*_____. 'Orientations actuelles des études lucaniennes', *Revue de theologie et de philosophie 26* (1976), pp. 161-90.

*Cadbury, Henry J. *The Making of Luke–Acts.* New York: Macmillan, 1927.

*Dibelius, Martin. *The Book of Acts: Form, Style and Theology.* Edited by K.C. Hanson. Minneapolis: Fortress Press, 2004.

*_____. *Studies in the Acts of the Apostles.* Edited by Heinrich Greeven. Translated from the German edition by Mary Ling. New York: Scribner, 1951.

*Foakes-Jackson, F. J. and Kirsopp Lake (eds.), *The Beginnings of Christianity.* 5 vols. London: Macmillan, 1919-1933.

*Gasque, Ward. *A History of the Interpretation of the Acts of the Apostles.* Rev. ed. Peabody: Hendrickson, 1989.

*Green, Joel B. and Michael C. McKeever. *Luke–Acts and the New Testament Historiography.* Institute of Biblical Research Bibliographies 8. Grand Rapids: Baker Books, 1994.

*Jervell, Jacob. *The Theology of the Acts of the Apostles.* New Testament Theology. Edited by James D.G. Dunn. Cambridge: Cambridge University Press, 1996

*Marshall, I. Howard. *Luke: Historian and Theologian.* Exeter: Paternoster Press, 1970.

*Mattill, Andrew J. and Mary B. Mattill. *A Classified Bibliography of Literature on the Acts of the Apostles.* New Testament Tools and Studies 7. Leiden: Brill, 1966.

Mittelstadt, Martin William. 'Review of Martin Dibelius, The Book of Acts: Form, Style and Theology'. *Pneuma* 27.2 (2005), pp. 393-95.

*Penner, Todd. 'Madness in the Method? The Acts of the Apostles in Current Study'. *Currents in Biblical Research* 2.2 (2004), pp. 223-93.

Powell, Mark Allan. *What are They Saying About Acts?* New York: Paulist Press, 1991.

_____. *What are They Saying About Luke?* New York: Paulist Press, 1989.

Trajectories of Pentecostal Theology in the Twentieth Century

Atkinson, William. 'Pentecostal Responses to Dunn's *Baptism in the Holy Spirit*: Luke–Acts'. *JPT* 6 (1995), pp. 87-131

_____. 'Pentecostal Responses to Dunn's *Baptism in the Holy Spirit*: Pauline Literature'. *JPT* 7 (1995), pp. 49-72.

Bundy, David D. 'Bibliography and Historiography of Pentecostalism Outside of North America'. Pages 405-417 in *NIDPCM*. Rev ed. Edited by Stanley M. Burgess. Grand Rapids: Zondervan, 2002.

Bruner, Frederick Dale. *A Theology of the Holy Spirit: The Pentecostal Experience and the New Testament Witness.* Grand Rapids: Eerdmans, 1970.

Cerillo, Augustus and Grant Wacker. 'Bibliography and Historiography of Pentecostalism in the United States'. Pages 382-405 in *NIDPCM*. Rev ed. Edited by Stanley M. Burgess. Grand Rapids: Zondervan, 2002.

Dunn, James. 'Baptism in the Spirit: A Response to Pentecostal Scholarship on Luke–Acts'. *JPT* 3 (1993), pp. 3-27.

Flokstra, Gerald J. 'Sources for the Initial Evidence Discussion: A Bibliographic Essay'. *AJPS* 2 (1999), pp. 243-59.

Hollenweger, Walter J. 'The Critical Tradition of Pentecostalism'. *JPT* 1 (October 1992), pp. 7-17.

Jacobsen, Douglas. 'Knowing the Doctrines of Pentecostals: The Scholastic Theology of the Assemblies of God, 1930-1955'. Paper presented at the annual meeting of the Society for Pentecostal Studies. Guadalajara, Mexico, November 11-13, 1993.

_____. *Thinking in the Spirit: Theologies of the Early Pentecostal Movement*. Bloomington: Indiana University Press, 2003.

Lederle, Henri. *Treasures Old and New: Interpretations of the Spirit Baptism in the Charismatic Renewal Movement*. Peabody: Hendrickson, 1988.

_____ and Mathew Clark et. al. *What is distinctive about Pentecostal Theology?* Pretoria: University of South Africa, 1983.

Lewis, Paul. 'Reflections on a Hundred Years of Pentecostal Theology'. *CPCR* 12 (February 2003): http://www.pctii.org/cyberj/cyberj12/lewis.html.

Ma, Wonsuk. 'Biblical Studies in the Pentecostal Tradition: Yesterday, Today, and Tomorrow'. Pages 52-69 in *Globalization of Pentecostalism*. Edited by Murray Dempster, Byron Klaus, and Douglas Petersen. Irvine, CA: Regnum Press, 1999.

MacArthur, John. *Charismatic Chaos*. Grand Rapids: Zondervan, 1992.

Macchia, Frank. 'The Struggle for Global Witness: Shifting Paradigms in Pentecostal Theology'. Pages 8-29 in *Globalization of Pentecostalism: A Religion Made to Travel*. Edited by Murray Dempster, Byron Klaus, and Douglas Petersen. Irvine, CA: Regnum Press, 1999.

Moore, Rickie, John Christopher Thomas, and Steven Land. 'Editorial'. *JPT* 1 (1992), pp. 3-6.

Packer, J. I. *Keep in Step with the Spirit*. Old Tappan, NJ: F. H. Revell, 1984.

Ramm, Bernard. 'Varieties of Christian Belief: Acts, Chapter Two'. *Eternity* (May 1982), pp. 45-46.

Spittler, Russell P. 'Theological Style among Pentecostals and Charismatics'. Pages 291-318 in *Doing Theology in Today's World*. Edited by John D. Woolbridge and Thomas Edward McComiskey. Grand Rapids: Zondervan Publishing House, 1991.

Stott, John R. W. *The Baptism and Fullness: The Work of the Holy Spirit Today*. London: Inter-Varsity Press, 1964.

Thomas, John Christopher. '1998 Presidential Address: Pentecostal Theology in the Twenty-First Century'. *Pneuma* 20 (1998), pp. 3-19.

PART II: History and Trajectory of Pentecostal Contributions to Luke–Acts Research

1. Stage 1—Pre-1970

Fisher, Elmer Kirk. *The Upper Room*, vol. 1, no. 1 (June 1909), p. 3. Repr., *Bridegroom's Messenger* (June 15, 1909), p. 2.

Horton, Stanley. *Reflections of an Early American Pentecostal*. Baguio City: APTS Press, 2001.

Seymour, William J., ed. *The Azusa Street Papers: A Reprint of the Apostolic Faith Mission Publications, Los Angeles, California, 1906-1908*. Foley, AL: Together in the Harvest Publications, 1997.

1.1 Acts Sets the Standard

Dutko, Joseph. 'This-Worldly Explanations for Otherworldly Growth: Vitality in an Ozarks Megachurch'. Unpublished MA thesis, Missouri State University, 2008.

Hudson, Neil. 'Strange Words and Their Impact on Early Pentecostals: A Historical Perspective'. Pages 52-81 in *Speaking in Tongues: Multi-Disciplinary Perspectives*. Edited by Mark J. Cartledge. *Studies in Pentecostal and Charismatic Issues*. Waynesboro: Paternoster Press, 2006.

McGee, Gary. 'Historical Backgrounds'. Pages 9-38 in *Systematic Theology: A Pentecostal Perspective*. Edited by Stanley Horton. Springfield: Logion Press, 1994.

_____. *Initial Evidence: Historical and Biblical Perspectives on the Pentecostal Doctrine of Spirit Baptism*. Edited by Gary McGee. Peabody: Hendrickson, 1991.

Wacker, Grant. *Heaven Below: Early Pentecostals and American Culture*. Cambridge, Mass.: Harvard University Press, 2001.

1.1.1 Charles Parham

Nelson, Douglas J. 'For Such a Time as This: The Story of William J. Seymour and the Azusa Street Revival'. Ph.D. diss., University of Birmingham, 1981.

Goff, James R. *Fields White Unto Harvest: Charles F. Parham and the Missionary Origins of Pentecostalism*. Fayetteville: University of Arkansas Press, 1988.

Parham, Charles F. *The Everlasting Gospel*. Baxter Springs, KS: Apostolic Faith Bible College, 1911.

Parham, Robert L., ed. *Selected Sermons of the Late Charles F. Parham, Sarah E. Parham: Co-Founders of the Original Apostolic Faith Movement*. Baxter Springs, KS: Apostolic Faith Bible College, 1941.

Parham, Sarah E. *The Life of Charles F. Parham*. Joplin, MO: Tri-State Printing Co., 1930. Repr., Birmingham, AL: Commercial Printing Co., 1977.

1.1.2 Azusa Street

Archer, Kenneth. 'Early Pentecostal Biblical Interpretation' *JPT* 18 (2001), pp. 32-70. Previously, a paper presented at the annual meeting of the Society for Pentecostal Studies. Kirkland, WA, March 16-18, 2000.

Bartleman, Frank. *How 'Pentecost' Came to Los Angeles—As It Was in the Beginning*. Los Angeles: the author, 1925. Repr., *Another Wave Rolls In*. Northridge, CA: Voice Publications, 1962. Repr., *Azusa Street: An Eyewitness Account*. Gainesville, FL: Bridge-Logos, 2006.

_____. 'Present Day Conditions'. *Weekly Evangel* 5 (1915), p. 3.

Brumback, Carl. *Suddenly… from Heaven: A History of the Assemblies of God*. Springfield, MO: Gospel Publishing House, 1961.

Robeck, Cecil M. *The Azusa Street Mission and Revival: The Birth of the Global Pentecostal Movement*. Nashville: Thomas Nelson, Inc., 2006

_____. 'Azusa Street Revival'. Pages 344-350 in *NIDPCM*. Edited by Stanley Burgess. Grand Rapids: Zondervan, 2002.

_____. 'Seymour, William Joseph'. Pages 1053-1058 in *NIDPCM*. Edited by Stanley Burgess. Grand Rapids: Zondervan, 2002.

Wilkinson, Michael. 'Religion and Global Flows'. Pages 375-89 in *Religion, Globalization and Culture*. Edited by Peter Beyer and Lori Beaman. Boston: Brill Academic, 2007.

1.1.3   Early Pioneers

Barratt, Thomas Ball. 'The Baptism of the Holy Ghost and Fire: What Is the Scriptural Evidence?' Evangel Tract No. 953. Springfield, MO: Gospel Publishing House, n.d.

_____. *In the Days of the Latter Rain*. London: Simpkin, Marshall, Hamilton, Kent & Co., Ltd., 1909.

Flower, J. R. *Is it Necessary to Speak in an Unknown Tongue?* Toronto: Full Gospel Publishing House, n.d.

Greenwalt, Alwyn. 'One Heart—One Soul'. *The Bridal Call*, (February 1927), pp. 16-17.

Lindsay, Gordon. *Acts in Action*. 5 vols. Dallas: Christ For the Nations, 1975.

Kerr, D. W. 'The Bible Evidence of the Baptism with the Holy Ghost'. *Pentecostal Evangel* 11 (August 1923), p. 2.

King, Joseph Hillery. 'How I Obtained Pentecost'. *Cloud of Witnesses to Pentecost in India* 2 (September 1907), pp. 48-52.

Lupton, Levi. *The New Acts* 3, no. 1. (February, 1907).

McGee, Gary. 'Early Pentecostal Hermeneutics: Tongues as Evidence in the Book of Acts'. Pages 96-118 in *Initial Evidence: Historical and Biblical Perspectives on the Pentecostal Doctrine of Spirit Baptism*. Peabody: Hendrickson, 1991.

McPherson, Aimee Semple. 'Dorcas'. *The Bridal Call* (February 1929), pp. 9-10, 31-32.

_____. 'God's Pattern for a Model Revival'. *The Bridal Call* (February 1929), pp. 7-8, 30.

_____. 'The Story of My Life'. *The Bridal Call* (January 1925), pp. 12-13.

_____. 'The Story of My Life'. *The Bridal Call* (March 1925), pp. 16-19.

_____. *This is That: Personal Experiences, Sermons, and Writings of Aimee Semple McPherson*. Los Angeles: Echo Park Evangelistic Association, 1923.

Nelson, P. C. *Testimony of P. C. Nelson To His Healing and His Baptism in the Holy Spirit*. Enid, OK: Southwestern Press, 1920.

Osborn, T. L. *3 Keys to the Book of Acts*. Tulsa: T. L. Osborn Publications, 1960.

Taylor, George Floyd. *The Spirit and the Bride: A Scriptural Presentation of the Operations, Manifestations, Gifts and Fruit of the Holy Spirit in His Relation to the Bride with special references to the 'Latter Rain' Revival*. Falcon, NC: Falcon Printing Co.,

1907. Repr. *Three Early Pentecostal Tracts*. Edited by Donald Dayton. New York: Garland, 1985.

Woodworth Etter, Maria. *Acts of the Holy Ghost or The Life, Work and Experience, of Mrs. M. B. Woodworth-Etter, Evangelist. Complete, Including Sermons*. Dallas: John F. Worley Printing Co., 1912.

1.2   Acts as the Center for Dissent

1.2.1   The New Issue

Ewart, Frank. *The Revelation of Jesus Christ*. Portland, OR: Apostolic Book Publishers, n.d.

_____. *The Phenomenon of Pentecost: A History of the Latter Rain*. Rev. ed. Hazelwood, MO: Word Aflame Press, 1975.

Haywood, G. T. *The Birth of the Spirit in the Days of the Apostles*. Indianapolis: Christ Temple Book Store, n.d.

Reed , David. 'In Jesus' Name': The History and Beliefs of Oneness Pentecostals*. Dorset, England: Deo Publishing, 2007.

_____. 'Oneness Pentecostalism'. Pages 936-44 in *NIDPCM*. Rev ed. Edited by Stanley M. Burgess. Grand Rapids: Zondervan, 2002.

Spittler, Russell P. 'Are Pentecostals and Charismatics Fundamentalists? A Review of American Uses of These Categories'. Pages 103-116 in *Charismatic Christianity As a Global Culture*. Edited by Karla Poewe. Columbia, SC: The University of South Carolina Press, 1994.

1.2.2   Tongues and the Bible Evidence

Atterberry, Thomas. 'They Shall Speak With New Tongues'. *Pentecostal Evangel* 320/321 (December 27, 1919), pp. 2-3.

Bell, E. N. 'Questions and Answers'. *Pentecostal Evangel* 300/301 (August 9, 1919), p. 5.

_____. 'Questions and Answers'. *Pentecostal Evangel* 394/395 (May 28, 1921), p. 10.

_____. 'Return to Pentecost'. *Pentecostal Evangel* 460/461 (September 2, 1922), p. 5.

Bosworth, F. F. *Do All Speak With Tongues? 1 Cor. 12:30. An Open Letter to the Ministers and Saints of the Pentecostal Movement*. New York: Christian Alliance Publishing Co., n.d.

Frodsham, Arthur W. 'What Is the Use of Speaking in Tongues?' *Pentecostal Evangel* 509 (August 11, 1923), pp. 6-7.

Gaston, W.T. 'The Sign and the Gift of Tongues'. Tract No. 4664. Springfield, MO: Gospel Publishing House, n.d.

Kerr, Daniel W. 'The Basis for Our Distinctive Testimony'. *Pentecostal Evangel* 460/461 (September 2, 1922), p. 4.

_____. 'The Bible Evidence of the Baptism with the Holy Ghost'. *Pentecostal Evangel* 509 (August 11, 1923), pp. 2-3.

_____. 'The Bosworth Meetings'. *Pentecostal Evangel* 386/387 (April 2, 1921), p. 7.

_____. 'Not Ashamed'. *Pentecostal Evangel* 386/387 (April 2, 1921), p. 5.

McGee, Gary. 'Initial Evidence'. Pages 788-790 in *NIDPCM*. Edited by Stanley Burgess. Grand Rapids: Zondervan, 2002.

_____. *Readings on the Doctrine of the Initial Evidence*. Unpublished Text for Assemblies of God Theological Seminary, n.d.

McPherson, Aimee Semple. 'What is the Evidence of the Baptism of the Holy Ghost?' *Pentecostal Evangel* 312/313 (November 1, 1919), pp. 6-7.

Minutes of the Sixth Annual Meeting of the General Council of the Assemblies of God in the United States of America, Canada, and Foreign Lands held at Springfield, Missouri Sept. 4-11, 1918. Springfield, MO: Gospel Publishing House, 1918.

Moffat, F. M. 'All May Speak with Tongues'. *Pentecostal Evangel* 540 (March 29, 1924), pp. 6-7.

Nelson, P. C. *Did They Speak With Tongues in Samaria?* Enid, OK: Southwestern Press, 1939.

Seymour, William. *Doctrines and Disciplines of the Azusa Street Apostolic Faith Mission of Los Angeles, California*. Edited by Larry Martin. The Complete Azusa Street Library 7. Joplin, MO: Christian Life Books, 2000.

1.3   Acts and Preservation

The Acts of the Holy Spirit among the Baptists Today. Los Angeles: Full Gospel Business Men's Fellowship International, 1971.

The Acts of the Holy Spirit among the Nazarenes Today. Los Angeles: Full Gospel Business Men's Fellowship International, 1973.

Acts: Today's News of the Holy Spirit's Renewal. Los Angeles: Acts Publishers, 1967.

Acts 29: Where we are Now in the Continuing Acts of the Holy Spirit (The Newsletter of the Episcopal Charismatic Fellowship). Denver: Episcopal Charismatic Fellowship, 1973-1994.

Author Unidentified. 'Signs and Wonders: Can the Present Church Fight the Increasing Antichristian Forces with Less Power than the Apostles of Old?' *Pentecostal Testimony* 32 (June 1951), p. 6.

Bennett, Dennis. *Nine O' Clock in the Morning*. South Plainfield, N.J.: Bridge Publishing Inc., 1970.

'Book of Acts Reading Set on April 24'. *Springfield Newsleader* (Sunday, Feb. 20, 1955). Also published as 'CA Youth Group to Sponsor Bible Reading Project'. *Springfield Advertiser* (Thursday, Feb. 24, 1955).

*Borgman, Paul. *The Way according to Luke: Hearing the Whole Story of Luke–Acts*. Grand Rapids: Eerdmans, 2006.

Dalton, Robert Chandler. *Tongues Like As of Fire: A Critical Study of Modern Tongue Movements in the Light of Apostolic and Patristic Times*. Springfield: Gospel Publishing House, 1945.

*Filson, Floyd. 'Journey Motif in Luke–Acts'. Pages 68-77 in *Apostolic History and the Gospel*. Edited by W. Gasque and R. Martin. Exeter: Paternoster, 1970.

Gee, Donald. *Pentecost*. Springfield, Mo.: Gospel Publishing House, 1932.

Land, Steven. *Pentecostal Spirituality: A Passion for the Kingdom*. JPTSup 1. Sheffield: Sheffield Academic Press, 1997.

Lindford, Aaron. 'The Initial Sign'. *The Pentecostal Testimony* 54 (September 1973), p. 3.

Lash, Nicholas. 'Performing the Scriptures'. *Theology on the Way to Emmaus*. London: SCM, 1986.

Luce, Alice E. 'Paul's Missionary Methods'. *Pentecostal Evangel* 374/375 (January 8, 1921), pp. 6-7.

_____. 'Paul's Missionary Methods'. *Pentecostal Evangel* 376/377 (January 22, 1921), pp. 6, 11.

_____. 'Paul's Missionary Methods'. *Pentecostal Evangel* 378/379 (February 5, 1921), pp. 6-7.

Marek, Karel. 'Acts 29'. *The Pentecostal Testimony* 70 (December 1989), pp. 24-5.

Nelson, P.C. *Bible Doctrines*. Springfield, MO: Gospel Publishing House, 1934.

Pearlman, Myer. *Through the Bible Book by Book: New Testament Gospels and Acts—Part III*. Springfield, MO: Gospel Publishing House, 1935.

Slauenwhite, David. *Fresh Breezes: An Historical Perspective on the Pentecostal Assemblies of Canada*. Mississauga: PAOC Dept. of Spiritual Life, 1996.

*Vanhoozer, Keith. *The Drama of Doctrine: A Canonical-Linguistic Approach to Christian Theology*. Louisville: Westminster John Knox, 2005.

Ward, C.M. 'I Saw The Holy Spirit Move in These Meetings'. *Pulpit Series 22*. Springfield, MO: Assemblies of God, 1956.

Williams, E.S. *My Sermon Notes: The Gospels and Acts*. Springfield, MO: Gospel Publishing House, 1967.

Womack, David, ed. *ReACTion: A Quarterly Newsletter Calling for a Fresh Revival of Book-of-Acts Christianity* 1-6 (2001-2006).

*Wright, N.T. *The New Testament and the People of God*. Minneapolis: Fortress Press, 1992.

Yong, Amos. *Hospitality & the Other: Pentecost, Christian Practices, and the Neighbor*. Maryknoll, NY: Orbis Books, 2008.

1.4 Summary

Gee, Donald. 'The Initial Evidence of the Baptism in the Holy Spirit'; Evangel Tract No. 961. Springfield, MO: Gospel Publishing House, n.d.

Rice, John R. *Speaking in Tongues*. Wheaton, IL: Sword of the Lord, n.d.

Robeck, Cecil. 'National Association of Evangelicals'. Pages 922-925 in *NIDPCM*. Edited by Stanley Burgess. Grand Rapids: Zondervan, 2002.

2. Stage 2—The Dunn Factor: Pentecostals Enter the Academic Marketplace

Archer, Kenneth J. 'Pentecostal Hermeneutics: Retrospect and Prospect'. *JPT* 8 (April 1996), pp. 63-81.

Atkinson, William. 'Pentecostal Responses to Dunn's *Baptism in the Holy Spirit*: Luke–Acts'. *JPT* 6 (1995), pp. 87-131.

_____. 'Pentecostal Responses to Dunn's *Baptism in the Holy Spirit*: Pauline Literature'. *JPT* 7 (1995), pp. 49-72.

Bruner, Frederick. *A Theology of the Holy Spirit*. Grand Rapids: Eerdmans, 1970.

Dunn, James D.G. *The Acts of the Apostles*. Epworth Commentary Series. London: Epworth Press, 1996.

_____. 'Baptism in the Spirit: A Response to Pentecostal Scholarship on Luke–Acts'. *JPT* 3 (1993), pp. 3-27.

_____. 'Baptism in the Holy Spirit … yet once more'. Paper presented at the annual meeting of the European Pentecostal Theological Association. Matterey Hall, England, 1998. *JEPTA* 18 (1998), pp. 3-25.

_____. *Jesus and the Spirit: A Study of the Religious and Charismatic Experience of Jesus and the First Christians as Reflected in the New Testament.* Philadelphia: Westminster Press, 1975.

_____. 'Spirit-Baptism and Pentecostalism'. *Scottish Journal of Theology* 23 (1970), pp. 397-407.

_____. *Unity and Diversity in the New Testament: An Inquiry into the Character of Earliest Christianity.* 3d ed. London: SCM Press, 2006.

Hacking, Keith. *Signs and Wonders, Then and Now: Miracle-Working Commissioning, and Discipleship.* Nottingham: Apollos/IVP, 2006.

Macchia, Frank. 'Salvation and Spirit Baptism: Another Look at James Dunn's Classic'. *Pneuma* 24 (2002), pp. 1-6.

Menzies, Robert P. 'Luke and the Spirit: A Reply to James Dunn'. *JPT* 4 (1994), pp. 115-38.

_____. Review of Keith Hacking, *Signs and Wonders, Then and Now: Miracle-Working Commissioning, and Discipleship. Evangelical Quarterly* 79.3 (2007), pp. 261-65.

Pinnock, Clark. Foreword to *Charismatic Theology*, by Roger Stronstad. Peabody: Hendrickson, 1984.

Spittler, Russell P. 'Suggested Areas for Further Research in Pentecostal Studies'. *Pneuma* 5 (Fall 1983), pp. 39-56.

2.1   Responses

2.1.1   Gordon Fee

Fee, Gordon D. 'Acts: The Question of Historical Precedent'. Pages 94-112 in *How to Read the Bible for All Its Worth.* 2nd ed. Edited by Gordon Fee and Douglas Stuart. Grand Rapids: Zondervan, 1993.

_____. 'Baptism in the Holy Spirit: The Issue of Separability and Subsequence'. Paper presented at the annual meeting of the Society for Pentecostal Studies. South Hamilton, MA, November 15-17, 1984. Later published in *Pneuma* 7 (Fall 1985), pp. 87-99.

_____. *God's Empowering Presence: The Holy Spirit in the Letters of Paul.* Peabody: Hendrickson, 1994.

_____. 'Hermeneutics and Historical Precedent: A Major Issue in Pentecostal Hermeneutics'. Pages 83-104 in *Gospel and Spirit: Issues in New Testament Hermeneutics.* Peabody: Hendrickson, 1991.

_____ and Douglas Stuart. *How to Read the Bible for All Its Worth.* Grand Rapids: Zondervan, 1981.

Keener, Craig S. *Gift Giver: The Holy Spirit for Today.* Grand Rapids: Baker, 2001.

_____. *The Spirit in the Gospels and Acts: Divine Purity and Power.* Peabody: Hendrickson, 1997.

_____. *Three Crucial Questions on the Holy Spirit.* Grand Rapids: Baker, 1996.

Noel, Bradley Truman. 'Gordon Fee and the Challenge to Pentecostal Hermeneutics: Thirty Years Later'. *Pneuma* 26 (2004), pp. 60-80.

2.1.2   Roger Stronstad

Burge, Gary M. Review of Roger Stronstad, *The Charismatic Theology of St. Luke.* *Pneuma* (Spring 1986), pp. 65-67.

Carson, Donald A. *Showing the Spirit: A Theological Exposition of 1 Corinthians 12-14.* Grand Rapids: Baker, 1987.

Stronstad, Roger. 'Affirming Diversity: God's People as a Community of Prophets'.*Affirming Diversity.* Presidential address at the annual meeting of the Society for Pentecostal Studies. Wheaton, IL, November 10-12, 1994. Published later in *Pneuma* 17.2 (1995), pp. 145-57.

_____. *Baptized and Filled with the Spirit.* Springfield, MO: Africa's Hope Publications, 2004.

_____. 'The Biblical Precedent for Historical Precedent'. Paper presented at the annual meeting of the Society for Pentecostal Studies. Springfield, MO, November 12-14, 1992.

_____. *The Charismatic Theology of St. Luke.* Peabody: Hendrickson, 1984.

_____. 'The Charismatic Theology of St. Luke *Revisited* (Special Emphasis Upon Being Baptized in the Holy Spirit)'. Pages 101-122 in *Defining Issues: Classical and Emergent.* Edited by Steven Studebaker. McMaster Theological Studies Series. Eugene: Pickwick, 2008.

_____. ''Filled with the Spirit' Terminology in Luke–Acts'. Paper presented at the annual meeting of the Society for Pentecostal Studies. Fresno, CA, November 16-18, 1989. Repr. Pages 1-14in *The Holy Spirit in the Scriptures and the Church: Essays Presented to Leslie Thomas Holdcroft on his 65th Birthday.* Edited by Roger Stronstad and Laurence M. Van Kleek. Clayburn, BC: Western Pentecostal Bible College, 1987.

_____. 'Hermeneutics of Lucan Historiography'. *Paraclete* 22 (Fall 1988), pp. 5-17. Repr. Pages 31-52 in *Scripture and Theology.* Baguio City, Philippines: Asia Theological Seminary Press, 1995.

_____. 'The Holy Spirit in Luke–Acts: A Synthesis of Luke's Pneumatology- Part 3'. *Paraclete* 23 (Winter 1989), pp. 8-13.

_____. 'The Holy Spirit in Luke–Acts: A Synthesis of Luke's Pneumatology- Part 3 (continued)'. (Spring 1989), pp 18-26. Repr. Pages 132-168 in *Spirit, Scripture and Theology.* Baguio City, Philippines: Asia Theological Seminary Press, 1995.

_____. 'The Influence of the Old Testament on the Charismatic Theology of St. Luke'. *Pneuma* 2 (Spring 1980), pp. 32-50.

_____. 'Pentecostal Experience and Hermeneutics'. *Paraclete* 26 (Winter 1992), pp. 14-30. Repr. Pages 53-78 in *Spirit, Scripture and Theology.* Baguio City, Philippines: Asia Theological Seminary Press, 1995.

_____. 'Pentecostal Hermeneutics' (Review of Gordon D. Fee, *Gospel and Spirit: Issues in New Testament Hermeneutics*). *Pneuma* 15 (1993), pp. 215-22.

_____. 'Pentecostalism, Experiential Presuppositions and Hermeneutics'. Paper presented at the annual meeting of the Society for Pentecostal Studies. Dallas, TX, November 8-10, 1990.

_____. 'The Prophethood of All Believers: A Study in Luke's Charismatic Theology'. Pages 60-79 in *Pentecostalism in Context: Essays in Honor of William W. Menzies.* Ed. Wonsuk Ma and Robert Menzies. JPTSup 11. Sheffield: Sheffield Academic Press, 1997.

_____. 'The Prophethood of All Believers'. Pages 1-50 in *Contemporary Issues in Pentecostal Theology*. Edited by William Menzies. Baguio City: Asia Theological Seminary Press, 1993.

_____. *The Prophethood of All Believers: A Study in Luke's Charismatic Theology*. JPTSup 16. Sheffield: Sheffield Academic Press, 1999.

_____. 'Prophets and Pentecost'. *The Pentecostal Testimony* 57 (March 1976), p. 5.

_____. *Signs on the Earth Beneath: A Commentary on Acts 2:1-21*. Springfield: Life Publishers International, 2003.

_____. 'Signs on the Earth Beneath: Interpreting Luke–Acts'. Paper presented at the annual meeting of the Society for Pentecostal Studies. Lakeland, FL, November 7-9, 1991.

_____. *Spirit, Scripture and Theology*. Baguio City, Philippines: Asia Theological Seminary Press, 1995.

_____. 'Trends in Pentecostal Hermeneutics'. *Paraclete* 3 (Summer 1988), pp. 1-12. Repr. Pages 11-31 in *Scripture and Theology*. Baguio City, Philippines: Asia Theological Seminary Press, 1995.

_____. 'Unity and Diversity: Lucan, Johannine, and Pauline Perspectives on the Holy Spirit'. *Paraclete* 23 (Summer 1989), pp. 15-28. Repr. Pages 169-192 in *Scripture and Theology*. Baguio City, Philippines: Asia Theological Seminary Press, 1995.

Turner, Max. 'Does Luke Believe Reception of the 'Spirit of Prophecy' Makes all 'Prophets'? Inviting Dialogue with Roger Stronstad'. *JEPTA* 20 (2000), pp. 3-24.

2.1.3   Howard Ervin

Dorman, David A. Review of Howard M. Ervin, *Conversion-Initiation and the Baptism in the Holy Spirit*. *Pneuma* 8 (Spring 1986), pp. 60-4.

Ervin, Howard. *Conversion-Initiation and the Baptism in the Holy Spirit: An Engaging Critique of James D.G. Dunn's Baptism in the Holy Spirit*. Peabody: Hendrickson, 1984.

_____. 'An Excursus on Acts 4.8, 31; 13.9'. Paper presented at the annual meeting of the Society for Pentecostal Studies. Pasadena, CA, November 18-20, 1982.

_____. 'Hermeneutics: A Pentecostal Option'. Pages 23-35 in *Essays on Apostolic Themes*. Edited by Paul Elbert. Peabody, MA: Hendrickson, 1995.

_____. *Spirit Baptism: A Biblical Perspective*. Peabody: Hendrickson, 1987.

_____. *These are Not Drunken as Ye Suppose (Acts 2.15)*. Plainsfield, NJ: Logos, 1968.

_____. *This Which Ye See and Hear: A Layman's Guide to the Holy Spirit*. Plainfield: Logos, 1972.

Isgrigg, Daniel D. 'Pilgrimage into Pentecost: The Pneumatological Legacy of Howard M. Ervin'. Paper presented at the annual meeting of the Society for Pentecostal Studies, Tulsa, OK, 2008.

Petts, David. Review of Howard M. Ervin, *Conversion-Initiation and the Baptism in the Holy Spirit*. *JEPTA* 6 (1987), pp. 16-17.

2.1.4   James Shelton

Menzies, Robert. James Shelton's *Mighty in Word and Deed*: A Review Article. *JPT* 2 (1993), pp. 105-15.

Shelton, James. 'A Reply to James D.G. Dunn's 'Baptism in the Spirit: A Response to Pentecostal Scholarship on Luke–Acts'.' *JPT* 4 (1994), pp. 139-43.

_____. 'Epistemology and Authority in the Acts of the Apostles: An Analysis and Test Case Study of Acts 15.1-19'. Paper presented at the annual meeting for the Society of Pentecostal Studies. Springfield, MO, 1999.

_____. ''Filled with the Holy Spirit' and 'Full of the Holy Spirit': Lucan Redactional Phrases'. Pages 81-107 in *Faces of Renewal: Studies in Honor of Stanley M. Horton. Presented on His 70ᵗʰ Birthday*. Edited by Paul Elbert. Peabody: Hendrickson, 1988.

_____. *Mighty in Word and Deed: The Role of the Holy Spirit in Luke–Acts*. Peabody: Hendrickson Publishing, 1991.

Thomas, John Christopher. Review of James Shelton *Mighty in Word and Deed: The Role of the Holy Spirit in Luke–Acts. Pneuma* 15 (Spring 1993), pp. 125-28.

2.1.5   Robert Menzies

Menzies, Robert. 'The Baptist's Prophecy in Lukan Perspective: A Redactional Analysis of Luke 3.16'. Paper presented at the annual meeting of the Society for Pentecostal Studies. Dallas, TX, 1990.

_____. 'Complete Evangelism' (Review of Pedrito U. Maynard-Reid, *Complete Evangelism: The Luke–Acts Model). JPT* 13 (1998), pp. 133-42.

_____. *The Development of Early Christian Pneumatology with Special Reference to Luke–Acts*. Journal for the Study of the New Testament: Supplement Series 54. Sheffield: Sheffield Academic Press, 1991.

_____. 'The Distinctive Character of Luke's Pneumatology'. *Paraclete* 25 (1991), pp. 17-30.

_____. *Empowered for Witness: The Spirit in Luke–Acts*. JPTSup 6. Sheffield: Sheffield Academic Press. 1994.

_____. 'Evidential Tongues: An Essay on Theological Method'. *AJPS* 1 (1998), pp. 1-9.

_____. 'Exegesis: A Reply to James Dunn'. Pages 63-68 in *Spirit and Power*. Edited by William W. Menzies and Robert Menzies. Grand Rapides: Zondervan, 2000.

_____. 'Hermeneutics: Luke's Distinctive Contribution'. Pages 47-62 in *Spirit and Power*. Edited by William W. Menzies and Robert Menzies. Grand Rapides: Zondervan, 2000.

_____. 'Jumping off the Postmodern Bandwagon'. *Pneuma* 16 (1994), pp. 115-20. Repr. Pages 63-68 in *Spirit and Power*. Edited by William W. Menzies and Robert Menzies. Grand Rapides: Zondervan, 2000.

_____ and William W. Menzies. *Spirit and Power: Foundations of Pentecostal Experience*. Grand Rapids: Zondervan, 2000.

Stronstad, Roger. Review of Robert Menzies *Empowered for Witness: The Spirit in Luke–Acts. Pneuma* 20 (Spring 1998), pp. 116-19.

2.1.6   Max Turner

Atkinson, William P. 'The Prior Work of the Spirit in Luke'. *Australasian Pentecostal Studies* 5/6 (2002): n.p. Online: http://aps.webjournals.org/articles/1/04/2002/2991.htm?id={ED4C92D8-DC69-4076-AE07-4F678C173FC0}

Cho, Youngmo. *Spirit and Kingdom in the Writings of Luke and Paul: An Attempt to Reconcile these Concepts*. Paternoster Biblical Monographs. Waynesboro, GA: Paternoster, 2005.

_____. 'Spirit and Kingdom in Luke–Acts: Proclamation as the Primary Role of the Spirit in Relation to the Kingdom of God in Luke–Acts'. *AJPS* 6 (2003), pp. 173-97.

Menzies, Robert. 'Exegesis: A Reply to Max Turner'. Pages 87-108 in *Spirit and Power*. Edited by William W. Menzies and Robert Menzies. Grand Rapids: Zondervan, 2000.

_____. 'Spirit and Power in Luke–Acts: A Response to Max Turner'. *Journal for the Study of the New Testament* 49 (1993), pp. 11-20.

_____. 'The Spirit of Prophecy, Luke–Acts and Pentecostal Theology: A Response to Max Turner' (review of Max Turner, *Power from on High: The Spirit in Israel's Restoration and Witness in Luke–Acts* and *The Holy Spirit and Spiritual Gifts: Then and Now*). *JPT* 15 (October 1999), pp. 49-74.

_____. 'Paul and the Universality of Tongues: A Response to Max Turner'. *AJPS* 2 (1999), pp. 283-95.

Mittelstadt, Martin. 'Review of Youngmo Cho, *Spirit and Kingdom in the Writings of Luke and Paul: An Attempt to Reconcile these Concepts*'. *JPT* 16.2 (2008), pp. 103-12.

Shelton, James. Review of Max Turner, *Power From on High: the Spirit in Israel's Restoration and Witness in Luke–Acts*. *Pneuma* 21 (Spring 1999), pp. 161-62.

Thomas, John Christopher. Max Turner's *The Holy Spirit and Spiritual Gifts: Then and Now* (Carlisle: Paternoster, 1996): An Appreciation and Critique. *JPT* 12 (April 1998), pp. 3-21.

Turner, Max. "Empowerment for Mission'? The Pneumatology of Luke–Acts' (An Appreciation and Critique of James B. Shelton's *Mighty in Word and Deed*). *Vox Evangelica* 24 (1994), pp. 103-22.

_____. *The Holy Spirit and Spiritual Gifts in the New Testament Church*. Peabody: Hendrickson, 1998.

_____. 'Jesus and the Spirit in Lucan Perspective'. *TynB* 32 (1981), pp. 3-42.

_____. 'Interpreting the Samarians of Acts 8: The Waterloo of Pentecostal Soteriology and Pneumatology?' *Pneuma* 23 (2001), pp. 265-86.

_____. 'Luke and the Spirit: Studies in the Significance of Receiving the Spirit in Luke–Acts'. PhD thesis, Cambridge University, 1980.

_____. *Power from on High: The Spirit in Israel's Restoration and Witness in Luke–Acts*. JPTSup 9. Sheffield: Sheffield Academic Press, 1996.

_____. 'Readings and Paradigms: A Response to John Christopher Thomas'. *JPT* 12 (1998), pp. 23-38.

_____. 'Receiving Christ and Receiving the Spirit: In Dialogue with Dawson [reply, J.D. Pawson, pp 33-48]'. *JPT* 15 (1999), pp. 3-31.

_____. 'A Response to the Responses of Menzies and Chan'. *AJPS* 2 (1999), pp. 297-308.

_____. 'The Significance of Receiving the Spirit in Luke–Acts: A Survey of Modern Scholarship'. *TrinJ* 2 (1981), pp. 131-158.

_____. 'Spirit Endowment in Luke–Acts: Some Linguistic Considerations'. *Vox Evangelica* 12 (1981), pp. 45-63.

_____. 'The Spirit and the Power of Jesus' Miracles in the Lucan Conception'. *NovT* 33 (1991), pp. 124-52.

_____. 'The Spirit of Prophecy and the Power of Authoritative Preaching in Luke–Acts: A Question of Origins'. *NTS* 38 (1992), pp. 66-88.

_____. 'Spiritual Gifts: Then and Now'. *Vox Evangelica* 15 (1985), pp. 7-64.

Westfall, Cynthia L. 'Paul's Experience and a Pauline Theology of the Spirit' Pages 123-143 in *Defining Issues in Pentecostalism: Classical and Emergent.* Eugene, OR: Pickwick Publications, 2007.

2.2   Pressing Issues

2.2.1   Cessationism

Elbert, Paul. 'Pentecostal/Charismatic Themes in Luke–Acts at the Evangelical Theological Society: The Battle of Interpretative Method'. *JPT* 12 (2004), pp. 181-215.

Harris, Ralph. *Acts Today: Signs and Wonders of the Holy Spirit.* Springfield: Gospel Publishing House, 1995.

Hertweck, Galen. 'The Holy Spirit in the Eschatology of Acts'. *Paraclete* 16 (Summer 1982), pp. 26-28.

Grudem, Wayne, ed. *Are the Miraculous Gifts for Today? Four Views.* Grand Rapids: Zondervan, 1996.

Kydd, Ronald. *Charismatic Gifts In the Early Church.* Peabody: Hendrickson. 1984.

McDonnell, Kilian and George Montague. *Christian Initiation and the Baptism in the Holy Spirit: Evidence from the First Eight Centuries.* Collegeville: The Liturgical Press, 1991.

_____ (eds.), *Fanning the Flame: What does Baptism in the Holy Spirit Have to Do with Christian Initiation?* Collegeville: The Liturgical Press, 1991.

_____. *Presence, Power, Praise: Documents on the Charismatic Renewal.* 3 vols.; Collegeville: The Liturgical Press, 1980).

Penney, John Michael. 'The Testing of New Testament Prophecy'. *JPT* 10 (1997), pp. 35-84.

Robeck, Cecil M. 'The Gift of Prophecy in Acts and Paul, Part I'. *Studia Biblica et Theologica* 5.1 (1975), pp. 15-38.

_____. 'The Gift of Prophecy in Acts and Paul, Part II'. *Studia Biblica et Theologica* 5.2 (1975), pp. 37-54.

Ruthven, Jon. '"The Imitation of Christ" in Christian Tradition: Its Missing Charismatic Emphasis', *JPT* 16 (2000), pp. 60-77.

_____. *On the Cessation of the Charismata: The Protestant Polemic on Postbiblical Miracles.* JPTSup 3. Sheffield: Sheffield Academic Press, 1993.

Suurmond, Jean-Jacques. *Word & Spirit at Play: Towards a Charismatic Theology.* Grand Rapids: Eerdmans, 1994.

Wadholm, Robert. 'An Apologetic of Signs and Wonders in Luke–Acts'. MA Thesis, Global University, 2005.

_____. 'The Role of Experience in the Interpretation of Miracles Narratives in Lucan Literature'. Paper presented at the annual meeting of the Society for Pentecostal Studies. Cleveland, TN, March 2007.

2.2.2.   Spirit Baptism

Aker, Ben C. 'Acts 2 as Paradigmatic Narrative for Luke's Theology of the Spirit'. Paper presented at the annual meeting of the Evangelical Theological Society, 1998. Online: http://www.agts.edu/faculty/faculty_publications/articles/aker_acts2.pdf.

_____. 'Breathed: A Study on the Biblical Distinction Between Regeneration and Spirit Baptism'. *Paraclete* 17 (Summer 1983), pp. 13-16.

_____. 'New Directions In Lucan Theology: Reflections on Luke 3:21-22 and Some Implications'. Pages 108-27 in *Faces of Renewal*. Edited by Paul Elbert. Peabody: Hendrickson, 1988.

Arrington, French L. 'The Indwelling, Baptism, and Infilling with the Holy Spirit: A differentiation of Terms'. *Pneuma* 3.2 (Fall 1981), pp. 1-10.

Baer, Richard. 'Quaker Silence, Catholic Liturgy, and the Pentecostal Glosso-lalia—Some Functional Similarities'. Pages 150-64 in *Perspectives on the New Pentecostalism*. Edited by Russell P. Spittler. Grand Rapids: Baker, 1976.

Barney, K.D. 'Joel and Peter'. *Paraclete* 19 (Winter 1985), pp. 1-4.

Cartledge, Mark J. 'The Purpose of Glossolalia: A Case Study'. Paper presented at the annual meeting of the Society for Pentecostal Studies. Cleveland, TN, 1998.

Chan, Simon. 'Evidential Glossolalia and the Doctrine of Subsequence'. *AJPS* 2 (1999), pp. 195-211.

_____. 'The Language Game of Glossolalia, Or Making Sense of the 'Initial Evidence'.' Pages 80-95 in *Pentecostalism in Context: Essays in Honor of William W. Menzies*. Edited by Wonsuk Ma and Robert Menzies. JPTSup 11. Sheffield: Sheffield Academic Press, 1997.

Chuen, Lim Yeu. 'Acts 10: A Gentile Model For Pentecostal Experience'. Paper presented and published in pages 73-84 in *Contemporary Issues in Pentecostal Theology* from the First Annual Pentecostal Lectureship Series. Baguio City: APTS, 1993. Repr. *AJPS* 1 (1998), pp. 1-9.

Cheung, Tak-Ming. ' Understandings of Spirit-Baptism'. *JPT* 8 (April 1996), pp. 115-128.

Cotton, Roger. 'The Pentecostal Significance of Numbers 11'. *JPT* 10 (2001), pp. 3-10.

Cox, R.L. 'Is Acts 2.4 Divisive?' *Paraclete* 7 (Winter 1973), pp. 11-14.

Dorman, David A. 'The Purpose of Empowerment in the Christian Life'. *Pneuma* 7 (Fall 1985), pp. 147-65.

Elbert, Paul. 'Towards an Understanding of Luke's Expectations for Theophilus Regarding the Lukan Gift of the Holy Spirit'. Paper presented at the annual meeting of the Society for Pentecostal Studies. Kirkland, WA, 2000.

Edwards, James. 'Initial Evidence of Holy Spirit Baptism and Pentecostal Type-Scenes in Acts'. Paper presented at the annual meeting of the Society for Pentecostal Studies. South Hamilton, MA, 1984.

Everts, Jenny. 'Tongues or Languages? Contextual Consistency in the Translation of Acts 2'. *JPT* 4 (April 1994), pp. 71-80.

Flokstra, Gerald. 'Sources for the Initial Evidence Discussion: A Bibliographic Essay'. *AJPS* 2.2 (1999), pp. 243-59.

Giblet, Jean. 'Baptism in the Spirit in the Acts of the Apostles' *One in Christ: A Catholic Ecumenical Review* 10.2 (1974), pp. 162-71.

Graves, Robert W. 'Use of *gar* in Acts 10.46'. *Paraclete* 22 (Spring 1988), pp. 15-18.

_____. 'The Jerusalem Council and the Gentile Pentecost'. *Paraclete* 18 (Winter 1984), pp. 4-8.

Grimes, L.R. 'When or After?' *Paraclete* 20 (Summer 1986), pp. 26-30.

Hamill, James E. 'The Pentecostal Experience: Acts 2.37-41'. *Paraclete* 14 (1980), pp. 1-3.

Hildebrandt, Wilf. *An Old Testament Theology of the Spirit of God.* Peabody: Hendrickson, 1995.

Ho, Melvin. 'A Comparison of Glossolalia in Acts and Corinthians'. *Paraclete* 20 (1986), pp. 15-19.

Holdcroft, L. Thomas. *The Holy Spirit: A Pentecostal Interpretation.* Springfield: Gospel Publishing House, 1962.

_____. 'Receiving the Baptism in the Holy Spirit'. *Paraclete* 14 (Winter 1980), pp. 4-7.

Holman, Charles. 'Spirit Reception in Acts and Paul'. Paper presented at the annual meeting of the Society for Pentecostal Studies. Toronto, ON, March 7-9, 1996.

Horner, Jerry. 'The Credibility and the Eschatology of Peter's Speech at Pentecost'. *Pneuma* 2 (Spring 1980), pp. 22-31.

Horton, Harold. *The Baptism in the Holy Spirit: A Challenge to Whole-Hearted Seekers After God.* Nottingham: Assemblies of God Publishing House, 1961.

Horton, Stanley. *What The Bible Says About The Holy Spirit.* Springfield: Gospel Publishing House, 1976.

Hunter, Harold. *Spirit Baptism: A Pentecostal Perspective.* Lanham: University Press of America, 1983.

Hurtado, Larry. 'Normal, But Not a Norm: 'Initial Evidence' and the New Testament'. Pages 189-201 in *Initial Evidence: Historical and Biblical Perspectives on the Pentecostal Doctrine of Spirit Baptism.* Edited by Gary McGee. Peabody: Hendrickson, 1991.

Lee, Mark. 'An Evangelical Dialogue on Luke, Salvation and Spirit Baptism'. *Pneuma* 26 (2004), pp. 81-98.

Leeper, Gregory J. 'The Nature of the Pentecostal Gift with Special Reference to Numbers 11 and Acts 2'. *AJPS* 6 (2003), pp. 23-38.

Levang, R.K. 'The Content of an Utterance in Tongues'. *Paraclete* 23 (Winter 1989), pp. 14-20.

Linzey, Verna M. *The Baptism with the Holy Spirit: The Reception of the Holy Spirit as Confirmed by Speaking in Tongues.* Longwood, FL: Xulon Press, 2004.

Ma, Wonsuk. 'The Empowerment of the Spirit of God in Luke–Acts: An Old Testament Perspective'. Pages 28-40 in *The Spirit and Spirituality: Essays in Honor of Russell P. Spittler.* JPTSup 24. Edited by Wonsuk Ma and Robert P. Menzies. London: T & T Clark, 2004.

Macchia, Frank. 'Sighs Too Deep for Words: Toward a Theology of Glossolalia'. *JPT* 1 (1992), pp. 47-72.

_____. 'Groans Too Deep for Words: Toward a Theology of Tongues as Initial Evidence'. *AJPS* 1.2 (1998), pp. 149-73.

MacDonald, William. *Glossolalia in the New Testament.* Springfield: Gospel Publishing House, 1964.

McGee, Gary, ed. *Initial Evidence: Historical and Biblical Perspectives on the Pentecostal Doctrine of Spirit Baptism.* Peabody: Hendrickson Publishing, 1991.

Menzies, Glen. 'Pre-Lucan Occurrences of the Phrase "Tongues of Fire".' *Pneuma* 22 (2000), pp. 27-60.

Menzies, Robert. 'Spirit Baptism and Spiritual Gifts'. Pages 48-59 in *Pentecostalism in Context: Essays in Honor of William W. Menzies.* Edited by Wonsuk Ma and Robert Menzies. JPTSup 11. Sheffield: Sheffield Academic Press, 1997.

Menzies, William. 'The Initial Evidence Issue: A Pentecostal Response'. *AJPS* 2 (1999), pp. 261-78.

Palma, Anthony D. *Baptism in the Holy Spirit.* Springfield, Gospel Publishing House, 1999.

*Patillon, Michael. *Aelius Théon Progymnasmata: Texte établi et traduit.* Collection des Universités de France. Paris: Les Belles Lettres, 1997.

Petts, David. *The Baptism in the Holy Spirit in Relation to Christian Initiation.* MTh diss., Nottingham University, 1984.

Robeck, Cecil M., Jr. 'Baptism in the Holy Spirit: Its Purpose(s)'. *Pneuma* 7 (Fall 1985), pp. 83-86.

_____. 'The Church: A Unique Movement of the Spirit' *Paraclete* 16 (1982), pp. 1-4.

Wessels, Roland. 'How is the Baptism in the Holy Spirit to be Distinguished from Receiving the Spirit at Conversion? A Problem in the Assemblies of God'. Paper presented at the annual meeting of the Society for Pentecostal Studies. Lakeland, FL, November 7-9, 1991.

Williams, J. Rodman. 'Pentecostal Spirituality'. *One in Christ: A Catholic Ecumenical Review* 10.2 (1974), pp. 180-92.

2.2.3   Hermeneutics

Aker, Ben. 'Streams in the Desert: Sources on the Spirit for Pentecostal Preachers'. *Encounter: Journal for Pentecostal Ministry* 1 (2004), pp. 1-5.

Arrington, French. 'The Use of the Bible by Pentecostals'. *Pneuma* 16 (1994), pp. 101-17.

Camery-Hoggatt, Jerry. *Speaking of God: Reading and Preaching the Word of God.* Peabody: Hendrickson, 1995.

Cargal, Timothy. 'Beyond the Fundamentalist-Modernist Controversy: Pentecostals and Hermeneutics in a Postmodern Age'. *Pneuma* 15 (1993), pp. 163-87.

Dempster, Murray W. 'Paradigm Shifts and Hermeneutics: Confronting Issues Old and New'. *Pneuma* 15 (1993), pp. 129-35.

Elbert, Paul. 'Pentecostal/Charismatic Themes in Luke–Acts at the Evangelical Theological Society: The Battle of Interpretative Method'. *JPT* 12.2 (2004), pp. 181-215.

_____. 'Possible Literary Links Between Luke–Acts and Pauline Letters Regarding Spirit-Language'. Pages 226-54 in *Intertextuality in the New Testament: Explorations of Theory and Practice*. Edited by T. L. Brodie, D. R. MacDonald, and S. E. Porter. New Testament Monographs 16. Sheffield: Sheffield-Phoenix Press, 2006.

Jacobsen, Douglas. 'Pentecostal Hermeneutics in Comparative Perspective'. Paper presented at the annual meeting of the Society for Pentecostal Studies. Cleveland, TN, March 12-14, 1998.

Johnston, Robert K. 'Pentecostalism and Theological Hermeneutics: Evangelical Options'. *Pneuma* 6 (Spring 1984), pp. 51-66.

Kärkkäinen, Veli-Matti. 'Reading in the Spirit in Which It Was Written: Pentecostal Bible Reading in Dialogue with Catholic Interpretation'. Paper presented at the annual meeting of the Society for Pentecostal Studies. Cleveland, TN, March 12-14, 1998.

Kydd, Ronald A. 'A Prolegomenon to Pentecostal Theologizing'. Paper presented at the annual meeting of the Society for Pentecostal Studies. Cleveland, TN, March 12-14, 1998.

Lewis, Paul. 'Reflections for Pentecostal Charismatic Research'. *CPCR* 12 (February, 2003): www.pctii. org/cyberj/index.html.

_____. 'Toward a Pentecostal Epistemology: The Role of Experience in Pentecostal Hermeneutics'. *The Spirit and Church* 2 (2000), pp. 95-125.

Menzies, Robert. 'Hermeneutics: Luke's Distinctive Contribution'. Pages 37-46 in *Spirit and Power: Foundations of Pentecostal Experience*. Edited by William and Robert Menzies. Grand Rapids: Zondervan, 2000.

_____. 'Hermeneutics: The Quiet Revolution'. Pages 87-108 in *Spirit and Power: Foundations of Pentecostal Experience*. Edited by William W. Menzies and Robert Menzies. Grand Rapids: Zondervan, 2000.

Menzies, William. 'The Methodology of Pentecostal Theology: An Essay on Hermeneutics'. Pages 1-14 in *Essays on Apostolic Themes*. Edited by Paul Elbert. Peabody: Hendrickson, 1985.

Sheppard, Gerald. 'Biblical Interpretation after Gadamer'. *Pneuma* 16 (1994), pp. 121-41.

_____. 'Pentecostals and the Hermeneutics of Dispensationalism: The Anatomy of an Uneasy Relationship'. *Pneuma* 6 (1984), pp. 5-33.

Spittler, Russell. 'Scripture and the Theological Enterprise: View from a Big Canoe'. Pages 56-77, 223-6 in *The Use of the Bible in Theology: Evangelical Options*. Edited by Robert Johnston. Atlanta: John Knox Press, 1985.

3. Stage 3—Out of the Shadows

3.1 The Triumph of Narrative Theology

Archer, Kenneth J. 'Early Pentecostal Biblical Interpretation'. Paper presented at the annual meeting of the Society for Pentecostal Studies. Kirkland, WA, March 16-18, 2000. Revised and reprinted as 'Early Pentecostal Biblical Interpretation: Blurring the Boundaries'. *JPT* 18 (2001), pp. 32-70.

_____. *A Pentecostal Hermeneutic for the Twenty-First Century: Spirit, Scripture and Community*. JPTSup 6. London/New York: T & T Clark International, 2004.

_____. 'A Pentecostal Hermeneutical Strategy: Spirit, Community and Scripture'. Paper presented at the annual meeting of the Society for Pentecostal Studies. Wilmore, KY, March 20-22, 2003.

_____. 'Pentecostal Story: The Hermeneutical Filter for the Making of Meaning'. *Pneuma* 26 (Spring 2004), pp. 36-59

Arrington, French. *The Acts of the Apostles: Introduction, Translation and Commentary*. Peabody, MA: Hendrickson, 1988.

Dowd, Michael B. 'Contours of a Narrative Pentecostal Theology and Practice'. Paper presented at the annual meeting of the Society for Pentecostal Studies. Gaithersburg, MD, November, 1985.

Elbert, Paul. 'Acts 2.38c Reconsidered: The Syntax of Imperative-Future and Imperative-Present Participle Combinations in Luke–Acts and Implications in Light of the Narrative-Rhetorical Tradition'. Paper presented at the International Meeting of the Society of Biblical Literature. Rome, 2001.

_____. 'Acts of the Holy Spirit: Hermeneutical and Historigraphical Reflections'. *Refleks: Med Karismatisk Kristendom i Focus* 4/1 (2005), pp. 48-97.

_____. 'An Observation on Luke's Composition and Narrative Style of Questions'. *CBQ* 66 (2003), pp. 98-109.

_____. 'Luke's Fulfillment of Prophecy Theme: Introductory Exploration of Joel and the Last Days'. Paper presented at the annual meeting of the Society for Pentecostal Studies. Milwaukee, WI, March 11-13, 2004.

_____. 'Paul of the Miletus Speech and 1 Thessalonians: Critique and Considerations'. *ZNW* 95/2 (2004), pp. 258-68.

_____. 'Pentecostal/Charismatic Themes in Luke–Acts at the Evangelical Theological Society: The Battle of Interpretative Method'. *JPT* 12.2 (2004), pp. 181-215.

_____. 'Possible Literary Links Between Luke–Acts and Pauline Letters Regarding Spirit-Language'. Pages 226-54 in *Intertextuality in the New Testament: Explorations of Theory and Practice*. Edited by T.L. Brodie, D. R. MacDonald, and S. E. Porter. New Testament Monographs 16. Sheffield: Sheffield University Press, 2006.

_____. 'Probable Literary Connections Between Luke–Acts and Pauline Letters Regarding Spirit-Language'. Paper presented at the annual meeting of the Society for Pentecostal Studies. Pasadena, CA, March 23-25, 2006.

_____. 'Toward a Pentecostal Hermeneutic: Observations on Archer's Progressive Proposal'. *AJPS* 9.2 (2006), pp. 320-28.

Ellington, Scott. 'History, Story and Testimony: Locating Truth in a Pentecostal Hermeneutic'. Paper presented at the annual meeting of the Society for Pentecostal Studies. Kirkland, WA, March 16-18, 2000.

Gause, R. Hollis. 'The Lukan Transfiguration Account: Luke's Pre-Crucifixion Presentation of the Exalted Lord in the Glory of the Kingdom of God'. Ph.D. diss., Emory University, 1975.

Goldingay, John. 'Biblical Story and the Way It Shapes Our Story'. Paper presented that the annual meeting of the European Pentecostal Theological Association. Nantwich, England, 1997. Published in *JEPTA* 17 (1997), pp. 5-15.

Kurz, William S. 'Acts 3.19-26 as a Test of the Role of Eschatology in Lukan Christology'. *Society of Biblical Literature Seminar Papers* 16 (1977), pp. 309-23.

_____. 'Effects of Variant Narrators in Acts 10-11'. *NTS* 43 (1997), ppl 570-86.

_____. *Farewell Addresses in the New Testament*. Zacchaeus Studies: New Testament. Collegeville: Liturgical Press, 1990.

_____. *Following Jesus: A Disciple's Guide to Luke and Acts*. Rev. ed. Ann Arbor: Servant Books, 2003.

_____. 'The Function of Christological Proof from Prophecy for Luke and Justin'. PhD diss., Yale University, 1976.

_____ and Luke Timothy Johnson. *The Future of Catholic Biblical Scholarship: A Constructive Conversation*. Grand Rapids: Eerdmans, 2002.

_____. 'Hellenistic Rhetoric in the Christological Proof of Luke–Acts'. *CBQ* 42 (1980), pp. 171-95.

_____. 'Intertextual Use of Sirach 48.1-16 in Plotting Luke–Acts'. Pages 308-24 in *The Gospels and Scriptures of Israel*. Edited by Craig A. Evans and W. Richard Stegne. Journal for the Study of New Testament Supplement Series 104. Sheffield, England: Sheffield Academic Press, 1994.

_____. 'Journey with Jesus (in Luke)'. *God's Word Today* 3.12 (1981), pp. 37-43. Partial repr., 'Journey with Jesus (in Luke)'. *The Sooner Catholic* 10/26 (December 18, 1983), p. 9.

_____. 'Luke 3.23-38 and Greco-Roman and Biblical Genealogies'. Pages 169-87 in *Luke- Acts: New Perspectives from the Society of Biblical Literature Seminar*. Edited by Charles H. Talbert. New York: Crossroad, 1984.

_____. 'Luke 22:14-38 and Greco-Roman and Biblical Farewell Addresses'. *JBL* 104/2 (1985), pp. 251-68.

_____. 'Luke–Acts'. Pages 268-271 in *New Catholic Encyclopedia: Volume XVIII*. 2nd ed. Edited by Berard L. Marthaler, et al. New Catholic Dictionary Supplemental Series 3. Farmington Hills, Mich.: Gale Group, 2002.

_____. 'Luke–Acts and Historiography in the Greek Bible'. *Society of Biblical Literature Seminar Papers* 19 (1980), pp. 283-300.

_____. 'Luke the Artist'. *Continuum* 1 (Autumn 1990), pp. 180-182.

_____. 'Narrative Approaches to Luke–Acts'. *Biblica* 68.2 (1987), pp. 195-220.

_____. 'Narrative Models for Imitation in Luke–Acts'. Pages 171-189 in *Greeks, Romans, and Christians: Essays in Honor of Abraham J. Malherbe*. Edited by David l. Balch, Wayne A, Meeks, Everett Ferguson. Minneapolis: Fortress, 1990.

_____. 'The Open-Ended Nature of Luke and Acts as Inviting Canonical Actualization'. *Neotestamentica* 31.2 (1997), pp. 289-308.

_____. 'The Problem with Prophecy—Part I'. *New Covenant* 23.2 (September 1993), pp. 11-13

_____. 'The Problem with Prophecy—Part II: Every Prophecy Must Be Discerned'. *New Covenant* 23.3 (October 1993), pp. 23-26.

_____. 'Promise and Fulfillment in Hellenistic Jewish Narratives and in Luke and Acts'. Pages 147-170 in *Jesus and the Heritage of Israel: Luke's Narrative Claim upon Israel's Legacy*. Edited by David P. Moessner. Vol. 1 of *Luke the Interpreter of Israel*. Harrisburg, PA: Trinity Press International, 1999.

_____. *Reading the Bible as God's Own Story: A Catholic Approach for Bringing Scripture to Life*. Ijamsville, MD: Word Among Us Press, 2007.

_____. *Reading Luke–Acts: Dynamics of Biblical Narrative*. Louisville: Westminster/John Knox Press, 1993.

Kydd, Ronald. *I'm Still There! A Reaffirmation of Tongues as the Initial Evidence of the Baptism in the Holy Spirit*. Toronto: Pentecostal Assemblies of Canada, 1977.

McNally, Randal G. 'Text, Narrative and Pentecostal Understanding: A Reading of Paul Ricoeur'. Paper presented at the annual meeting of the Society for Pentecostal Studies. Springfield, MO, November 12-14, 1992.

McGee, Gary. '"More Than Evangelical": The Challenge of the Evolving Identity of the Assemblies of God'. Pages 35-45 in *Church, Identity and Change: Theology and Denominational Structures in Unsettled Times*. Edited by David Roozen & James Nieman. Grand Rapids: Eerdmans, 2005.

Menzies, William. 'Coming to Terms with an Evangelical Heritage: Pentecostals and the Issue of Subsequence'. Pages 97-108 in *Contemporary Issues in Pentecostal Theology*. Paper presented at the First Annual Pentecostal Lectureship Series. Baguio City: Asia Pacific Theological Seminary, 1993.

*Patillon, Michael. *Aelius Théon Progymnasmata: Texte établi et traduit*. Collection des Universités de France; Paris: Les Belles Lettres, 1997.

Shelton, James. 'Epistemology and Authority in the Acts of the Apostles: An Analysis and Test Case Study of Acts 15:1-29'. Paper presented at the annual meeting of the Society for Pentecostal Studies. Springfield, MO, March 11-13, 1999.

Thomas, John Christopher. 'Reading the Bible from Our Tradition: A Pentecostal Test Case'. Pages 108-122 in *Between Two Horizons: Spanning New Testament Studies and Systematic Theology*. Edited by Joel Green and Max Turner. Grand Rapids: Eerdmans, 2000.

_____. 'Women, Pentecostals and the Bible: An Experiment in Pentecostal Hermeneutics', *JPT* 5 (1994), pp. 41-56.

*Walton, Steve. *Leadership and Lifestyle: The Portrait of Paul in the Miletus Speech and 1 Thessalonians*. Society for New Testament Studies Monograph Series 108. Cambridge: Cambridge University Press, 2000.

3.2   Missiology

Amstutz, John. 'Beyond Pentecost: A Study of Some Sociological Dimensions of New Testament Growth From the Book of Acts'. Pages 208-25 in *Essays on Apostolic Themes: Studies in Honor of Howard M. Ervin*. Peabody: Hendrickson, 1990.

Bagalawis, Manuel A. '"Power" in Acts 1:8; Effective Witnessing Through Signs and Wonders'. *Asian Journal of Mission* 3 (2001), pp. 1-13.

Barclift, M.A. 'Supernatural Guidance in Acts 16:6-10'. *Paraclete* 18 (Fall 1984), pp. 8-10.

Brooks, M.P. 'The Spirit and Mission in Acts'. *Paraclete* 25 (Winter 1991), pp. 14-23.

Charette, Blaine. 'Restoring the Kingdom to Israel: Kingdom and Spirit in Luke's Thought'. Paper presented at the annual meeting of the Society for Pentecostal Studies. Cleveland, TN, March 2007.

_____. "Tongues as of Fire': Judgment as a Function of Glossolalia in Luke's Thought'. Paper presented at the annual meeting of the Society for Pentecostal Studies. Tulsa, OK, March 8-10, 2001.

Cho, Youngmo. 'Spirit and Kingdom in Luke–Acts: Proclamation as the Primary Role of the Spirit in Relation to the Kingdom of God in Luke–Acts'. *AJPS* 6 (2003), pp. 173-97.

Cheum, David Chee Wai. 'The Spirit and Mission in the Book of Acts'. *Journal of Asian Mission* 6.1 (2004), pp. 3-15.

dela Cruz, Roli G. 'Luke's Application of Joel 2:28-32 in Peter's Sermon in Acts 2'. *CPCR* 4 (1998): np. Online: http://www.pctii.org/cyberj/cyberj4/cruz.html.

Dempster, Murray W. 'Pentecostal Social Concern and the Biblical Mandate of Social Justice'. *Pneuma* 9 (Fall 1987), pp. 129-53.

Grizzle, Trevor. 'Purity and Power According to the Acts of the Apostles'. Paper presented at the annual meeting of the Society for Pentecostal Studies. Cleveland, TN, March 12-14, 1998.

Hertweck, G.F. 'The Holy Spirit in the Eschatology of Acts'. *Paraclete* 16 (1982), pp. 26-28.

Hodges, M.L. 'Acts 1--Bridge to an Apostolic Ministry'. *Paraclete* 12 (Summer 1978), pp. 29-31.

Holman, Charles L. 'Isaiah's Servant of Yahweh and Christian Mission in Luke–Acts'. Paper presented at the annual meeting of the Society for Pentecostal Studies. Kirkland, WA, March 16-18, 2000.

May, F.J. *The Book of Acts and Church Growth*. Cleveland, TN: Pathway Press, 1990.

Munyon, Tim. 'Two Criteria for Revival in Acts 1-8'. *Paraclete* 25 (Winter 1991), pp. 10-13.

Parker, David. 'Situating the Spirit in the Preface of the Acts Narrative'. *Australasian Pentecostal Studies* 5/6 (2006): np. Online: http://aps.webjournals.org/articles/1/03/2006/6664.htm?id={040F588A-17ED-484A-93CD-51C5827A B5D9}.

Penney, John Michael. *The Missionary Emphasis of Lukan Pneumatology*. JPTSup 12. Sheffield: Sheffield Academic Press, 1997.

Poirier, John. 'The Day of Pentecost as the Birthday of the Church'. Paper presented at the annual meeting of the Society for Pentecostal Studies. Cleveland, TN, March 2007.

Postlethwait, D. Michael. 'The Soteriological Language and Experience of Luke's Gospel as They Relate to a Lukan Pneumatology and its Impact on Pentecostal Theology'. Paper presented at the annual meeting of the Society for Pentecostal Studies. Pasadena, CA, March 23-25, 2006.

Roberts, Jerry. *Discerning God's Will: Spiritual Guidance from an Acts-Luke Perspective*. Kearney, NB: Morris Publishing, 2005.

Scheffer, Norman. 'The Biblical Imperative for Church Planting'. *African Journal of Pentecostal Studies* 2 (2004), pp. 23-34.

Simpson, A.B. *The Fourfold Gospel*. Harrisburg, PA: Christian Publications, 1887.

Stacey, Jeff. 'Does the Historical Phenomenon of Revival Have a Recognizable 'Pattern' of Characteristic, Observable Features?' *Australasian Pentecostal Studies*

8 (2004): np. Online: http://aps.webjournals. org/Issues.asp?index=216&id= {040F588A-17ED-484A-93CD-51C5827AB5D9}

Tipei, John F. 'The Function of Laying on of Hands in the New Testament'. *JEPTA* 20 (2000), pp. 93-115.

Tipei, John F. *The Laying on of Hands in the New Testament: Its Significance, Techniques, and Effects*. Lanham, MD: University Press of America, 2008.

Wagner, C. Peter. *Spreading the Fire: A New Look at Acts—God's Training Manual for Every Christian*. Vol. 1 of *Acts of the Holy Spirit*. Ventura, Calif.: Regal Publishing, 1994.

Williams, L. 'The Basic Pattern for Church Growth'. *Paraclete* 22 (Spring 1988), pp. 27-30.

Wilson, Mark. 'The Role of the Holy Spirit in Paul's Ministry Journeys'. Paper presented at the annual meeting of the Society for Pentecostal Studies. Wilmore, KY, March 20-22, 2003.

3.3   Healing & Exorcism

Elbert, Paul. A Review of John Christopher Thomas, *The Devil, Disease and Deliverance: Origins of Illness in New Testament Thought*. *AJPS* 3 (2000), pp. 139-54.

Ervin, Howard M. *Healing: Sign of the Kingdom*. Peabody, Mass.: Hendrickson, 2002.

Gen, Raymond M. 'The Phenomena of Miracles and Divine Infliction in Luke–Acts: Their Theological Significance'. *Pneuma* 11 (Fall 1989), pp. 3-19.

Grant, W. V. *Luke was a Physician and Six Other Deliverance Sermons*. Dallas: the Author, n.d.

Hayford, Jack W. 'The Finger of God'. Pages 199-254 in *A Reader on the Holy Spirit: Anointing, Equipping and Empowering for Service*. Edited by Eloise Clarno. Los Angeles: International Church of the Foursquare Gospel, 1993.

Pilch, John J. *Visions and Healing in the Acts of the Apostles: How the Early Believers Experienced God*. Collegeville, MN: Liturgical Press, 2004.

Powell, T.M. 'The Spirit of Healing'. *Paraclete* 18 (Winter 1984), pp. 9-11.

Thomas, John Christopher. *The Devil, Disease and Deliverance: Origins of Illness in New Testament Thought*. JPTSup 13. Sheffield: Sheffield Academic Press, 1998.

Twelftree, Graham. 'Beelzebub'. Pages 417-8 in vol. 1 of *New Interpreter's Dictionary of the Bible*. Edited by Katharine D. Sakenfeld. 5 vols. Nashville, TN: Abingdon, 2006.

_____. 'Blasphemy'. 75-77 in *Dictionary of Jesus and the Gospels*. Edited by Joel B Green, Scot McKnight, and I. Howard Marshall. Downers Grove, IL: Intervarsity Press, 1992.

_____. 'But What is Exorcism?' *New Times* (March 1993), p. 14.

_____. *Christ Triumphant: Exorcism Then and Now*. London: Hodder and Stoughton, 1984.

_____. 'Church Agenda: The Lucan Perspective'. Pages 59-73 in *Evangelism and Preaching in Secular Australia: Essays in Honour of Arthur Jackson*. Edited by R. Dean Drayton. Melbourne: JBCE, 1989.

_____. 'Demon, Devil, Satan'. 163-172 in *Dictionary of Jesus and the Gospels*. Edited by Joel B Green, Scot McKnight, and I. Howard Marshall. Downers Grove, IL: Intervarsity Press, 1992.

_____. 'The Demonic'. Pages 296-7 in *New Dictionary of Christian Ethics and Pastoral Theology*. Edited by David J. Atkinson and David Field. Downers Grove, IL: Intervarsity Press, 1995.

_____ and James Dunn. 'Demon Possession and Exorcism in the New Testament'. *Churchman* 94 (1980), pp. 10-25. Repr., Pages 170-86 in vol. 2 of *The Christ and the Spirit: Collected Essays of James D.G. Dunn*. 2 vols. Edinburgh: T & T Clark, 1998.

_____. 'Devil and Demons'. Pages 196-98 in *New Dictionary of Theology*. Edited by Sinclair B. Ferguson and David F. Wright. Downers Grove: Intervarsity Press, 1988.

_____. 'Exorcism'. Pages 244-6 in *New Dictionary of Theology*. Edited by Sinclair B. Ferguson and David F. Wright. Downers Grove: Intervarsity Press, 1988.

_____. 'Exorcism in the New Testament and in Contemporary Ministry: A Reader's Guide'. *Christian Book Newsletter* 5 (8 November 1987), pp. 7-11.

_____. 'The History of Miracles in the History of Jesus'. Pages 191-208 in *The Face of New Testament Studies: A Survey of Recent Research*. Edited by Scot McKnight and Grant R. Osborne. Grand Rapids: Baker Academic, 2004.

_____. 'If I Cast Out Demons?' Pages 361-400 in *The Miracles of Jesus*. Gospel Perspectives 6. Edited by David Wenham and Craig Blomberg. Sheffield: Sheffield Academic Press, 1986.

_____. *In The Name of Jesus: Exorcism Among Early Christians*. Grand Rapids: Baker Academic, 2007.

_____. 'Jesus as an Exorcist'. *New Times* (May 1987), pp. 9-10.

_____. 'Jesus the Exorcist and Ancient Magic'. Pages 57-86 in *A Kind of Magic: Understanding Magic in the New Testament and its Religious Environment*. Edited by Michael Labahn and Bert Jan Lietaert Peerbolte. Library of New Testament Studies 306. New York: T&T Clark, 2007.

_____. *Jesus the Exorcist: A Contribution to the Study of the Historical Jesus*. Peabody, Mass.: Hendrickson, 1993.

_____. *Jesus the Miracle Worker: A Historical and Theological Study*. Downers Grove: InterVarsity, 1999.

_____ and James Dunn. 'La possession démoniaque et l'exorcisme dans le Nouveau Testament', *Hokhma* 51 (1992), pp. 34-52.

_____'.The Miracles of Jesus: Marginal or Mainstream?' *Journal for the Study of the Historical Jesus* 1 (2003), pp. 104-24.

_____. 'The Place of Exorcism in Contemporary Ministry'. *Anvil* 5 (1988), pp. 133-50.

_____. 'The Place of Exorcism in Contemporary Ministry'. *St Mark's Review* 127 (September 1986), pp. 25-39.

_____. 'Prayer and the Coming of the Spirit in Acts'. *Expository Times* 117 (2006), pp. 271-76.

_____. 'Signs and Wonders'. Pages 775-81 in *New Dictionary of Biblical Theology*. Edited by T. D. Alexander and Brian S. Rosner. Downers Grove: Intervarsity Press, 2000.

_____. 'Spiritual Powers'. Pages 796-802 in *New Dictionary of Biblical Theology*. Edited by T.D. Alexander and Brian S. Rosner. Downers Grove: Intervarsity Press, 2000.

_____. 'Temptation of Jesus'. Pages 821-27 in *Dictionary of Jesus and the Gospels*. Edited by Joel B Green, Scot McKnight, and I. Howard Marshall. Downers Grove, IL: Intervarsity Press, 1992.

_____. 'Testing'. Pages 814-15 in *New Dictionary of Biblical Theology*. Edited by T.D. Alexander and Brian S. Rosner. Downers Grove: Intervarsity Press, 2000.

Warrington, Keith. 'Healing Then: Healing Now'. Paper presented at the annual meeting of the Society for Pentecostal Studies. Milwaukee, WI, March 11-13, 2004.

Wilson, John A. 'Ministry to the Sick as Described in the Acts of the Apostles'. Paper presented at the annual meeting of the Society for Pentecostal Studies. Virginia Beach, VA, November 12-14, 1987.

Yong, Amos. 'Academic Glossolalia? Pentecostal Scholarship, Multi-disciplinarity, and the Science-Religion Conversation'. *JPT* 14.1 (2005), pp. 63-82.

3.4 Women

Alexander, Estelda and Amos Yong (eds.), *Philip's Daughters: Women in Pentecostal-Charismatic Leadership*. Princeton Theological Monograph Series 104. Eugene, OR: Pickwick Publications, 2009.

Arlandson, James Malcolm. *Women, Class, and Society in Early Christianity: Models from Luke–Acts*. Peabody: Hendrickson, 1997.

Cunningham, Loren and David Joel Hamilton. *Why Not Women? A Fresh Look at Scripture on Women in Missions, Ministry and Leadership*. Seattle: YWAM Publishing, 2000.

Elbert, Paul. *Pastoral Letter to Theo: An Introduction to Interpretation and Women's Ministries*. Eugene, OR: Wipf & Stock, 2008.

Estrada, Nelson P. 'Praise for Promise Fulfilled: A Study on the Significance of the Anna the Prophetess Pericope'. *AJPS* 2 (1999), pp. 5-18.

Gill, Deborah and Barbara Cavaness. *God's Women: Then and Now*. Springfield, MO: Gospel Publishing House, 2004.

General Presbytery of the Assemblies of God. 'The Role of Women in Ministry as Described in Holy Scripture'. *Assemblies of God Position Papers*. Springfield, MO: General Council of the Assemblies of God, 1990. Online: http://ag.org /top/Beliefs/Position_Papers/pp_downloads/pp_4191_women_ministry. pdf.

Powers, Janet Everts. '"Your Daughters Shall Prophesy" Pentecostal Hermeneutics and the Empowerment of Women'. Pages 313-37 in *The Globalization of Pentecostalism: A Religion Made to Travel*. Edited by Murray Dempster, Byron Klaus, and Douglas Petersen. Irvine, CA: Regnum Press, 1999.

Thomas, John Christopher. 'Women, Pentecostals and the Bible: An Experiment in Pentecostal Hermeneutics'. *JPT* 5 (1994), pp. 41-56.

Wacker, Grant. *Heaven Below: Early Pentecostals an American Culture*. Cambridge: Harvard University Press, 2001.

*Webb, William. *Slaves, Women & Homosexuals: Exploring the Hermeneutics of Cultural Analysis*. Downers Grove: IVP: 2000.

Williamson, Rick L. 'Female/Male Pairs in Luke: Gender Balance in Proclaiming the Word of God'. Paper presented at the annual meeting of the Society for Pentecostal Studies. Cleveland, TN, March 12-14, 1998.

3.5 Spiritual Formation

Choi, M. H. 'An Examination of the Existing Paradigm for the 21st Century Pentecostal Spirituality and Movement'. Paper presented at the annual meeting of the Society for Pentecostal Studies. Tulsa, OK, March 8-10, 2001.

Cullen, Peter. 'Euphoria, Praise and Thanksgiving: Rejoicing in the Spirit in Luke–Acts'. *JPT* 6 (1995), pp. 13-24.

Ford, J. Massyngberde. 'The Social and Political Implications of the Miraculous in Acts'. Pages 137-160 in *Faces of Renewal*. Edited by Paul Elbert. Peabody: Hendrickson, 1988.

Hertweck, G. F. 'The Holy Spirit in the Eschatology of Acts'. *Paraclete* 16 (1982), pp. 26-28.

Kim, Dongsoo. 'Lukan Pentecostal Theology of Prayer: Is Persistent Prayer Not Biblical?' *AJPS* 7 (2004), pp. 205-17.

Ruthven, John. 'Jesus as Rabbi: A Mimesis Christology: The Charismatic Pattern of Discipleship in the New Testament'. Paper presented at the annual meeting of the Society for Pentecostal Studies. Cleveland, TN, March 12-14, 1998.

Shelton, James B. 'Epistemology and Authority in the Acts of the Apostles; An Analysis and Test Case Study of Acts 15:1-19'. Paper presented at the annual meeting of the Society for Pentecostal Studies. Springfield, MO, March 11-13, 1999.

Thomas, John Christopher. 'The Charismatic Structure of Acts'. Paper presented at the annual meeting of the Society for Pentecostal Studies. Wilmore, KY, March 20-22, 2003. Repr., *JPT* 13 (2004), pp. 19-30.

_____. 'Discipleship in Mark's Gospel' Pages 64-79 in *Faces of Renewal: Studies in Honor of Stanley M. Horton. Presented on His 70th Birthday*. Edited by Paul Elbert. Peabody: Hendrickson, 1988. Repr. Pages 62-76 in *The Spirit of the New Testament*. Leiden: Deo Publishing, 2005. Originally "Discipleship in the Synoptic Gospels". Paper presented at the annual meeting of the Society for Pentecostal Studies. Cleveland, TN, November, 1983.

_____. 'The Spiritual Situation of the Disciples Before Pentecost'. Paper presented at the annual meeting of the Society for Pentecostal Studies. South Hamilton, MA, November 15-17, 1984.

Twelftree, Graham. 'Prayer and *Heilsgeschichte* in Acts: A Reassessment'. Paper presented at the annual meeting of the Society for Pentecostal Studies. Wilmore, KY, March 20-22, 2003.

_____. 'Prayer and the Coming of the Spirit in Acts', *Expository Times* 117 (2006), pp. 271-76.

3.6 Oneness Theology

Acts 2:38: The Original New Testament Plan of Salvation (Tract). Hazelwood, MO: Word Aflame Press, 1983.

Arnold, Marvin M. Pentecost [Acts 2:38] *Before Azusa: 2000 Years of Revival in All Nations*. Jackson, MS: Arno Publications, 1991.

Bass, Kenneth. 'Baptism in the Canon: Can/Should We Still Harmonize the Baptismal Formulae in Matthew and Acts?' Paper presented at the annual meeting of the Society for Pentecostal Studies. Cleveland, TN, March 2007.

_____. 'The Normativity of Acts'. Paper presented at the annual meeting of the Society for Pentecostal Studies. Virginia Beach, VA, March 10-12, 2005.

Bernard, David. *In the Name of Jesus*. Hazelwood, MO: Word Aflame Press, 1992.

_____. *The New Birth*. Hazelwood, MO: Pentecostal Publishing House, 1993.

_____. *The Oneness of God. Series in Pentecostal Theology* 1. Hazelwood, MO: Word Aflame Press, 1983.

_____. *The Oneness View of Jesus Christ*. Hazelwood, MO: Word Aflame Press, 1994.

Gillespie, Bernie. *Faith is the Essential Response to Acts 2:38*. Published by the author, 2002.

Macchia, Frank. 'The Oneness-Trinitarian Pentecostal Final Report, 2002-2007'. *Pneuma* 30.2 (2008), pp. 203-24.

Perkins, Jonathan Ellsworth. *An Honest Effort to Harmonize Matthew 28:19 With Acts 2:38 in Relation to Water Baptism*. Los Angeles: The Author, n.d.

Zampino, David. 'Normative, Descriptive, or Formulaic?: A Critique of Kenneth Bass' Theology of Jesus' Name Baptism in the Acts of the Apostles'. *Memories of The Azusa Street Revival: Interrogations and Interpretations*. Paper presented at the annual meeting of the Society for Pentecostal Studies. Pasadena, CA, March 23-25, 2006.

4.   Stage 4—Old Story, Enduring Message: Luke–Acts for the Twenty-First Century

4.1   Social Justice

*Cnaan, Ram A. *The Invisible Caring Hand: American Congregations and Provision of Welfare*. New York: New York University Press, 2002.

Dempster, Murray W. 'Christian Social Concern in Pentecostal Perspective: Reformulating Pentecostal Eschatology'. *JPT* 2 (1993), pp. 51 -64.

_____. 'The Church's Moral Witness'. *Paraclete* 23 (Winter 1989), pp. 1-7.

_____. 'Holistic Mission in the Pentecostal Kingdom Paradigm'. Paper presented at the annual meeting of the Society for Pentecostal Studies. Wilmore, KY, March 20-22, 2003.

_____. 'Pentecostal Social Concern and the Biblical Mandate of Social Justice'. *Pneuma* 9 (Fall 1987), pp. 129-53.

_____. 'Soundings in the Moral Significance of Glossolalia'. Paper presented at the annual meeting for the Society for Pentecostal Studies. Cleveland, TN, November 3-5, 1983. Repr., 'The Structure of a Christian Ethic Informed by Pentecostal Experience: Soundings in the Moral Significance of Glossolalia'. Pages 108-141 in *The Spirit and Spirituality: Essays in Honor of Russell P. Spittler*. JPTSup 24. Edited by Wonsuk Ma and Robert P. Menzies. London: T & T Clark, 2004.

Hernando, James D. 'The Church as a Transformational Agent in Society: The Parable of the Good Samaritan, Luke 10:25-27'. *Encounter* 1.2 (Fall 2004): np. Online: http://www.agts.edu/encounter/articles/ 2004_fall /hernando.htm.

_____. 'The Church as a Transformational Agent in Society: The Story of Zacchaeus, Luke 19:1-10. Part 1' *Encounter* 1.1 (Summer 2004): np. Online: http://www.agts.edu/encounter/articles/2004_summer/zac cheus.pdf.

Hittenberger, Jeff and Martin William Mittelstadt. 'Power and Powerlessness in Pentecostal Theology' (review of Amos Yong, Theology and Down Syndrome: Reimagining Disability in Late Modernity). *Pneuma* 30 (2008), pp. 137-45.

*Johnson, Luke Timothy. *The Literary Function of Possessions in Luke–Acts.* Society of Biblical Literature Dissertation Series 39. Missoula: Scholars, 1977.

Jones, C.E. 'Tinney, James Steven'. Page 1143 in *NIDPCM*. Rev ed. Edited by Stanley M. Burgess. Grand Rapids: Zondervan, 2002.

Kydd, Ronald. 'To See is to be Called'. *Pentecostal Testimony* 77 (January 1996), p. 11.

Miller, Donald E. *Global Pentecostalism: The New Face of Christian Social Engagement.* Los Angeles: University of California Press, 2007.

Mouw, Richard J. 'Life in the Spirit in an Unjust World'. *Pneuma* 9 (Fall 1987), pp. 109-28.

Sato, Timothy. 'The S Factor: A Conversation about Pentecostalism with Donald E. Miller'. *Book and Culture: A Christian Review* (Posted 7/10/2009). Online: http://www.christianitytoday.com/bc/2009/julaug/thesfactor.html.

*Tennant, Agnieszka. 'Tallying Compassion'. *Christianity Today* 47 (February, 2003), p. 56.

Thomas, John Christopher. 'Unity and Diversity: Obstacle or Opportunity.' Pages 71-84 in *Ministry and Theology: Studies for the Church and Its Leaders.* Cleveland, TN: Pathway Press, 1996.

Tinney, James. 'What Doth Hinder Me? The Conversion of a Black Homosexual as Recorded by St. Luke'. Sermon delivered at the Metropolitan Church of Philadelphia, November 15, 1981. Typescript available from the Associated Mennonite Biblical Seminary Library, Elkhart, Ind.

Volf, Miroslav. 'On Loving With Hope: Eschatology and Social Responsibility'. *Transformation* 7 (July/Sept 1990), pp. 28-31.

_____. Work in the Spirit: Toward a Theology of Work. Eugene: Wipf & Stock, 2001.

Wenk, Matthias. 'Community Forming Power: Reconciliation and the Spirit in Acts'. *JEPTA* 19 (1999), pp. 17-33.

_____. *Community-Forming Power: The Socio-Ethical Role of the Spirit in Luke–Acts.* JPTSup 19. Sheffield: Sheffield Academic Press, 2000.

_____. 'The Holy Spirit as Transforming Power Within a Society: Pneumatological Spirituality and Its Political/Social Relevance for Western Europe'. *JPT* 11 (2002), pp. 130-42.

Yong, Amos. *The Spirit Poured Out on All Flesh: Pentecostalism and the Possibility of a Global Theology.* Grand Rapids: Baker, 2005.

_____. Theology and Down Syndrome: Reimagining Disability in Late Modernity. Waco, TX: Baylor University Press, 2007.

4.2   The Good News of Peace

Alexander, Paul. *Peace to War: Shifting Allegiances in the Assemblies of God.* C. Henry Smith Series 9. Telford, Penn.: Cascadia Publishing House, 2009.

_____. 'Spirit-Empowered Peacemaking as Opportunity: Toward a Pentecostal Charismatic Peace Fellowship'. Paper presented at the annual meeting of the Society for Pentecostal Studies. Lakeland, FL, March 14-16, 2002.

_____. 'Spirit-Empowered Peacemaking: Toward a Pentecostal Peace Fellowship'. *JEPTA* 22 (2002), pp. 78-102.

_____. 'A Theology for Pentecostal Peacemaking'. Paper presented at the annual meeting of the Society for Pentecostal Studies. Lakeland, FL, March 14-16, 2002.

Beaman, Jay. *Pentecostal Pacifism: The Origin, Development, and Rejection of Pacific Beliefs among the Pentecostals.* Hillsboro, KS: Center for Mennonite Brethren Studies, 1989.

Ford, J. Massyngbaerde. *My Enemy is My Guest: Jesus and Violence in Luke.* Maryknoll, NY: Orbis, 1984.

*Hauerwas, Stanley. *Christian Existence Today.* Durham, NC: Labyrinth, 1988.

*Kilgallen, John. ''Peace' in the Gospel of Luke and Acts of the Apostles'. *Studia Missionalia* 38 (1989), pp. 55-79.

Mittelstadt, Martin William. 'Spirit and Peace in Luke–Acts: Possibilities for Pentecostal/Anabaptist Dialogue'. Paper presented at the annual meeting of the Society for Pentecostal Studies. Eugene OR, March 26-28, 2009.

Moltmann, Jürgen. *The Spirit of Life: A Universal Affirmation.* Minneapolis: Fortress, 2001.

Reid, Robert G. ''Savior' and 'Lord' in the Lukan Birth Narrative: A Challenge to Caesar?' Paper presented at the annual meeting of the Society for Pentecostal Studies. Cleveland, TN, March 2007.

Shuman, Joel. 'Pentecost and the End of Patriotism: A Call for the Restoration of Pacifism among Pentecostal Christians'. *JPT* 9 (1996), pp. 70-96.

*Swartley, Willard M. *Covenant of Peace: The Missing Peace in New Testament Theology and Ethics.* Grand Rapids: Eerdmans, 2006.

4.3   Suffering + Persecution

Bradley, James E. 'Miracles and Martyrdom in the Early Church: Some Theological and Ethical Implications'. *Pneuma* 13 (Spring 1991), pp. 65-81.

Dunn, Peter Wallace. 'The Charismatic Gifts in the *Acts of Paul*: Second Century Trends'. Paper presented at the annual meeting of the Society for Pentecostal Studies. Kirkland, WA, March 16-18, 2000.

Elbert, Paul. 'Spirit, Scripture and Theology Through a Lukan Lens: A Review Article'. *JPT* 13 (1998), pp. 55-75.

Gallagher, Robert L. 'From Doingness to Beingness: A Missiological Interpretation of Acts 4:23-31'. Paper presented at the annual meeting of the Society for Pentecostal Studies. Tulsa, OK, March 8-10, 2001.

_____. 'Hope in the Midst of Trial: A Missiological Interpretation of Acts 12:1-11'. Paper presented at the annual meeting of the Society for Pentecostal Studies. Milwaukee, WI, March 11-13, 2004.

_____ and Paul Hertig (eds.), *Mission in Acts: Ancient Narratives in Contemporary Context*. American Society of Missiology 34. Maryknoll: Orbis Books, 2004.

Holm, Randall. 'Acts 7 and the Destiny of the Holy Spirit'. Paper presented at the annual meeting of the Society for Pentecostal Studies. Wilmore, KY, March 20-22, 2003.

Mittelstadt, Martin William. 'Life in the Spirit and the Way of the Cross'. *Enrich: A Journal for Pentecostal Ministry* 4:2 (Fall 2005), pp. 26-30

_____. 'Spirit and Suffering in Contemporary Pentecostalism: The Lukan Epic Continues'. Pages 144-174 in *Defining Issues in Pentecostalism: Classical and Emergent*. Eugene, OR: Pickwick Publications, 2007.

_____. *The Spirit and Suffering in Luke–Acts: Implications for a Pentecostal Pneumatology*. JPTSup 26. London: T & T Clark, 2004.

Newton, Jon. 'Toward a Pentecostal Martyrology'. *Australasian Pentecostal Studies* (2008): np. Online: http://pcbc.webjournals.org/Issues. asp?index=358&id= {9960F980-CE81-42AA-8AAD-5F4CD4F27103}.

Wesley, Luke. 'Is the Chinese Church Predominantly Pentecostal?' *AJPS* 7 (January 2004), pp. 225-54.

_____. *The Church in China: Persecuted, Pentecostal and Powerful*. Asian Journal of Pentecostal Studies Supplement Series 2. Baguio: Asian Journal of Pentecostal Studies Books, 2004.

_____. *Stories from China: Fried Rice for the Soul*. Waynesboro, GA: Authentic Media, 2005.

Warrington, Keith. 'A Spirit Theology of Suffering'. Pages 24-36 in *The Suffering Body: Responding to the Persecution of Christians* . Edited by Cecil M. Robeck and Harold Hunter. Peabody: Paternoster Press, 2006.

4.4   Ecumenism and Interreligious Dialogue

Anderson, Allan. 'Diversity in the Definition of 'Pentecostal/Charismatic' and its Ecumenical Implications'. Paper presented at the annual meeting of the Society for Pentecostal Studies. Lakeland, FL, March 14-16, 2002.

Cantalamessa, Raniero. *Mary: Mirror of the Church*. Translated by Frances Lonergan Villa. Collegeville, MN: Liturgical Press, 177.

Clifton, Shane. Review of Amos Yong, *The Spirit Poured Out on All Flesh: Pentecostalism and the Possibility of Global Theology*. *Australasian Pentecostal Studies* 9 (2006): np. Online: http://aps.webjournals.org/articles/1/03 /2006/6669.htm?id= {ED4C92D8-DC69-4076-AE07-4F678C173FC 0}.

Del Colle, Ralph. 'Mary, The Unwelcome (?) Guest in Catholic/Pentecostal Dialogue'. Paper presented at the annual meeting of the Society for Pentecostal Studies. Milwaukee, WI, March, 2004.

Finger, Thomas. 'The Possibilities of a Lucan Hermeneutic: Some Mennonite Reflections on Amos Yong's Theology'. Paper presented at the annual meeting of the Society for Pentecostal Studies. Durham, NC, March 13-15, 2008.

'Final Report of the Dialogue between the Secretariat for Promoting Christian Unity of the Roman Catholic Church and some classical Pentecostals, 1977-1982'. *Pneuma* 12.2 (Fall 1990), pp. 97-115.

Macchia, Frank D. 'Sighs too Deep for Words: Toward a Theology of Glossolalia'. *JPT* 1 (1992), pp. 47-73.

_____. 'The Tongues of Pentecost: A Pentecostal Perspective on the Promise and Challenge of Pentecostal/Roman Catholic Dialogue'. *Journal of Ecumenical Studies* 35 (1998), pp. 1-18.

Menzies, Robert. 'Luke's Understanding of Baptism in the Holy Spirit: A Pentecostal Perspective'. *PentecoStudies* 6 (2007), pp. 108-126.

Moltmann, Jürgen. *The Church in the Power of the Spirit*. San Francisco: Harper and Row, 1975.

Robeck, Cecil M. Jr. 'The Church: A Unique Movement of the Spirit'. *Paraclete* 16 (Fall 1982), pp. 1-4.

Van der Kooi, Cornelius. 'The Wonders of God: A Reformed Perspective on Luke's Baptism in the Holy Spirit'. *PentecoStudies* 7 (2008), pp. 34-45.

Yong, Amos. *Beyond the Impasse: Toward a Pneumatological Theology of Religions*. Grand Rapids: Baker Academic, 2004.

_____. *Hospitality & the Other: Pentecost, Christian Practices, and the Neighbor*. Maryknoll, NY: Orbis Books, 2008.

_____. 'Poured out on All Flesh: The Spirit, World Pentecostalism, and the Renewal of Theology and Praxis in the 21st Century'. *PentecoStudies* 6.1 (2007), pp. 16-46.

4.5   Global Readings—'To the Ends of the Earth'

Akinsanya, 'Gbolohan Olukayode. You Shall Receive Power': The Establishment of the Pentecostal Movement in the Nigerian Context. PhD diss., Drew University, 2000.

Anderson, Allan. *An Introduction to Pentecostalism*. Cambridge: Cambridge University Press, 2004.

_____. 'The Pentecostal Gospel and Third World Cultures'. Paper presented at the annual meeting of the Society for Pentecostal Studies. Springfield, MO, March 11-13, 1999 .

Dempster, Murray. 'Paradigm Shifts and Hermeneutics: Confronting Issues Old and New'. *Pneuma* 15 (1993), pp. 129-35.

Everts, Jenny. 'Missionary Tongues?' Paper presented at the annual meeting of the Society for Pentecostal Studies. Guadalajara, Mexico, Nov. 11-13, 1993.

Gräbe, Peter. 'The Pentecostal Discovery of the New Testament Theme of God's Power and Its Relevance to the African Context'. *Pneuma* 24 (2002), pp. 225-42.

Hollenweger, Walter J. 'Evangelism: A Non-Colonial Model'. *JPT* 7 (1995), pp. 107-28.

Hunter, Harold D. 'Two Movements of the Holy Spirit in the 20th Century? A Closer Look at Global Pentecostalism and Ecumenism'. Paper presented at the annual meeting of the Society for Pentecostal Studies. Lakeland, FL, March 14-16, 2002.

Jenkins, Philip. *The Next Christendom: The Coming of Global Christianity*. New York: Oxford University Press, 2002.

Macchia, Frank. 'Babel and the Tongues of Pentecost: Reversal or Fulfillment?—A Theological Perspective'. Pages 34-51 in *Speaking in Tongues: Multi-Disciplinary Approaches*. Edited Mark J. Cartledge. Studies in Pentecostal and Charismatic Issues. Waynesboro: Paternoster Press, 2006.

_____. 'Tongues as a Sign: Towards a Sacramental Understanding of Pentecostal Experience'. *Pneuma* 15 (1993), pp. 61-76.

Mesfin, Melisachew. 'To the Ends of the earth': Exposition of the Book of *Acts* (Amharic). Addis Abada, Ethiopia: Melisachew Mesfin, 2006.

Petersen, Douglas. *Not By Might Nor By Power: A Pentecostal Theology of Social Concern in Latin America*. Irvine, CA: Regnum Books, 1996.

Price, Lynne. *Theology Out of Place: A Theological Biography of Walter J. Hollenweger*. JPTSup 23. Sheffield: Sheffield University Press, 2003.

Samuel, Vinay. 'Pentecostalism as a Global Culture: A Response'. Pages 253-258 in *The Globalization of Pentecostalism: A Religion Made to Travel*. Edited by Murray Dempster, Byron Klaus, and Douglas Petersen. Irvine, CA: Regnum Press, 1999.

Satyavrata, Ivan. 'Contextual Perspectives on Pentecostalism as a Global Culture: A South Asian View'. Pages 201-221 in *The Globalization of Pentecostalism: A Religion Made to Travel*. Edited by Murray Dempster, Byron Klaus, and Douglas Petersen. Irvine, CA: Regnum Press, 1999.

Solivan, Samuel. 'Cultural Glossolalia in Acts 2: A Theological Reassessment of the Importance of Culture and Language'. Paper presented at the annual meeting of the Society for Pentecostal Studies. Wheaton, IL, November 10-12, 1994.

_____. *The Spirit, Pathos and Liberation: Toward an Hispanic Pentecostal Theology*. JPTSup 14. Sheffield: Sheffield Academic Press, 1998.

Yong, Amos. *Beyond the Impasse: Toward a Pneumatological Theology of Religions*. Grand Rapids: Baker Academic, 2003.

_____. '"Not Knowing Where the Wind Blows…". On Envisioning a Pentecostal-Charismatic Theology of Religions'. *JPT* 14 (April 1999), pp. 81-112.

_____. 'The Inviting Spirit: Pentecostal Beliefs and Practices Regarding the Religions Today'. Pages 29-45 in *Defining Issues in Pentecostalism: Classical and Emergent*. Edited by Steven Studebaker. McMaster Theological Studies Series; Eugene: Pickwick, 2008.

Young, Brad. 'The Power of Pentecost: Word and Spirit as Points of Convergence for Christianity and Judaism in the First Century'. Paper presented at the annual meeting of the Society for Pentecostal Studies. Tulsa, OK, March 8-10, 2001.

4.6　Luke–Acts in a Postmodern Age

Ayers, Adam. 'Can the Behavior of Tongues Utterance Still Function as Ecclesial Boundary? The Significance of Art and Sacrament'. *Pneuma* 22 (2000), pp. 271-301.

Camery-Hoggatt, Jerry. 'Moral Terror of the Inner Life: The Four Horsemen of the Inner Apocalypse'. Pages 148-61 in *Grapevine: The Spirituality of Gossip*. Scottsdale, PA: Herald Press, 2002.

Charette, Blaine. 'Messiah Without Anointing: A Missing Element in Cinematic Portrayals of Jesus'. Paper presented at the annual meeting of the Society for Pentecostal Studies. Wilmore, KY, March 20-22, 2003.

Clark, Mathew S. 'Pentecostal Hermeneutics: The Challenge of Relating To (Post)-Modern Literary Theory'. *AJPS* 1 (2002), pp. 67-92.

Cox, Harvey. Introduction to *Religion in the Secular City: Essays in Honor of Harvey Cox*. Edited by Arvind Sharma. Harrisburg, PA: Trinity Press International, 2001.

_____. '"Pentecostalism and Global Market Culture": A Response to Issues Facing Pentecostalism in a Postmodern World'. Pages 386-95 in *The Globalization of Pentecostalism: A Religion Made to Travel*. Edited by Murray Dempster, Byron Klaus, and Douglas Petersen. Irvine, CA: Regnum Press, 1999.

_____. 'The Market as God'. *The Atlantic* 283.3 (March 1999): np. Online: http://www.theatlantic.com/issues/99mar/marketgod.htm. Repr., Cited 15 April 2009. Online: http://speakingoffaith.publicradio.org /programs/atheism-religion/cox_marketasgod.shtml.

Ellington, Scott. 'Pentecostals and the Authority of Scripture'. *JPT* 9 (1997), pp. 16-38.

Hollenweger, Walter. *Besuch bei Lukas*. Munich: Chr. Kaiser Verlag, 1986.

_____. *Das Wagnis des Glaubens: Ein Spiel über die Mission für Sprecher, Instrumentalisten, Bewegungstheater und Gemeinde*. Munich: Chr. Kaiser Verlag, 1986.

Johns, Jackie David. 'Pentecostalism and the Postmodern Worldview'. *JPT* 7 (1995), pp. 73-96.

Kärkkäinen, Veli-Matti. 'Pentecostal Hermeneutics in the making: On the Way From Fundamentalism to Postmodernism'. *JEPTA* 18 (1998), pp. 76-115.

Lewis, Paul W. 'Postmodernity and Pentecostalism: A Survey and Assessment'. *AJPS* 1 (2002), pp. 34-66.

McDonnell, Killian. *God Drops and Loses Things*. Collegeville, Minn.: St. John's University Press, 2009.

_____. *Swift, Lord, You Are Not*. Collegeville, Minn.: St. John's University Press, 2003.

_____. *Yahweh's Other Shoe*. Collegeville, Minn.: St. John's University Press, 2006.

Turnage, Marc. 'The Early Church and the Axis of History and Pentecostalism facing the 21st Century: Some Reflections'. *JEPTA* 23 (2003), pp. 4-29.

The Current Status of Luke–Acts Research: Observations and Possibilities

*Conzelmann, Hans. *Acts of the Apostles*. Hermenia: A Critical and Historical Commentary on the Bible. Translated by James Limburg et al. Edited by Helmut Koester. Philadelphia: Fortress Press, 1987.

*Elliot, Matthew. *Faithful Feelings: Rethinking Emotion in the New Testament*. Grand Rapids: Kregel Publications, 2006.

*Haenchen, Ernst. *The Acts of the Apostles: A Commentary*. Translated by Bernard Noble and Gerald Shinn. Edited by R. McL. Wilson. Philadelphia: Westminster, 1971.

*Gilbert, Gary. 'The List of Nations in Acts 2: Roman Propaganda and the Lukan Response'. *JBL* 121.3 (2002), pp. 427-529.

Jenkins, Phillip. *The New Faces of Christianity: Believing the Bible in the Global South*. New York: Oxford University Press, 2006.

_____. *The Next Christendom: The Coming of Global Christianity*. New York: Oxford University Press, 2002.

Martin, David. 'Undermining the Old Paradigms: Rescripting Pentecostal Accounts'. *PentecoStudies* 5.1 (2006), pp. 18-36.

Moltmann, Jürgen. *The Church in the Power of the Spirit: A Contribution to Messianic Ecclesiology*. New York: Harper & Row, 1977.

*Parsons, Mikeal C. and Richard I. Pervo. *Rethinking the Unity of Luke–Acts*. Minneapolis: Fortress, 1993.

Reid, Robert G. "'Savior' and 'Lord' in the Lukan Birth Narrative: A Challenge to Caesar?' Paper presented at the annual meeting of the Society for Pentecostal Studies. Durham, NC, March 13-15, 2008.

Robinson, Anthony B. and Robert W. Wall. *Called To Be Church: The Book of Acts for a New Day*. Grand Rapids: Eerdmans, 2006.

*Smith, David E. *The Canonical Function of Acts: A Comparative Analysis*. Collegeville: Liturgical Press, 2002.

Volf, Miroslav. *Work in the Spirit: Toward a Theology of Work*. Eugene: Wipf & Stock, 2001.

*Wall, Robert W. 'The Acts of the Apostles in the Context of the New Testament Canon'. *Biblical Theological Bulletin* 18 (1988), pp. 15-23.

_____. 'Purity and Power According to Acts of the Apostles'. Paper presented at the annual meeting of the Society for Pentecostal Studies. Cleveland, TN, March 12-14, 1998.

Yong, Amos. *The Holy Spirit in Luke–Acts & the Public Square*. Brewster, MA: Paraclete Press, Forthcoming.

_____. 'Pentecostalism and the Theological Academy'. *Theology Today* 64 (2007), pp. 244-50.

A Not So Final Word

*Bakhtin, Mikhail. *Speech Genres and Other Late Essays*. Edited by Caryl Emerson and Michael Holquist. Translated by Vern W. McGee. Austin: University of Texas Press, 1986.

*Coates, Ruth. *Christianity in Bakhtin: God and the Exiled Author*. Cambridge: Cambridge University Press, 1998.

Johns, Cheryl Bridges. 'The Adolescence of Pentecostalism: In Search of a Legitimate Sectarian Identity'. *Pneuma* 17 (1995), pp. 3-17.

*Newbigin, Leslie. *The Gospel in a Pluralist Society*. Grand Rapids, MI: Eerdmans, 1989.

Postlethwait, D. Michael. 'Drunk No More: The Biblical Case For Sobriety and Intellectual Awareness in Acts 2'. Paper presented at the annual meeting of the Society for Pentecostal Studies. Eugene, OR, March 2009.

Commentaries

Adeyemo, Tokunboh, ed. *Africa Bible Commentary: A One Volume Commentary Written by 70 African Scholars*. Grand Rapids: Zondervan, 2006.

Arrington, French. 'Acts'. Pages 535-693 in *Life in the Spirit New Testament Commentary*. Edited by French Arrington and Roger Stronstad. Grand Rapids: Zondervan, 1999.

_____. The Acts of the Apostles: Introduction, Translation and Commentary. Peabody, MA: Hendrickson, 1988.

_____. 'Luke'. Pages 375-534 in *Life in the Spirit New Testament Commentary*. Edited by French Arrington and Roger Stronstad. Grand Rapids: Zondervan, 1999.

_____. *The Spirit-Anointed Church: A Commentary on the Acts of the Apostles*. Cleveland, TN: Pathway Press, 2008.

_____. *The Spirit-Anointed Jesus: A Study of the Gospel of Luke*. Cleveland, TN: Pathway Press, 2008.

Conn, Charles. *The Acts of the Apostles*. Cleveland: Pathway Press, 1965.

Holman, Charles L. 'Review of French L. Arrington, *The Acts of the Apostles: An Introduction and Commentary*'. Paper presented at the annual meeting of the Society for Pentecostal Studies. Fresno, CA, November 16-18, 1989.

Horton, Stanley. *Acts. The Complete Biblical Library* 6. Springfield, MO: Gospel Publishing House, 1987.

_____. *Acts*. The Logion Press Commentary. Springfield, MO: Logion Press, 2001.

_____. *The Book of Acts. The Radiant Commentary of the New Testament*. Springfield, MO: Gospel Publishing House, 1981.

_____. *The Book of Acts: The Wind of the Spirit* [Russian]. Republic of Belarus: Life Publishers International, 2002.

_____, ed. *Luke. The Complete Biblical Library* 4. Springfield, MO: Gospel Publishing House, 1988.

Kurz, William S. *The Acts of the Apostles*. Collegeville Bible Commentary 5. Collegeville, MN: Liturgical Press, 1983.

Michaels, J. Ramsey. 'Luke–Acts'. Pages 544-61 in *Dictionary of Pentecostal and Charismatic Movements*. Edited by Stanley Burgess, Gary McGee and Patrick Alexander. Grand Rapids: Zondervan, 1988.

Montague, George. *The Holy Spirit: Growth of a Biblical Tradition. A Commentary on the Principal Texts of the Old and New Testaments*. New York: Paulist Press, 1976.

Roberts, Oral. *Matthew, Mark, Luke, John. The New Testament Comes Alive: A Personal New Testament Commentary* 1. Tulsa: Oral Roberts, 1984.

Rea, John, ed. *The Layman's Commentary on the Holy Spirit*. Plainfield, NJ: Logos, 1972.

Swaggart, Jimmy. *Acts. Jimmy Swaggart Bible Commentary* 11. Baton Rouge, Louisiana: World Evangelism Press, 1997.

_____. *Luke. Jimmy Swaggart Bible Commentary* 9. Baton Rouge, Louisiana: World Evangelism Press, 1996.

*Talbert, Charles H. *Reading Acts: A Literary and Theological Commentary on the Acts of the Apostles*. Reading the New Testament Series. New York: Crossroad, 1997.

* _____. *Reading Luke: A Literary and Theological Commentary on the Third Gospel*. Reading the New Testament Series. New York: Crossroad, 1982.

*Tannehill, Robert. *The Narrative Unity of Luke–Acts: A Literary Interpretation*. 2 vols. Philadelphia: Fortress Press, 1986 & 1990.

Tourville, Robert E. *The Acts of the Apostles: A Verse-By-Verse Commentary from the Classical Pentecostal Point of View*. New Wilmington, PA: House of Bonn Giovanni, 1983.

Popular Pastoral Tools

Armstrong, Hart R. *The Book of Acts: Correspondence Course*. 7 vols. Springfield: Gospel Publishing House, 1952.

Balliet, Emil. *Acts*. Great Themes of the Christian Faith. Springfield: Gospel Publishing House, 1972.

_____. *Acts: To the Ends of the Earth*. Spiritual Discovery Series. Springfield: Gospel Publishing House, 1996.

Barney, Kenneth. *It Began in an Upper Room: The Pentecostal Explosion of the First Century*. Springfield: Radiant Books, 1979.

Bard, Balthasar Theodor. *The Acts of the Apostles*. Unpublished Teaching Notes, ca. 1935.

Brandt, R. L. *The Acts Pattern*. San Diego: Segen Books, 2003.

Burkhart, Rob. *The Acts Story: The Teacher's Guide*. Springfield: Gospel Publishing House, 1988.

Carlson, G. Raymond. *The Acts Today: The Work of the Holy Spirit in the Early Church*. Springfield: Gospel Publishing House, 1978.

Carlstrom, Paul and Kathern. *Acts in Action: A Bible Study Manual for the Deaf*. Springfield: Gospel Publishing House, 1978.

Copley, A.S. *The Church of Christ Founded: Spiritual-Studies in The Acts*. Kansas City: Grace and Glory, n.d.

Cunningham, Robert. *Getting Together With Luke and Acts: A Guide to Group Bible Study*. Springfield: Gospel Publishing House, 1972.

Grizzle, Trevor. *Church Aflame: An Exposition of Acts 1-12*. Cleveland, TN: Pathway Press, 2000.

Hummel, Charles E. *Fire in the Fireplace: Contemporary Charismatic Renewal*. Downers Grove: Intervarsity Press, 1978.

Hurst, D.V. and T.J. Jones. *The Church Begins: A Study Manual on the First 12 Chapters of the Acts*. Springfield: Gospel Publishing House, 1959.

Jones, Gwen, ed. *Conference on the Holy Spirit Digest: A Condensation of Plenary Sessions and Seminars of the Conference on the Holy Spirit in Springfield, Missouri, August 16-18, 1982*. 2 Vols. Springfield: Gospel Publishing House, 1983.

Ohrnell, Arvid. *The Book of Acts: A Bible Study Course*. Springfield: Home Missions Department of the Assemblies of God, 1962.

_____ and Paul Markstrom. *The Book of Acts: A Bible Study Course*. Rev. ed. Springfield: Home Missions Department of the Assemblies of God, 1962.

Stewart, Marjorie. *Looking at Jesus with Luke: Studies in the Life of Christ*. Springfield: Gospel Publishing House, 1978.

Ward, C. M. *Sermons From Luke*. Tulsa, Okla.: Harrison House, 1982.

Witherspoon, Jet. *Born in the Fire: A Study Course on the Book of the Acts of the Apostles*. Hazelwood, MO: General Home Missions Division United Pentecostal Church International, n.d.

Author Index

Adeyemo, T. 169
Aker, B. 70, 79
Akinsanya, G.B. 139-40
Alexander, E. 106
Alexander, Patrick. 169
Alexander, Paul. 124-26
Alter, R. 83
Amstutz, J. 95
Anderson, A. 132, 138
Archer, K. 24, 33-34, 43-44, 47, 85
Arlandson, J.M. 105
Arnold, M. 111
Arrington, F. 69, 78, 86, 166, 168-69
Atkinson, 13, 47, 61, 71
Atterberry, T. 37
Ayers, A. 146-47
Baer, R. 77
Bagalawis, M. 94
Bakhtin, M. 164
Balch, D. 90
Barclift, M. 93
Bard, B.T. 166
Barnes, A. 72
Barratt, T.B. 29-30
Barrett, C.K. 8
Bartleman, F. 24-25
Bass, K. 112-13
Baur, F.C. 7
Beacham, A.D. 167
Beaman, J. 122
Beaman, L. 26
Beardslee, W. 83
Bell, E.N. 37
Bennett, D. 41
Bergant, D. 89
Bernard, D. 110-11, 113
Beyer, P. 26
Blomberg, C. 101

Boddy, J.T. 35
Borgman, P. 43, 124
Bosworth, F.F. 22, 34-35, 37
Bovon, F. 10-11, 82
Bradley, J. E. 130
Brodie, T. 78
Brooks, P. 92
Brown, R.A. 35
Bruce, F.F. 7
Brumback, C. 26
Bruner, F.D. 15, 49, 53
Bundy, D. 13
Burgess, S. 5, 22
Burkitt, W. 72
Cadbury, H.J. 7-8, 86
Camery-Hoggatt, J. 78-79, 81, 148
Cantalamessa, R. 133
Cargal, T. 78
Carson, D.A. 54, 88
Cartledge, M. 19, 141
Cavaness, B. 103-104, 106
Cerillo, A. 13
Chan, S. 77
Charette, B. 96-97, 147
Cheum, D.C.W. 92
Cheun, L.Y. 71
Cheung, T. 69
Cho, Y. 62-63, 93
Choi, M. 107
Christenson, L. 42
Clarke, A. 72
Clarke, M. 74, 144
Clarno, E. 102
Clifton, S. 135
Comblin, J. 143
Conn, C. 165
Conzelmann, H. 150
Cook, G. 24

Copley, A.S. 165
Cotton, R. 74
Cox, H. 144-45
Cox, R. 77
Cullen, P. 110
Cunningham, L. 104
Dalton, R.C. 38
Dayton, D. 1, 27
Del Colle, R. 113, 133
Dela Cruz, R.G. 74, 92
Dempster, M. 12, 14, 78, 92, 106,
    116-17, 120, 138, 140, 144
Derstine, G. 42
Dibelius, M. 8, 150
Dippold, D. 167
Dorman, D. 56
Dowd, M. 81, 83-84
Drane, J. 56
Drayton, R.D. 101
Dunn, J.D.G. 3-4, 8-10, 13, 15, 47-
    53, 55-58, 60, 62-64, 68, 70-71,
    78-79, 81, 101, 166
Dunn, P.W. 128
DuPlessis, D. 42
Dutko, J. 20
Edwards, Jm. 72-73
Edwards, Jn. 95
Elbert, P. 56, 58, 68, 70, 75-76, 78,
    81, 85-89, 91, 104, 108, 127
Ellington, S. 84, 144
Elliot, M. 152
Emerson, C. 164
Ervin, H. 4, 48, 55-57, 99
Estrada, N. 104
Evans, C.A. 91
Everts, J. 73, 142
Ewart, F. 32-33
Fee, G. 4, 48-50, 54, 68, 84
Ferguson, E. 90
Filson, F. 43
Finger, T. 135
Fisher, E. 25-26
Flokstra, G. 16, 68
Flower, J.R. 26
Foakes Jackson, F.J. 150
Foakes Jackson, F.J. 7
Ford, J.M. 108-109, 122-23

Frei, H. 83
Frey, E. 103
Frodsham, A.W. 37
Frye, N. 83
Gaffin, R. 67
Gallagher, R. 127-28
Gasque, W. 7-10, 43
Gaston, W.T. 35, 37
Gause, R.H. 83
Gee, D. 41, 44, 122
Gen, R. 99
Giblet, J. 76
Gilbert, G. 155
Gill, D. 103-104, 106
Gillespie, B. 111
Gilman, T. 167
Goff, J. 21
Goldingay, J. 82, 84
Gräbe, P. 142-43
Grant, W.V. 98
Graves, R. 71
Green, J. 9, 85
Greenwalt, A. 29
Greeven, H. 8
Grimes, L. 70
Grizzle, T. 96, 166
Grudem, W. 67
Hacking, K. 48
Haenchen, E. 150
Hamill, J. 75
Hamilton, D.J. 104
Hamman, C.A. 110
Haney, K. 113
Hanson, K.C. 8
Harris, R.W. 67
Hartman, D. 167
Hauerwas, S. 123
Hayford, J. 102
Haywood, G.T. 32-33
Henry, M. 72
Hernando, J. 120
Hertweck, G. 67
Hildebrandt, W. 75
Hittenberger, J. 119
Ho, M. 75
Hodges, M. 93-94
Holdcroft, L.T. 69

Hollenweger, W. 1, 16, 138-39, 142, 147
Holm, R. 127
Holman, C. 70, 96, 166
Holquist, M. 164
Horton, S. 19, 25, 58, 69, 166-67
Hudson, N. 19
Hunter, H. 74, 140
Hurtado, L. 72-73
Isgrigg, D. 56
Jacobsen, D. 16, 44-45, 78-79
Jenkins, P. 138, 152-53
Jervell, J. 9
Johns, C.B. 162
Johnson, J.A. 113
Johnson, L.T. 91, 118
Johnston, R.K. 78
Jones, C.E. 119
Kärkkäinen, V. 78, 143-44
Karris, R. 89
Keener, C. 50
Kerr, D.W. 29-30, 34-35, 37
Kilgallen, J. 124
Kim, D. 110
King, J.H. 27
Klaus, B. 12, 106, 138, 144
Koester, H. 150
Krause, M. 167
Kurz, W. 89-91
Kydd, R. 67-68, 78, 83, 120-21, 163
Labahn, M. 101
Lake, K. 150
Lake, K. 7
Land, S. 12-13, 42-43
Lash, N. 43
Lederle, H. 16
Lee, M. 69
Leeper, G. 74-75
Leonard, T.K. 35
Lewis, P. 14-16, 78, 144
Lightfoot, J.B. 7
Lim, D. 74
Limburg, J. 150
Lindford, A. 40
Lindsay, G. 30
Ling, M. 8
Ling, T.M. 74

Linzey, V. 72
Luce, A.E. 39
Lupton, L. 27-28
Luther, M. 1, 30
Ma, W. 14, 16, 53, 74-75, 116
MacArthur, J. 15
Macchia, F. 12, 47, 74, 76-77, 113, 126, 132-33, 141-42
MacDonald, D.R. 78
MacDonald, W.G. 69
Malherbe, A. 90
Marek, K. 40
Marshall, I.H. 8, 58
Martin, D. 154
Martin, L. 36
Martin, R. 43
Mattill, A.J. 7
Mattill, M.B. 7
May, F.J. 95
Maynard-Reid, P.U. 59
McAlister, R.E. 31-32
McCaslin, K. 167
McComiskey, T.E. 15
McDonnell, K. 67, 114-15, 148-49
McGee, G. 19, 31-32, 34, 37, 44, 73, 88, 169
McGee, V.W. 164
McKeever, M. 9
McKinney, K. 10
McLaren, A. 72
McPherson, A.S. 28-29, 37, 98
Meeks, W.A. 90
Menzies R.P. 9, 48, 53, 56, 58-62, 74-75, 78, 116-17, 134, 167
Menzies, G. 75
Menzies, W. 14, 53-54, 58, 60, 74-75, 78, 84, 113
Mesfin, M. 143
Michaels, J.R. 169
Miller, D.E. 115
Mittelstadt, M.W. 63, 119, 130, 167
Moessner, D.P. 91
Moffat, F.M. 37
Moltmann, J. 126, 135, 155
Montague, G. 67, 169
Moody, D.L. 30
Moore, R. 12-13

Mouw, R. 117
Munyon, T. 94
Nelson, P.C. 15, 29
Newbigin, L. 162
Newton, J. 131
Nieman, J. 88
Noble, B. 150
Noel, B.T. 50
Ong, W. 83
Osborn, T.L. 30
Oss, D. 67
Ozman, A.N. 21
Packer, J.I. 15
Palma, A. 73-74
Parham, C.F. 14, 20-21
Parham, R.L. 20
Parham, S.E. 21
Parker, D. 97
Parsons, M. 158
Patillon, M. 86
Peake, A.S. 72
Pearlman, M. 15, 39, 44, 165
Peerboldt, B.J.L. 101
Penner, T. 9
Penney, J.M. 10, 66, 94, 167
Perkins, J.E. 110
Pervo, R.I. 158
Petersen, D. 12, 106, 138, 143-44
Petts, D. 70-71
Pilch, J. 102-103
Pinnock, C. 46-47
Poewe, K. 33
Poirier, J. 97-98
Pope, W.H. 35
Porter, S.E. 78
Postlethwait, D.M. 163
Powell, M.A. 9
Powell, T. 98-99
Powers, J.E. 105-106
Price, L. 139
Ramm, B. 12
Ramsey, W.M. 7
Reed, D. 34, 113
Reid, R. 122
Rice, J.R. 44
Ricoeur, P. 84

Robeck, C.M. 22, 24, 45, 65-66, 68, 74
Roberts, J. 93
Roberts, O. 165
Robinson, A.B. 158-59
Roozen, D. 88
Rosselli, J. 35
Ruthven, J. 65, 107
Samuel, V. 138
Sato, T. 115
Satyavrata, I. 138
Saucy, R. 67
Schaff, P. 72
Scheffer, N. 96
Seagraves, D. 113
Seymour, W. 18, 22-24, 35-37
Shaka, R. 113
Shelton, J. 4, 9-10, 48, 56-59, 61, 85-86, 109, 167
Sheppard, G. 78
Shinn, G. 150
Shuman, J. 123
Simpson, A.B. 98
Slauenwhite, D. 41
Smith, D.E. 159
Solivan, S. 140-41
Spittler, R. 15, 33, 46, 50, 77-78, 116
Stacey, J. 95
Stegne, R. 91
Storms, C.S. 67
Stott, J.R.W 15, 49
Streeter, S. 167
Stronstad, R. 4, 8-10, 46, 48, 51-59, 115-16, 157, 167-68
Stuart, D. 50
Studebaker, S. 55
Suurmond, J.J. 64
Swaggart, J. 165
Swartley, W. 124
Synan, V. 87
Talbert, C.H. 91, 167
Tannehill, R.C. 167
Taylor, G.F. 27
Tennant. A. 121
Thomas, J.C. 12-13, 16, 57, 84-85, 100, 106-108, 120, 167
Tinney, J. 119

Tipei, J. 95
Tourville, R. 166
Tuckett, C.M. 8
Tunmore, J. 35
Turnage, M. 145-46
Turner, M. 9-10, 54, 60-62, 68, 74,
    85, 110, 117
Twelftree, G. 100-101, 110
Van Belle, G. 8
Van der Kooi, C. 134
Van Der Maas, E.M. 5
Van Kleek, L.M. 52
Van Segbroeck, F. 8
Vanhoozer, K. 43
Verheyden, J. 8
Volf, M. 121, 155-56
Wacker, G. 13, 20, 103
Wadholm, R. 66
Wagner, C.P. 94
Wall, R.W. 158-59
Walton, S. 88
Ward, A.G. 38
Ward, C.M. 38
Warrington, K. 98, 131
Webb, W. 106
Wenham, D. 101
Wenk, M. 10, 117-18, 167
Wesley, J. 72
Wesley, L. 130
Westfall, C. 62-63
Whitefield, G. 30
Wilkinson, M. 2
Williams, E.S. 15, 39, 44, 165
Williams, J.R. 76
Williams, L. 95
Williams, M. 167
Williamson, R.L. 104-105
Wilser, J. 167
Wilson, J. 98
Wilson, M. 92
Wilson, R. 150
Womack, D. 42
Wood, G. 113
Woodworth-Etter, M. 27
Woolbridge, J.D. 15
Wright, N.T. 43

Yong, A. 43, 102-103, 106, 118-19,
    134-38, 150-51, 153
York, G. 167
Zampino, D. 112

SCRIPTURE INDEX

Genesis
2   141
11   141

Exodus
14   147

Numbers
11   74
11.14-17   52
11.16   101
11.25   52

2 Samuel
7.16   149

2 Kings
2.9   52
2.15   52

Isaiah
28.11-12   33
42.1-4   96
42.6   96
49.1-6   96
49.6   96
50.4-9   96
52.13-53.12   96
61.1-2   59

Joel
2   132
2.28-32   59, 75, 92, 115

Matthew
10.34   124
11.28   33
21.12-13   122

26.56   149
28.19   32, 110-12
28.19-20   32

Mark
1.29-34   100
5.34   124
11.15-19   122
15.40   149
16:16-19   36

Luke
1.1-4   168
1.1-2.17   167
1.5-25   99
1.5-79   105
1.5-3.38   168
1.15   51
1.15-17   116
1.17   94
1.20   100
1.22   116
1.26   149
1.31-33   149
1.35   94, 134
1.38   116
1.41   51
1.44   149
1.46-55   116
1.52-53   134
1.67   51, 116
1.76   116
1.79   124, 154
1.80   134
2.1   149, 154
2.1-14   147
2.8-12   66
2.11   154

2.14   124, 154
2.18-4.13   167
2.25-32   116, 134
2.25-35   128
2.25-38   105
2.29   116, 124
2.34   59, 105
2.34-35   66
2.52   134
3.1   154
3.15-16   129
3.16   51, 59
3.21-22   70, 134, 169
3.22   129
3.23-38   91
4   59, 121
4.1   125, 129, 134
4.1-13   124
4.1-9.50   168
4.2   169
4.4   125
4.14   125, 129, 134
4.14-15   94
4.14-7.18   167
4.15   107
4.16-20   128
4.16-21   117
4.16-30   118, 129, 169
4.18   97
4.18-19   117, 134
4.18-21   52
4.21   121
4.23-27   65
4.23-30   104
4.31-37   102
4.31-8.56   169
4.36   94
4.38-41   100
4.40   95
4.40-41   107
5.17   94, 101
5.29   122, 149
6.19   94, 107
6.20-21   134
6.24-25   134
6.27-36   123
7.19-8.40   167

7.20   100
7.36-50   79, 105
7.45   149
7.50   124
8.1-2   149
8.1-3   102
8.26-34   102
8.27   100
8.41-9.62   167
8.46   94, 101
8.48   124
9.1   94
9.1-2   107
9.1-6   101
9.2   107
9.11   107
9.37-42   102
9.38   101
9.51-56   122
9.51-19.44   168
9.51-22.53   169
10.1-12   101, 169
10.1-11.29   167
10:5   124
10:6   124
10.9   107
10.13   94
10.17-20   101
10.19   94
10.25-27   120
10.25-37   79
11.1-4   110
11.5-8   110
11.8   149
11.9-13   110
11.13   52, 76
11.14-20   66
11.20   100, 102
11:21   124
11.29-32   66
11.30-12.53   167
12   128
12.1-3   148
12.1-12   128-29
12.1-53   88
12.11-12   130
12.12   52

12.51   86, 124
12.54-14.35   167
13.1-9   122
13.10-17   102
13.11   100
13.13   95
13.16   100
13.32   100
13.33   107
14.32   124
15   149
15.1-17.9   167
15.1-2   122
15.1-10   104
15.8   149
15.11-32   39
15.12   148
15.15   148
15.18   148
15.20   149
15.28   149
15.29   149
15.30   149
15.32   149
17.18   86
17.20-19.27   167
18.1-14   104
19.1-10   120, 122, 147
19.9   121
19.28-21.16   167
19.37   94
19.38   124
19.42   124
19.45-46   122
19.45-21.38   168
21   128
21.5-36   66
21.14   66
21.14-15   52
21.26   94
21.27   94
22   90-91, 125
22.1-24.53   168
22.14-38   88, 90-91
22.39   91
22.47   149
22.63-23.56   167

22.69   94
23.8-11   66
23.34   122
23.46   134
23.49   149
23.55-24.35   105
24.1-53   167
24.19   56, 65
24.36   124
24.46-49   125
24.47   76
24.49   23, 76, 94

Acts
1   41
1-8   94
1-10   157
1-12   166
1.1   107, 117, 136, 162
1.1-5   108, 168
1.1-11   168
1.3   169
1.4-8   23
1.4-5   52
1.5   51
1.6-2.47   108
1.8   52, 73, 76, 93-94, 130, 138, 155
1.10   102
1.12-14   39
1.12-2.41   168
1.14   94-95
1.15-26   93
1.16   159
1.22   159
2   5, 20, 21, 25, 29, 41, 56, 70-75, 77, 92, 132, 140-41, 149, 157
2-19   95
2-28   41
2.1-4   66, 73, 155, 169
2.1-41   66
2.2-3   36
2.3   35, 75, 96
2.4   23-25, 29, 33, 35, 51, 73
2.5-11   154
2.7   103
2.12   86, 141

2.14   108
2.14-21   39, 65
2.14-40   169
2.15   41, 103
2.16-17   105
2.17   65, 105, 139
2.17-18   103, 117, 132
2.19-21   134
2.20   65
2.22   94
2.23   159
2.33   116
2.33b   70
2.34   23
2.37   86
2.38   31-33, 71, 76, 110-12, 134
2.39   65, 134, 136, 139
2.41   53
2.42   95
2.42-47   20, 66
2.42-6.7   168
2.46   94-95
3-5   128-29
3.1-10   98
3.1-6.7   108
3.1-12.17   169
3.4   102
3.12   94
3.19-21   134
3.19-26   91
3.21   159
4   72, 127
4.1-22   66
4.7   94
4.8   51, 56, 128-29
4.8-12   66
4.23   39
4.23-31   66, 93, 127, 131
4.24   94
4.28   159
4.30-31   108
4.31   51, 53, 56, 66, 129
4.32-37   117
4.33   94
5.1-11   96, 100
5.1-14   99
5.7-10   104

5.12   94-95
5.12-16   66, 101
5.14   103
5.29   122, 131
5.31   154
6   94
6.1-7   118, 120
6.3   53, 66
6.3-5   61
6.4   95
6.5   53, 66
6.6   95
6.8   94
6.8-10   66
6.8-9.31   108
6.8-12.24   168
6.10   66
6.15   103
6.16   134
7   127-129
7.22   56
7.26   124
7.35-39   66
7.55   102, 130
7.56   127
8   56, 61, 72, 143, 157
8-9   157
8.1-4   136
8.3   104
8.4-8   101
8.4-25   118
8.6   94
8. 5-13   66
8.10   94
8.12   103
8.13   94-95
8.13-24   96
8.14   61
8.14-16   112
8.14-17   108
8.16   111
8.26-40   118
8.30   86
8.36   86
9   56, 72, 103, 157
9.1-21   99
9.2   104

9.3-6   103
9.8-9   100
9.9-12   103
9.17   51, 95
9.17-18   134
9.26-28   118
9.31   61, 124
9.32-11.21   108
10   23, 56, 71-73, 118, 139, 157
10-11   91
10.10   103
10.10-43   66
10.34   139
10.34-48   117
10.36   124, 154
10.38   94
10.42   159
10.44-46   36
10.44-47   73
10.44-48   25, 108, 112
10.45-46   23, 35
10.46   23, 71, 73
10.48   111
11.1-18   93
11.9-20   136
11.14   134
11.16   51
11.19-21   96
11.22-12.24   108
11.24   53, 61, 118
11.24-28   108
11.25-26   96
11.27-28   154
11.27-30   65, 93
11.28   66
12   100, 128
12.1-5   128
12.1-11   128
12.6-11   128
12.7   103
12.20   124
12.20-23   99
12.25-16.5   108
12.25-22.21   168
13   157
13.1-3   65-66, 103
13.1-4   93

13.1-19.20   169
13.2   66, 95
13.2-4   66
13.4-12   99
13.9   51, 56, 108
13.9-10   102
13.9-12   66
13.23   154
13.47   97
13.51-14.3   66
13.52   51
14.1-3   66
14.3   95
14.9   102
14.15b-17   140
15   85, 106, 118
15.1-29   109
15.1-35   93
15.12   66
15.22   118
15.32   61
15.32-35   65
15.33   124
15.36-41   118
16.3-5   104
16.6   66, 93
16.6-7   93
16.6-19.20   108
16.7   93
16.9   66
16.10   5
16.14-15   134
16.16-18   101
16.16-34   131
16.31-33   134
16.36   124
17.4   103
17.26-27   142
17.34   103
18.2   154
18.8a   134
18.23-19.7   76
19   56, 70, 72-73, 144, 157
19.1-7   73, 108, 112
19.2   70, 86
19.5   111
19.6   23-25, 35, 36, 65, 73

19.11   94-95
19.21-21.26   169
19.21-28.31   108
20   91
20-17-30   90
20.18-35   88, 128-29
20.22   129
20.22-24   93
20.22-21.11   108
20.23   66
20.28   61
20.35   155
21.4   66
21.8-9   89
21.8-14   65
21.9   104
21.11   66
22.4-11   103
22.6-16   99
22.16   134
22.22-26.32   168
24.2   124
26.9-18   103
26.12-18   99
27.1-28.31   168
28   26, 41
28.8   95

Romans
2.29   59
8.14-17   59
8.15   70
10.9   111
14.17   59
15.16   59

1 Corinthians
2.12   70
6.11   59
12   34
12-14   54, 61, 75
12.3   111
12.13   51
13   36
14.3   66
14.18   30
14.21   35-36

2 Corinthians
1.21   70
5.5   70
6.4-11   147
11.4   70

Galatians
4.6   59
5.5   59
5.16-26   59

Ephesians
1.13   70
2.20   97
5.18   51

Philippians
2.11   111

Col
4.14   5

2 Timothy
4.10-11   5

Philemon
24   5

James
1.1   136

1 Peter
1.1   136
3.14   126

Revelation
7.9   123

Didache
7.1-3   112

Ignatius (Philippians)
2.20   112-13

Other Books from CPT Press

R. Hollis Gause, *Living in the Spirit: The Way of Salvation* (2009). ISBN 9780981965109

Kenneth Archer, *A Pentecostal Hermeneutic: Spirit, Scripture and Community* (2009). ISBN 9780981965116

Larry McQueen, *Joel and the Spirit: The Cry of a Prophetic Hermeneutic* (2009). ISBN 9780981965123

Lee Roy Martin, *Introduction to Biblical Hebrew* (2009). ISBN 9780981965154

Lee Roy Martin, *Answer Key to Introduction to Biblical Hebrew* (2009). ISBN 9780981965161

Roger Stronstad, *The Prophethood of All Believers: A Study in Luke's Charismatic Theology* (2010). ISBN 9780981965130

Printed in Great Britain
by Amazon.co.uk, Ltd.,
Marston Gate.